Feminists and Party Politics

Lisa Young

Feminists and Party Politics

UBCPress · Vancouver · Toronto

Printed in Canada on acid-free paper

ISBN 0-7748-0773-3

Canadian Cataloguing in Publication Data

Young, Lisa
   Feminists and party politics

   Includes bibliographical references and index.
   ISBN 0-7748-0773-3

   1. Women in politics – Canada. 2. Women in politics – United States. 3. Political parties – Canada. 4. Political parties – United States. 5. Feminism – Canada. 6. Feminism – United States. I. Title.
HQ1236.5.C2Y68 2000   324.2'082'0971   C99-911204-X

This book has been published with the help of a grant from the Humanities and Social Sciences Federation of Canada, using funds provided by the Social Sciences and Humanities Research Council of Canada.

UBC Press acknowledges the financial support of the Government of Canada through the Book Publishing Industry Development Program (BPIDP) for our publishing activities.

Canadä

We also gratefully acknowledge the support of the Canada Council for the Arts for our publishing program as well as the support of the British Columbia Arts Council.

UBC Press
University of British Columbia
2029 West Mall
Vancouver, BC V6T 1Z2
(604) 822-5959
Fax: (604) 822-6083
E-mail: info@ubcpress.ubc.ca
www.ubcpress.ubc.ca

For my parents, Audrey and David Young

Contents

Figures and Tables

Abbreviations

AFEAS	Association féminine d'éducation et d'action sociale
APSA	American Political Science Association
BPW	Business and Professional Women's Clubs
BQ	Bloc Québécois
CACSW	Canadian Advisory Council on the Status of Women
CAWP	Center for the American Woman and Politics
CCF	Co-operative Commonwealth Federation
CFA	Canada Family Action coalition
CWA	Concerned Women for America
CWPR	Canadian Women for Political Representation
DCCC	Democratic Congressional Campaign Committee
DNC	Democratic National Committee
DSCC	Democratic Senatorial Campaign Committee
DTF	Democratic Task Force (of the NWPC)
DWC	Democratic Women's Caucus
EMILY's	Early Money Is Like Yeast List
ERA	Equal Rights Amendment
FDR	Franklin Delano Roosevelt
FEC	Federal Election Commission
FFM	Fund for the Feminist Majority
FFQ	Fédération des femmes du Québec
FPC	Feminist Party of Canada
GOP	Grand Old Party (Republicans)
LEAF	Legal Education and Action Fund
LPC	Liberal Party of Canada
LWV	League of Women Voters
MP	Member of Parliament
NAC	National Action Committee on the Status of Women

NAFTA	North American Free Trade Agreement
NARAL	National Abortion Rights Action League
NPCBW	National Political Congress of Black Women
NDP	New Democratic Party
NFDW	National Federation of Democratic Women
NFRW	National Federation of Republican Women
NOW	National Organization for Women
NRCC	National Republican Coalition for Choice
NWAC	Native Women's Association of Canada
NWDN	National Women's Democratic Network
NWLC	National Women's Liberal Commission
NWPC	National Women's Political Caucus
PAC	Political Action Committee
PC	Progressive Conservative Party
PCWAC	Progressive Conservative Women's Association of Canada
PLQ	Parti libéral du Québec
POW	Participation of Women Committee (of the NDP)
PP	Planned Parenthood
RCERPF	Royal Commission on Electoral Reform and Party Financing
RCSW	Royal Commission on the Status of Women
REAL	Realistic, Equal and Active for Life Women
RFC	Republicans for Choice
RNC	Republican National Committee
RTF	Republican Task Force (of the NWPC)
VOW	Voice of Women
WCF	Women's Campaign Fund
WISH	Women in the Senate and House List
WLFC	Women's Liberal Federation of Canada
WPA	Women for Political Action
YWCA	Young Women's Christian Association

Acknowledgments

Several organizations and individuals made available materials that were essential to this research. A number of feminist and partisan activists in both the United States and Canada agreed to be interviewed for this research and were generous with their time and personal files. Both the Liberal and the New Democratic Parties of Canada granted permission to use closed archival collections that yielded valuable information, provided party documents, and made it possible to attend party conventions as an observer. In addition, the staff of the Canadian Women's Movement Archives at the University of Ottawa and at the National Archives of Canada were very patient with a novice archival researcher.

Data for Canadian party conventions were made available by George Perlin of the Centre for the Study of Public Opinion at Queen's University, Keith Archer of the University of Calgary, and Alan Whitehorn of Royal Military College. Data for American party conventions were made available by Denise Baer and by the Inter-University Consortium for Political and Social Research at the University of Michigan. Neither the collectors of the data nor the ICPSR bear any responsibility for the analyses or interpretations presented here. A special note of thanks to Laine Reuss of the University of Toronto Data Library, who was of great assistance in procuring the American data sets, and to Joanna Everitt, who was extraordinarily patient in her explanation of matters statistical.

This book began as a doctoral dissertation at the University of Toronto. The research for that dissertation was supported by the Social Sciences and Humanities Research Council of Canada through a doctoral fellowship, and a Queen Elizabeth Doctoral Fellowship from the government of Ontario gave me the luxury of an extra year to complete the research and writing. The American portion of this project would not have been possible had it not been for generous financial support in the form of a Canada-US Fulbright Scholarship and a University of Toronto Associates' travel grant. The additional research and writing required to turn my dissertation into a book were supported by a postdoctoral fellowship from the SSHRC and teaching release time from the University of Calgary.

The political science departments at the University of Toronto, University of British Columbia, and University of Calgary, and Green College at UBC have provided me with stimulating environments in which to complete the research and writing of this book. Emma Cross, Lawna Hurl, and Tracey Raney have all provided able research assistance, and I could not have asked for a more helpful editor than Emily Andrew. I am grateful to Joanna Everitt, Lawrence Hanson, Janine Clark, Linda White, Steven Bernstein, Ben Cashore, Shaun Narine, Michelle Cloutier, Neil Thomlinson, Jeff Heynen, Ken Carty, Bill Cross, Joanne Fiske, and Karen Murray for their encouragement when I was writing and revising the book.

I owe a special debt of thanks to the members of my supervisory committee at the University of Toronto. It was a privilege to work under the supervision of Sylvia Bashevkin, who was a careful and encouraging reader. I am in debt to her and to Jill Vickers for pioneering the study of women in politics in Canada and nurturing a new generation of feminist political scientists. David Rayside generously took time away from his own pioneering efforts to be a challenging reader, who taught me a great deal about professional writing (and its attendant agonies). The intellectual passion and social commitment that Richard Simeon brought to the study of politics made it a tremendous privilege to be his student.

Finally, I am grateful to my husband, Mike Griffin, for his encouragement while I revised this book and to my parents, Audrey and Dave Young, for their patient support and encouragement through this very long process.

Feminists and Party Politics

Introduction

The contemporary women's movement has transformed North American society. Change has been greatest in the realm of everyday life, but the insistence by feminists that "the personal is political" has challenged the substance and practice of politics. This book examines one aspect of the contemporary women's movement: the effort to bring feminism into the formal political arena through established political parties. Because parties occupy a central and privileged position in representative government, a study of parties' responses to feminism offers us the most direct means of understanding whether electoral democracy is open to reform by feminists.

There is nothing new about women's involvement in party politics. For years, ladies' auxiliaries performed many of the day-to-day tasks that sustained political machines. It was the mobilization of the contemporary women's movement in the late 1960s and early 1970s that gave women's participation in party politics a new context, however. Radical new ideas about women's place in society and in politics found their way from consciousness-raising groups and the feminist press into the formal political arena as women called on political parties to accept women as equal participants and to adopt new policies regarding women's equality, reproductive freedom, and child care.

This book examines the feminist effort to transform political parties in the United States and Canada from 1970 until 1997. Two major sets of questions structure this inquiry. First, how have organizations in the women's movement approached partisan and electoral politics? To what extent have they tried to change parties? Have they focused their attention on one party, or tried to influence all the major parties? What factors have shaped the approaches taken by these organizations?

Second, how have political parties responded to the mobilization of feminism? Have political parties taken steps to include women in elite cadres? Have they adopted as their own any of the policy stances advocated by organizations in the women's movement? Alternatively, have any of the political parties come to define themselves in opposition to feminism? Has the party system polarized in response to the women's movement? What factors have shaped parties' responses?

Can Feminists Transform Party Politics?

Before going on to consider these questions, we must consider a more fundamental issue: Can feminist activists reasonably expect to transform political party politics? Are political parties merely male-dominated, and thus transformable by women, or are they inherently patriarchal? Does feminist participation in the formal political arena hold the potential for changing the arena or its symbolic and policy outputs?

Feminist theorists, researchers, and activists are divided on these questions. The liberal feminist view holds that women can reform political institutions, and that integration of women into these institutions is an essential component of a campaign for political and social change. This view has spawned an extensive literature cataloguing barriers to women's entry into formal political institutions.[1] More recently, scholars working in this tradition have focused on evidence that women's participation in formal political arenas is distinctive from men's in both style and substance and thus holds a transformative potential.[2]

The liberal feminist view rests on two key underpinnings. First, it conceives of the state as a potential ally for feminists. Retaining the liberal focus on the individual and understanding political power in conventional terms, the liberal feminist project has zeroed in on ending gender-based discrimination, and putting women on an equal footing with men in all realms of social, economic, and political life. In this view, the state is not inherently patriarchal, but rather a neutral arbiter or potentially principled agency that could be deployed on behalf of women (Allen 1990, 29). As Vickers (1980, 67) notes, liberal feminists "believe that while the character of state power ... will be changed when men share power with women, they tend to view as utopian and counter-productive the insistence of other feminists that the very existence of state power and of hierarchical power relationships involving dominance must be questioned and challenged." Seeing the state and other political institutions as male-dominated rather than inherently patriarchal, liberal feminism can conceive of the potential for women's participation to transform them.

This notion illuminates the second assumption underlying the liberal feminist view: that the categories "woman" and "feminist" are substantially overlapping. Much of the research examining the extent to which women in the public or in political elites hold feminist views has been conducted in the hope of finding women to be feminists.[3] To a certain extent, this has proven to be the case. Ultimately, however, efforts to equate women and feminism have foundered on the presence of anti-feminist and non-feminist women, and the problem of the irreducibility of women's interests into one single gender-based interest.

The alternative school of thought is grounded primarily in radical and postmodernist feminism and has proponents within socialist feminism.[4] This approach characterizes formal political institutions not as male-dominated but as inherently patriarchal. The richest body of literature in this regard deals with the nature of the modern state. Historian Gerda Lerner (1986) argues that men appropriated women's sexual and reproductive capacity prior to the formation of private property and class society; the archaic states were then organized in the form of patriarchy. From its inception, the state had an essential interest in the maintenance of the patriarchal family and attendant social organization. Similarly, in her construction of a radical feminist theory of the state, Catharine MacKinnon (1989) argues that the rule of law and the rule of men are one thing, indivisible. The liberal state coercively and authoritatively constitutes the interest of men as a gender through its legitimating norms and policies. The state is therefore crucial to the maintenance of the patriarchal system and, consequently, inherently and inevitably patriarchal itself.

Radical feminist theorizing has not addressed the character of political parties in as much detail as it has the state, but certainly the logic that rejects the modern state as inherently patriarchal can be applied equally to political parties. Just as the state serves the interests of men, political parties allow different factions of men to exercise partial control over some state functions. A coherent radical feminist critique of mainstream political parties is offered by Lise Gotell and Janine Brodie, who argue that mainstream political parties can avoid and have avoided hard programmatic commitments to the women's movement by recruiting highly visible and like-minded women (Gotell and Brodie 1991).[5] The recruitment of these women cannot translate into changes in public policy because political parties, particularly those pursuing policy agendas inspired by neoconservatism, are unwilling to address the structural sources of women's oppression.

At the heart of this debate among feminists lies the question of political elites. Are elites inevitable, and is the integration of women into political elites a worthy project for feminists? Certainly, some feminists would argue the very notion of a political elite is antithetical to feminism because of the hierarchy it implies. Elites, by definition, dominate non-elites, and this exercise of "power over" others represents precisely the kind of oppressive force that feminism seeks to eliminate. An alternative feminist understanding of the question is offered by Anna Jonasdottir (1988, 57), who argues that women share at least one objective interest: they require a political presence. By identifying political representation of women as a common interest, Jonasdottir implicitly argues that the formation of a feminist, or at least female, elite is an essential function of the women's movement.

If the formation of new elites, or the "circulation" into positions of power of a female elite, is in fact an integral part of the feminist political project, then political parties are a logical focus for activism. One of the primary functions of political parties is the recruitment of new elites. Moreover, as Duverger (1954, 426) observes, the distinctive contribution of political parties to democratic practice in Western Europe is that they provided the necessary framework for the emergence of an elite "sprung from" the working class. Baer and Bositis (1988, 89) echo this, arguing that parties promote democracy by encouraging the development of new elites. In contemporary practice, this has meant elites "sprung from" other groups with a history of exclusion from political power, most notably women and ethnic minorities.

While accepting Duverger's argument that political parties serve democracy by facilitating the emergence of new elites, it is important to note his observations regarding the tendency towards psychological cohesion of political elites. Duverger (1954, 160) asserts that "the mentality of the leaders is never identical with that of the masses, even if the leaders are of the same social composition as the masses ... whatever may be their origins, leaders tend to draw closer together and constitute naturally a leader class."

On this point, Duverger echoes Michels's ([1915] 1962, 182) observation that elite cadres within political parties seldom "circulate" in the sense that one group entirely replaces another. Rather, there is a "reunion" of elites in which new members are integrating into the elite cadre and mute their difference with the older elite in an effort to retain their elevated position.

These observations speak to what radical feminists might call the danger of co-optation for women who assume positions of power in party politics. As will be discussed in this book, feminist activism in North American political parties was initially motivated by a desire to further a policy agenda, but over time policy has faded in importance while the drive to promote women has gained momentum. Women are not immune to the organizational imperatives and psychological tendencies that produce cohesion within political elite cadres, so it should come as no great surprise that the more contentious aspect of the feminist project inside the political parties – the pursuit of a feminist policy agenda – has been muted, while the less threatening calls for equal opportunity in the promotion of women within party elites have gained currency.

Logic of Comparison

The methodological approach employed in this study is comparative. The first dimension is comparison over time. The research spans the period from 1970, when Canadian and US women's movements began to organize in the formal political arena, to 1997. Over this period, both the orientations of the organizations within the feminist movement towards political parties and the parties' responses to feminism have evolved. By tracing these variations over a period of twenty-seven years, it is possible to identify and explain the moments when organizations in the women's movement and political parties were in close alliance and when any such alliances broke down.

The second dimension of comparison is cross-national. As liberal democracies with federal systems, constitutional guarantees of rights, single-member plurality electoral systems, small numbers of political parties, and relatively fixed party systems, Canada and the United States demonstrate many of the contextual similarities that facilitate close comparison. Moreover, the geographic proximity of the two countries and the extensive, if overwhelmingly unidirectional, communications links connecting them have fostered a degree of convergence in their politics. Although contextually similar and tending towards convergence, there remain significant differences between the two countries that justify a comparative project. Canadian federalism, for instance, is far more decentralized than its American counterpart, and because of the unique character of Quebec it is becoming asymmetrical in its arrangements. Moreover, the Canadian party system is less fixed than its American counterpart.

Women's Movements

Because of their complex array of similarities and differences, the US and Canadian women's movements invite comparison. Situating the two movements within the broader universe of feminist movements in advanced industrialized countries, we find the two North American movements more similar to one another than to any other national movements. In part, the similarity of the two movements can be traced to their common origins. Both began to emerge (or in some respects re-emerge) in the mid-1960s and were products of similar sets of forces, including greater access to higher education, the radical student movements of the era, and a growing resistance to the strictly enforced gender roles of the postwar era. Compounding the movements' similar origins, the influence of US feminism on Canada has fostered convergence. American women's movement politics have been played out through the mass media and the publication of mass-market books, both of which are readily accessible to Canadian women. The most significant similarity between the two movements has been the liberal feminist ideology that was dominant in both movements through the 1970s and early 1980s (Vickers et al. 1993, 31-51). Liberal feminism has remained dominant in the United States, but has coexisted with socialist feminism as prevailing ideological tendencies in the Canadian movement since the mid-1980s.

While we can acknowledge these similarities, closer comparison nonetheless yields a rich array of differences between the two movements. Unlike its US counterpart, the Canadian women's movement has always included a strong socialist feminist element. Socialist feminism was nurtured in the New Democratic party in the early 1970s, and has subsequently grown to be a dominant ideological tendency in the Canadian movement. The US women's movement, with its roots in the new left and anti-war protests, includes an anti-statist element absent from the Canadian movement.

The two movements are also very different in their organizational forms. The major national movement organization in the United States is the National Organization for Women (NOW), which is a membership-based group with state and local chapters. In Canada, there is no major membership-based women's organization at the federal level. Rather, the largest and most prominent pan-Canadian organization is the National Action Committee for the Status of Women (NAC), an umbrella organization made up of member groups.

Researching and comparing social movements is not a simple task. Social movements are amorphous, heterogeneous entities that encompass divergent ideological tendencies and strategic orientations and consequently defy easy generalizations. The task for research is to identify different strategic tendencies within each movement and to examine their relative strength. While recognizing that women's movements are more than the sum of their organizational parts, the primary focus in this book is major organizations at the federal level – NOW in the United States and NAC in Canada. These groups play a crucial role in defining the partisan meaning of the women's movement, and provide critical cues to adherents throughout the movement (Dalton 1994). A secondary focus of research is those women's movement organizations in both countries that are focused primarily on partisan and electoral politics. These include the National Women's Political Caucus (NWPC) and various women's political action committees (PACs) in the United States, and Women for Political Action (WPA) and the Committee for '94 in Canada. The accounts of the orientations of women's movement organizations towards partisan and electoral politics are based on documents from movement organizations, open-ended interviews with movement leaders, and secondary accounts.[6] In the American case, the activity of women's political action committees was documented using contribution records filed at the Federal Election Commission.

Because the focus of this research is major national-level women's organizations and groups focused primarily on electoral and partisan politics, the full diversity of the Canadian and US women's movements is not captured in this book. This is a necessary, albeit regrettable, aspect of the research design being employed. Of particular note are silences regarding visible minority women in both countries and African American women in the United States and Québécois feminists in Canada.[7] An additional consequence of this research design is that it limits the study of partisan responsiveness to the national, as opposed to sub-national, level.[8] There is considerable scope for further research in this respect in both countries.

Political Parties

In addition to allowing Canada-United States comparisons, a two-country/five-party (and later, seven-party) design employed in this research facilitates comparisons between political parties. The parties considered in this study – in the United States the Democratic and Republican parties and in Canada the New Democratic, Liberal, and Progressive Conservative parties, later joined by the Reform party and by the Bloc Québécois – differ in their internal organization, ideological predispositions, electoral success, internal cultures, and historical relationships with outside groups. These variations make it possible to determine whether cross-national differences have a greater effect than do cross-party differences. This in turn sheds light on the factors that affect the movement-party relationship.

The accounts of the five parties' responses to the mobilization of the women's movement are based on party documents[9] and secondary analyses of party convention survey data,[10] supplemented by interviews with partisan activists. In the accounts of party responsiveness to feminism, considerable emphasis is placed on the initial mobilization of the feminist movement in the early 1970s, as this period was crucial to establishing the pattern of relations that would persist throughout the period of study.

Overview

Chapter 1 lays out the theoretical framework for the book. Social movement theory structures the analysis of the approaches of the women's movements to party politics in the two countries. This analysis relies on the concept of a political opportunity structure that shapes social movement activity. In this conceptualization, the crucial determinants of movement behaviour are external to the movement, and include political institutions, alliances, and arrangements. Emphasis is placed on changes in opportunity structures, as political alliances shift or as new resources become available.

To understand how political parties in the two countries have responded to the mobilization of feminism, party theory is employed. The chapter reviews four approaches to the study of parties – ideological, competitive, organizational, and cultural – and suggests that all four may contribute to an explanation of diverging partisan responses to the mobilization of feminism.

Chapters 2 and 3 trace the involvement of American and Canadian women's movements in electoral politics from 1970 to the present. The US women's movement became involved in electoral politics in the early 1970s, and the degree of that involvement has increased over time. Since 1980, women's movement organizations have entered into partisan alliances with the Democratic party. They have, in fact, become an important internal constituency within that party. The Canadian women's movement was initially enthusiastic about engaging with the formal political process, but that enthusiasm waned in the mid-1980s. Although closer to the NDP than the other parties, the women's movement in Canada has never formed partisan alliances. From the mid-1980s on, it has grown sceptical of parties and allowed its ties to the established parties to erode.

In Chapters 4 and 5, the responses of US and Canadian parties to the mobilization of feminism are examined. Once again, there are significant differences between the two cases. American parties polarized in response to feminism, while Canadian parties (until 1993) responded with moderate endorsement of a liberal feminist policy agenda. In both countries, political parties have been more receptive to inclusion of women in political elites than to the feminist policy agenda.

Chapter 6 returns to the question of whether feminists can transform party politics. The evidence from the United States and Canada suggests that the responses of political parties to feminism are shaped by party ideology, anticipated electoral benefit, internal party policies, and the strategies pursued by movement organizations. In this sense, political parties are not inherently hostile to feminism. Rather, political parties are most open to change when it appears to promise electoral benefit. Organizations in the women's movement are most able to influence political parties when they are able to offer crucial resources – either money or votes – to the parties. Although the effort of North American feminists to transform political parties over the past thirty years cannot be judged entirely a success, it has not been a failure. By bringing women into the formal political arena on something beginning to approach an equal footing, feminists have begun to realize liberal democracy's promise of equal citizenship for women.

1
Theorizing Feminist Strategy and Party Responsiveness

The focus of this book is on the responses of political parties to the contemporary women's movement. Not all women are feminists, and many women involved in partisan politics would object to the idea that their political involvement is best understood as related to feminist efforts to reform political parties. Nonetheless, changes in the role of women inside political parties coincided with the rise of modern feminism, so it is reasonable to frame this discussion in that context.

This raises a crucial question: to what extent have feminist organizations in the United States and Canada engaged with political parties? If we are to understand parties' responses to feminism, we must first come to grips with the stimulus to which they are responding. The emphasis that women's movement organizations place on electoral politics, the movement's partisan orientation, and the character and intensity of ties between movement and party organizations may all affect partisan responses to feminism.

"New" social movement theory tells us that women's movements will eschew ties with political parties and other elements of formal politics. The primarily West European proponents of this approach argue that environmental, peace, and women's movements that have emerged since the "hot summer" of 1968 are qualitatively new phenomena that can be distinguished from earlier social movements in several ways.[1] First, they are ideologically distinct, advocating a new, "postmaterial" social paradigm. This leads to an emphasis on cultural and "quality of life" issues rather than issues of material well-being. According to Melucci (1989), submerged networks of movement activists act as cultural laboratories where new social meanings and relations are developed. Unlike the well-developed political program of earlier movements, the new movements lack a comprehensive vision or institutional design for a new society (Offe 1990, 234). Melucci characterizes new social movement activists as "nomads of the present" wandering the terrain of the social order and offering tentative alternatives within its framework. In this view, the construction of a collective identity is the most central task of new social movements. This construction is a negotiated process in which the "we" involved in collective action is elaborated and given meaning (Melucci 1989; Gamson 1992).

Second, these theorists insist that the new movements are primarily social, as opposed to political, in character. They are located mainly within civil society and tend to bypass the state and the institutions of formal politics. Finally, the new movements privilege means over ends, or more accurately understand "means" to be ends in and of themselves.[2] In other words, these new movements will privilege the ideological purity of the strategy over the outcome. These latter assertions – that new social movements are primarily social in character, privilege means over ends, and reject old-style politics – imply that movements will eschew ties with political parties and other elements of formal politics regardless of the potential benefit of such ties.

Even the most cursory reading of the history of North American women's movements tells us that social movement theory does not accurately predict movement behaviour. Feminist groups in both the United States and Canada have, to varying degrees, advocated the election of women and engaged with established parties in efforts to further a feminist policy agenda. To understand how and why women's movement organizations are sometimes drawn into the partisan political arena, a political opportunity structure approach proves helpful. In contrast to the new social movement literature that sees movement orientations as endogenously determined, the opportunity structure literature looks to exogenous factors to explain movement-party interaction. These exogenous variables make up the "political opportunity structure" – the set of constraints and opportunities that discourage or encourage movement behaviours and lead movements to favour certain forms of collective action over others (Tarrow 1989, 32). In contrast to new social movement theory, which presents activists as driven by ideological predisposition, an opportunity structure approach portrays activists as strategic actors making pragmatic choices in the face of fixed and semi-fixed structures.

Tarrow (1994) developed the concept of the political opportunity structure to explain why some societal groups mobilize to become social movements while others do not. He argues that resources external to the group – political opportunities – translate the potential for movement into mobilization. The crucial determinant, then, is the political opportunity structure, which refers to "consistent – but not necessarily formal, permanent, or national – dimensions of the political environment that either encourage or discourage people from using collective action" (ibid., 17). Tarrow emphasizes the importance of changes in opportunity structures, in particular the opening up of access to participation, shifts and instability in ruling alignments, the availability of influential allies, and cleavages among elites (ibid., 86-9). When these four factors work in combination, windows of opportunity open, even for resource-poor challengers. Although Tarrow's emphasis is on changes in opportunities, he also notes that stable institutional structures affect movement formation and strategy. This latter observation takes into account a growing body of empirical work emphasizing the role that institutions play in shaping movement characteristics and strategies (Katzenstein and Mueller 1987).

Although originally developed to explain movement mobilization, the political opportunity structure approach is also helpful in understanding what strategies movement organizations adopt once they have mobilized. Tarrow's approach constitutes a framework for analysis, rather than a theory. It asserts that external factors, including but not limited to institutional arrangements, shape movement behaviours. It does not, however, specify which external factors are important. This flexibility makes the political opportunity structure framework attractive, as it does not dictate the causal factors but rather forces us to consider which external factors are likely to shape movement outcomes and to weigh the evidence supporting these claims. Similarly, this framework does not predict what specific outcomes will result from a given institutional arrangement. For example, researchers using the framework have generated contradictory hypotheses regarding the rational movement response to different party systems. Costain and Costain (1987) and Tarrow (1989) contend that movement organizations are unlikely to ally with weak, unprincipled American political parties and will choose instead to pursue an interest group strategy. Garner and Zald (1985, 138) suggest, however, that when political parties are undisciplined, ideologically non-cohesive congeries of interest groups, movements will try to become interest groups within a party, possibly allowing the movement to influence party stands and national policy without making untenable compromises.

Elements of the Political Opportunity Structure

The least variable elements of the political opportunity structure are macro-level institutional arrangements, including (for the purpose of this study, at least) legislative systems, the legal environment, and electoral systems. These in turn shape the somewhat more variable political arrangements, including party systems and characteristics of parties. The most variable elements of the opportunity structure are the fluid moments of opportunity that arise spontaneously or can be created by actors in the movement.

Institutional Arrangements

Although both the United States and Canada are federal systems governed by liberal democratic regimes based on the rule of law, their macro-level institutional arrangements vary considerably. First, the two countries employ vastly different legislative arrangements. The US congressional system reflects the deliberate efforts of its founders to design institutions that would represent the will of the people but be limited in scope in order to prevent tyranny. The resulting institutional design is characterized by a fragmentation of power among institutions (most notably the presidency and Congress) and a set of institutional arrangements intended to check ambition with ambition. Thus, limited government and separated authority are fundamental values in the US system (Simeon and Willis 1997). The Canadian government is a parliamentary system of the Westminster variety. Its Parliament is bicameral, but the upper house is an appointed body with limited powers and substantially constrained political legitimacy. The principle of responsible government requires that the government maintain the support of a majority of members of the House of Commons on all significant votes, so party discipline in the House is strict (Franks 1987). There is no separation of powers, as the prime minister and members of the Cabinet hold seats in the House and are held accountable to the Commons on a daily basis. Power is consequently concentrated in the executive. Thus, concentrated authority, responsible government, and majority rule are fundamental guiding principles of the Canadian model of governance (Simeon and Willis 1997).

Because the courts under certain circumstances can offer an alternative political channel for equality-seeking groups, they are likely to represent part of the opportunity structure facing movement organizations. The courts were a fruitful route for US feminists in the 1970s because of the combination of an entrenched practice of judicial review with an activist, liberal-leaning Supreme Court. This resulted in several decisions favourable to the women's movement, most notably the landmark ruling in *Roe* v. *Wade*. With the election of Ronald Reagan to the presidency in 1980, however, the courts were gradually transformed into more conservative forces as Reagan, and after him George Bush, made a concerted effort to appoint judges with a conservative bent. In Canada, the adoption in 1982 of the Charter of Rights and Freedoms, entrenched in the Canadian Constitution, with explicit guarantees of gender equality, opened a new route for activists. Having won a highly visible battle over the wording of the equality provisions in it, many Canadian feminists had a sense of ownership of the Charter, and believed that judicial review of legislation held considerable promise (Razack 1991). Although this did yield some notable victories such as the *Morgentaler* decision (striking down the Criminal Code provisions regarding abortion), the early promise of the Charter has lost some of its appeal for Canadian feminists, particularly in light of several decisions that have championed the rights of the accused in cases concerning sexual assault.

Although both countries employ single-member plurality electoral systems, their specifics vary sufficiently to create different incentives for political parties and movements. The US electoral system is highly regulated, particularly by state governments. The internal workings of national parties are consequently determined in large part by state law. This is most clear in the legislated use of primary elections as a means for candidate selection in both presidential and congressional elections. By taking this function out of the hands of partisan activists, state regulation has made US political parties considerably less cohesive entities than they would otherwise be (McSweeney and Zvesper 1991). Moreover, the rules governing electoral financing serve to constrain the role political parties can play in assisting candidates (Alexander 1992). An extensive system of political action committees (PACs) has emerged, effectively making interest groups, including business, the primary sources of direct funding for candidates in congressional elections (ibid.). Because elections to the House of Representatives are biennial, there is a state of "permanent campaign" and all candidates, even incumbents, must devote considerable time and energy to fund-raising.

The Canadian electoral system, in contrast, fosters highly cohesive political parties. Even though political parties receive extensive public funding, there is virtually no public regulation of their candidate and leadership selection practices. Political parties have successfully resisted efforts to bring these contests under the aegis of the Canada Elections Act. The provision of extensive public funding for candidates and registered political parties through reimbursement of campaign expenses, as well as generous tax credits for political contributions, means that political parties are less reliant on outside interests for funding than they would otherwise be (Stanbury 1991). Finally, the Canada Elections Act invests considerable potential power in the hands of party leaders by requiring their signature for a candidate's nomination to be official. Although party leaders have been highly selective in their use of this power, it does give the national party an effective veto over the candidate nomination decision.

As single-member plurality systems, both the Canadian and American electoral systems present significant barriers to the entry of new parties. In addition, the regulatory regime surrounding electoral politics in the two countries arguably further heightens the barriers. In the US case, this refers mainly to the system of primaries and the institutionalization of the two-party system in voter registration, and in Canada to the extensive system of public financing of major registered parties (Katz and Mair 1995). The Canadian party system has periodically seen the emergence of regionally based political parties including the CCF-NDP, the Reform party, and the Bloc Québécois. Noting that a new political party must have a regional basis of support if it is to win seats serves to illuminate a barrier to entry that only feminist political parties would experience: such parties would presumably appeal mainly to women, and women tend not to live in geographic concentration (unlike members of ethnic groups who may congregate in neighbourhoods), so a women's political party is almost certainly a non-starter in a single-member plurality electoral system.[3]

Political Arrangements
The most fundamental difference between the Canadian and US party systems is the number of major parties. During the period covered by this study, the American system remained a stable two-party system protected from the emergence of new parties by the various institutional mechanisms discussed above. Although there is little scope for entry of new parties in congressional elections, independent candidates periodically make a strong showing in the presidential contests. The Canadian party system is somewhat more open to the entry of new parties, as demonstrated by the emergence of the CCF-NDP, and later the Reform party and Bloc Québécois. During most of the period of this study, however, the Canadian system was a stable system with three parties, two of which (the Liberals and Progressive Conservatives) rotated in and out of government and one (the NDP) maintained a strong position on the opposition benches. Because it was a party system in which two parties rotated in and out of office and the third remained a relatively minor force, the Canadian party system was best characterized as a two-and-a-half party system (Ware 1996, 161). Since 1993, the Canadian party system has changed profoundly. The 1993 and 1997 general elections have resulted in a multi-party system, with the governing Liberals holding a majority of the seats and the remaining seats divided among four opposition parties: the right-wing populist Reform party, the separatist Bloc Québécois, and the much-reduced Conservatives and NDP. The party system as it is currently emerging in Canada is highly regionalized, and at present the Liberals hold all but one of the seats in Ontario, and the two largest opposition parties in the House of Commons are based entirely in Western Canada (Reform) and in Quebec (the BQ).[4]

Party organizations in the two countries vary considerably. American national parties are essentially diffuse networks of activists and organizations with varying degrees of cohesion. Because of their unique characteristics, US political parties are not easily assimilated into comparative schema, so attempts to categorize them within comparative frameworks reflect this difficulty. Katz and Kolodny (1994, 24) advance the view that "from a structural perspective, American national parties are best understood as being two loose alliances, each consisting of three fundamentally independent organizations. From a more substantive perspective, each of the six organizations exhibits such a low degree of 'partyness' ... *that they do not, in fact, constitute national parties"* (emphasis added). Struggling to describe the same phenomenon in a way that would be meaningful to those more familiar with European political parties, Ware suggests that "the extremely loose connections between the different elements of the Democratic and Republican parties today, and especially the virtual autonomy of most candidates vis-à-vis party structures, mean that it is not a two-party system at all, but *a very complex multi-party system masquerading as two-partism"* (Ware 1996, 155, emphasis added). These disparate accounts demonstrate that US political parties are extremely loose coalitions, held together more by bonds of convenience or necessity than loyalty or shared ideological purpose. Several characteristics contribute to this American exceptionalism.

First, US political parties lack mass membership. Voters register as Democrats, Republicans, or Independents, but this has more in common with a statement of preference than with party membership as understood in other liberal democratic regimes. This absence of formal membership deprives US party organizations of discipline and resources (McSweeney and Zvesper 1991, 100). Party officials have no formal means for controlling entry into party activity, nor do they possess the means to control activists by revoking their membership.

Second, the national parties are confederal in origin and each unit of the party, down to the precinct level, possesses near autonomy.[5] Many state and local party organizations are creations of state law rather than party rules, so national party leaders cannot control them or threaten to disband them (ibid., 100). When combined with the absence of formal membership, this is an invitation for groups to capture party structures to further their goals. As the politics of patronage has fallen victim to regulation, party bosses no longer have selective benefits at their disposal to use as inducements to party loyalty.

Third, national and even local party organizations play only a limited role in election campaigns. The national party committees do not interfere in primary elections, so the national party has little control over which candidates will represent it in the general election. Because the resources the national parties can offer their candidates in the general election are restricted by the US Federal Election Campaign Act, candidates must develop extensive networks of campaign workers and must solicit financial contributions from other sources, which inevitably means PACs.

Groups that are able to supply human and financial resources are extremely important to candidates who can expect only limited support from their political party.

In terms of ideology, the regional, ethnic, religious, and political diversity of the American populace, when combined with a two-party system, has presented political parties with an imperative to build diverse coalitions that encompass cross-sections, rather than sections, of society (ibid., 11). This imperative has "often required in coalition managers a rhetorical tactfulness that can seem like willful blandness" (ibid.). Within US parties, distinct ideological factions can be identified. Within the Republican party, liberal Republicans were an identifiable faction for many years until they were all but forced out of the party by a new faction – Christian conservatives (see Rae 1989). Similarly, southern Democrats have been and continue to be a distinct right-of-centre faction among the Democrats (see Rae 1994).

In contrast to US parties, Canadian political parties are cohesive, disciplined organizations that are generally resistant to incursions by outside groups. They are membership-based, and only party members can participate in decisions concerning the party organization. Although the thresholds for such participation are low – a small membership fee and a brief waiting period between joining the party and being able to vote on delegate selection for leadership conventions or candidate nominations – there is little evidence to suggest that interest groups have successfully "captured" party organizations. The possible exception to this is Liberals for Life, an anti-abortion group that mobilized to nominate Liberal candidates in the 1988 and 1993 elections and that supported Tom Wappel's candidacy for the party's leadership in 1990.[6]

Moreover, national party organizations are able to exercise a considerable degree of control over local party activities. The Canada Elections Act requires that the party leader sign the nomination papers for all candidates running under the party's banner, effectively giving the leader veto power over candidate selection. The Liberal party in 1990 went so far as to give its leader the power to appoint candidates, and he used this power in both 1993 and 1997. To the extent that party nomination contests and leadership conventions are regulated, it is by the party itself rather than the state (as is the case in the United States).

In the Canadian case, the system of brokerage parties is even more fluid and pragmatic than its US counterpart. Unlike political parties in other industrialized democracies, which can rely on relatively stable patterns of support from defined social groups, Canadian brokerage parties must recreate their coalitions at each election, constantly competing for the same policy space and the same votes (Clarke et al. 1991, 9). Moreover, the absence of stable coalitions of voters means that "Canadian parties are most comfortable multiplying the number of politically relevant divisions" in the electorate. It follows from this that Canadian brokerage parties organize around leaders rather than principles and ideologies, and that a wide variety of conflicting and contradictory policy stances may coexist inside each brokerage party (ibid., 10).[7]

A final notable difference between the US and Canadian political party systems is the presence of a socialist party in Canada. Even though the New Democratic party espouses a very moderate democratic socialism (relative to socialist parties in Western Europe), the presence of the CCF-NDP in the Canadian party system has served periodically to shift politics in a leftward direction. As has been noted in an extensive body of literature dealing with American exceptionalism, the absence of a socialist party makes the US party system unique in comparative terms.

Windows of Opportunity

The final element of the opportunity structure model consists of windows of opportunity that open spontaneously or are created by movement mobilization. Tarrow (1989; 1994) suggests that collective action may shape political opportunity structures, essentially introducing a feedback loop into the model. It is conceivable that a movement might, through collective action, shape political institutions, thereby altering an otherwise relatively stable element of the political opportunity structure. It is more likely, however, that movement actions will shape the less fixed political elements of the structure. For example, the decision of Icelandic feminist women to form their own political party changed the Icelandic party system, thereby altering the array of political alternatives available to feminist women in that country. Collective action by one group can also present opportunities for other groups. For example, civil rights and anti-war activism within the American Democratic party in the late 1960s created opportunities for feminist activism in the party in the early 1970s. By the same token, collective action can create opportunities for a movement's opponents. One might argue that the activism of feminist women within the Democratic party in the 1970s may have created opportunities for anti-feminists within the Republican party in the 1980s.

Categorizing Movement Strategy

When characterizing the orientation of a movement towards political parties and the electoral system, two dimensions require examination: the importance of electoral or partisan activities relative to other movement undertakings, and the movement's choice among partisan, multipartisan, and apartisan orientations.

Social movements vary in the emphasis they place on political parties and electoral politics relative to other priorities. If partisan and electoral strategies are a regular element of movement activity over an extended period, and consume significant financial and human resources, then they can be considered core activities of the movement. If, however, the movement only expends effort and resources on these activities sporadically, and if the resources expended are minimal, then these activities can be considered peripheral activities of the movement.

The second dimension of a movement's orientation involves its stance towards the political party system. A movement that adopts a *partisan* stance enters into some form of exclusive relationship with one established political party. In its most regularized form this would entail a formal relationship between one or more major movement organizations and a particular political party such as that between unions and the British Labour party. Less institutionalized manifestations of a partisan stance would include movement organizations endorsing a party in elections, significant informal contact between movement leaders and party officials, financial support exclusively for the party and/or its candidates, movement involvement in internal party affairs, and organized efforts for movement adherents to become active in the party. To say that the movement has become partisan, it would be necessary to see evidence of several of these indicators over time.

A movement that is *multipartisan* in orientation engages with more than one political party. In this case, movement organizations avoid endorsing a single party and their leaders have meaningful contact with more than one party. If financial support is offered, it is divided among the parties. Movement organizations that are multipartisan may act like interest groups during elections, engaging in such activities as rating party platforms and staging debates on key issues.

A movement that is not engaged with political parties in any way can be termed *apartisan*. A distinction must be made, however, between movements or groups that are apartisan because they are apolitical, and politicized movements that have chosen not to engage with parties. Politicized apartisan movements may choose to form their own political parties to compete with other parties, or they may choose to work outside the electoral arena to achieve social change. Clearly, these are very different kinds of behaviours, yet they share an aversion to working within the confines of the existing political parties.

Party Responses

There are limits to what party theory can tell us about the responsiveness of political parties to women's movements. Few party scholars have considered the mobilization of contemporary feminism as a significant event for political parties, so the literature has not addressed the question explicitly. Moreover, most accounts of women's involvement in party politics have documented the participation of women in party affairs as individuals, rather than looking to the relationship between the feminist movement and the partisan involvement of women's organizations.[8] Although a fairly substantial body of literature deals with the "organic" or formal ties between labour unions and social democratic parties, it is of limited applicability to the informal ties between new social movements and political parties. Despite these limitations, a review of four approaches to the study of political parties provides the theoretical tools necessary to explain party responsiveness. None of these theoretical approaches is likely to offer a complete explanation for the pattern of party responsiveness to the women's movement. Rather, the explanation is likely to be found in some interaction of ideological, organizational, and competitive factors. A model of partisan responsiveness combining these three approaches is developed in Chapter 6.

Party Ideology

This approach understands political parties primarily as ideological in purpose or, more precisely, as the organizational forms that transmit coherent sets of ideas into the political sphere. A purely ideological explanation of party responsiveness to the women's movement would hold that partisan responsiveness is determined by the ideological congruence between movement and party.

In the North American context, the idea that political parties are ideological entities is not widely held. Most observers characterize Canadian and American political parties not as ideological, but as "brokers" that canvass and delineate the various interests of the electorate in the process of coalition-building (Clarke et al. 1991, 9). Despite strong evidence that North American political parties are brokers rather than ideologues, some researchers contend that the ideological elements of political parties must be taken into account.[9] In the US case, some argue that American political parties are "advocacy parties" whose activists are "true believers" motivated by ideological concerns (Kessel 1980; Bruce et al. 1991). In recent years, moreover, several observers have noted a trend through which US political parties have become more ideologically distinct from one another (Miller and Jennings 1986; Rae 1989). Writing about Canada prior to 1993, Christian and Campbell (1989) argue that the three major political parties were ideologically distinct, and that ideological debates among parties suffused Canadian political life.

Even accepting that North American political parties are brokers, it is evident that they can be distinguished from one another in terms of ideological tendencies if nothing else. The US Republican party, the Canadian Progressive Conservative party, and more recently the Canadian Reform party have occupied the right of the political spectrum. Through the 1980s, the Republican and Progressive Conservative parties shifted towards the right, but the Republicans under Reagan were generally neo-conservative (implying a social conservatism), while the PCs under Mulroney were predominantly neo-liberal (focusing on economic liberalization).[10] The Reform party is to the right of the Progressive Conservative party and espouses both fiscal and social conservatism. The Democrats and the Liberals occupy the centre of the political spectrum. Arguably, since the 1970s they have drifted rightward. The NDP clearly occupies the left of the political spectrum.[11] The sovereigntist Bloc Québécois is difficult to place on a left-right continuum, as it is above all else dedicated to Quebec nationalism.

Party Competition

Rational choice and neo-institutionalist approaches emphasize the competitive aspect of political parties.[12] These approaches characterize parties as vote maximizers that privilege the goal of winning elections above all else. In the words of Anthony Downs (1957, 28), "Parties formulate policies in order to win elections rather than win elections in order to formulate policies." In other words, the policy stances of political parties are best understood as means to electoral success, not as statements of deep-rooted belief.

It is unclear whether the logic of party competition would cause political parties to polarize around issues raised by the women's movement or to converge in a competition for the median voter, found at the centre of the political spectrum. Rational choice theory implies that this would depend on the distribution of public attitudes on these issues. If public attitudes were distributed normally (a bell curve), there would be policy convergence towards the median voter, but if attitudes were distributed bimodally, there would be a polarization of political parties.

A difficulty with the rational choice approach is that it sees parties as unitary rational actors, not as complex organizations within which individuals pursue different, and sometimes competing, agendas. Party leaders who accept the overarching objective of vote maximization will probably behave essentially as the theory predicts. A closer examination of internal party politics suggests, however, that not all partisan activists have simple loyalties, and organizations are not always able to behave in such a way as to maximize electoral benefit.

In an effort to come to terms with the limits of the rational choice approach, Tsebelis (1990) developed the idea of "nested games" – games involving conflict between different actors that are occurring within other games. Applying this to the study of political parties, he shows that British Labour activists who appear to be following a wholly irrational (in Downsian terms) strategy of replacing their MPs, thereby contributing to the party's defeat, are in fact behaving rationally because in the long run these actions enable the activists to create a reputation for toughness which means their views are later taken more seriously (Ware 1996, 328). Clearly, the concept of nested games is useful for understanding the actions of feminist activists within political parties, not least because it challenges the conception of political parties as coherent and homogeneous strategic players.

Party Organization
Organizational approaches look to the structural and organizational characteristics of political parties to explain their behaviour. An organizational approach would hold that the responsiveness of partisans to the mobilization of the women's movement is determined primarily by the organizational attributes of the party. The two organizational elements that are most relevant to this study are the party's permeability to outside interests and its internal cohesion. American political parties have no formal membership, operate in the context of publicly regulated primary elections, and have only loose organizational forms. Consequently, they are highly permeable to outside interests. In part because they are so open to a myriad of outside interests and because they operate in a political system that does not require disciplined legislative caucuses, US political parties have tended to be ideologically diverse coalitions encompassing distinct factions (Rae 1989; 1994). Canadian political parties, in contrast to this, are considerably less permeable to outside interests, as they have more coherent organizational forms and exert centralized control over most party functions. Moreover, operating in a parliamentary system that requires disciplined parties and that has made party loyalty a virtue, Canadian political parties are relatively coherent entities within which distinct factions are seldom tolerated.[13]

These differences suggest that both American political parties might be more open to feminist engagement than their Canadian counterparts. As will be seen in Chapters 4 and 5, however, this has not proven to be the case. The Republicans easily repelled the tentative overtures from the women's movement in 1972 (see Freeman 1987; Melich 1996), while the Democrats did not. It might be possible to explain this with reference to organizational differences between the two parties. The organizations that constitute the Republican party at the national level have retained far greater vitality than those of the Democrats (Ware 1996, 123; Aldrich 1995, 257; Katz and Kolodny 1994). The Republican party is financially healthier, and this has allowed party organizations to play a greater role in the recruitment of candidates and coordination of campaigns than has been the case for the Democrats. Nonetheless, the organizational differences between the two parties are not of sufficient magnitude to explain this difference. If the Republicans were so much stronger as an organization, then why would the party have succumbed to the extent that it has to the overtures of the Christian Coalition?[14] This contrast suggests that ideological goodness of fit, discussed above, also plays a part.

Party Culture

Within the literature dealing with US political parties, there is a small but growing school of thought that explains differences between the Democrats and the Republicans with reference to the distinct "cultures" of the two parties. This was pioneered by Jo Freeman (1987; 1994), who argues that the Democratic party's openness to feminism and the Republican party's hostility to it can be attributed to the distinct cultures of each party. The concept of party culture is similar to that of political culture as it encompasses the basic values and understandings of how decisions should be made. Using a similar approach, Klinkner (1994a; 1994b) argues that the Democratic party's focus on procedural matters stems, in large part, from a party culture that stresses inclusion and participation, while the Republican party's emphasis on organizational and managerial activities arises from a party culture that values the techniques and technologies of business enterprises.

Although Freeman and Klinkner have both produced rich, contextualized, and nuanced accounts of American party politics using a cultural approach, their accounts are not entirely convincing. Unpacking Freeman's concept of "party culture," it becomes clear that it is made up of both an organizational and a genuinely cultural element. The organizational aspect looks at the extent to which the political party is made up of constituencies that exist in organized form independent of the party.

The second element of Freeman's concept of party culture is more genuinely cultural. She notes that within the Democratic party, conflictual behaviour is an effective means of gaining some power for an internal constituency, whereas in the Republican party such tactics would be interpreted as evidence of disloyalty to party leaders. Extending this observation to a cross-national comparison, one can argue that the culture of Canadian political parties is more similar to that of the Republicans than the Democrats. Canadian political parties operate on norms of loyalty and muted internal conflict. These are important factors shaping party responses to social movements, though they can be traced back to the organizational imperatives for political parties working in two distinct political systems.

Party Responsiveness to Feminism

Party responsiveness to feminism is a two-dimensional concept. The first dimension, representational responsiveness, refers to both the numerical representation of women in partisan elites and the extent to which the party employs quotas or other representational guarantees for women. The second dimension is policy responsiveness, which includes the extent to which the party adopts or opposes the movement's policy agenda, as well as the attitudinal support for this agenda among partisan elites.

In gauging the two parties' policy responsiveness, the primary focus is on their responses to the original set of issues raised by the feminist movements of Canada and the United States in the early 1970s, namely, abortion, equal rights for women, and government-run child care programs. This does not reflect the diversity of the feminist agenda in the movement's early days, nor does it accurately reflect the scope of the current feminist agenda. Most significantly, it does not tap into feminist support for social welfare programs currently under attack. There are nonetheless two compelling reasons for focusing on this original set of issues. First, these issues constitute the unique contribution of the women's movement to the political agenda, as well as the issues most immediately associated with contemporary feminism. Second, these are the issues that, at least until recently, have formed the locus of conflict between feminists and the political establishment. For these reasons, it is justifiable to focus on the differences between the two political parties on these issues as a research question, although the broader matter of the relationship between neo-conservative economic policies and feminist agendas provides the backdrop for these comparisons.

Representational and policy responsiveness do not necessarily work in tandem. It is, for example, possible to conceive of a situation in which the political party is highly responsive in representational terms, but opposed to the women's movement's policy agenda. The pattern of possible responses is outlined in Table 1.1. A political party that is responsive to feminism will include women in partisan elites in significant numbers, may employ quotas or other measures guaranteeing women such

Table 1.1

Models of party responsiveness

	Responsive	Co-optive	Non-responsive	Oppositional
Representational	High or moderate	High or moderate	Low	Low
Policy	Positive	Negative	Neutral	Negative

representation, and will include significant elements of the movement's policy agenda in its platform. Conversely, a political party that makes little effort to include women in partisan elites and adopts stances in opposition to the women's movement can be understood to have an oppositional orientation. A low degree of representational responsiveness, when combined with a failure to respond to the movement's policy agenda in either a negative or positive manner, would suggest a non-responsive stance. If, however, a high degree of representational responsiveness is mixed with policy stances in direct opposition to those of the movement, then the pattern of party responsiveness is best understood as co-optation, as women are probably being included in partisan elites in an effort to mask or soften the party's stance on these issues.[15]

Theorizing Feminist Strategy and Party Responsiveness

Significant differences in institutional and political arrangements between Canada and the United States have the potential to shape the strategies of women's movement organizations in the two countries. Different basic institutional arrangements in the two countries affect the attractiveness of partisan engagement for political parties; the US two-party system offers a more constrained set of options than the Canadian multiparty system; the organizational characteristics of political parties in the two systems offer very different sets of incentives. Given these differences, it is reasonable to expect that the American and Canadian women's movements would adopt very different strategies. Moreover, changes in these arrangements, and in particular evolutions in the party system and party organization, may well cause change over time. It is to the strategies of the women's movements in the United States and Canada that we now turn.

2

Partisan Engagement: American Feminists and Party Politics

A defining characteristic of the contemporary American women's movement is the high priority it places on electoral and partisan politics. The absence of disagreement among major national women's organizations regarding the importance of electing women is, in comparative perspective, remarkable. When asked why the US movement was so interested in electoral politics, a woman active in national movement organizations for several years responded, "Well, what else is there?" a comment reflecting the centrality of an electoral strategy among national movement leaders (interview 02/23/95b). In fact, the American movement's commitment to an electoral strategy centred on electing women is unique among Anglo-American and Western European movements.

Like any social movement, the US women's movement has struggled with the question of strategy vis-à-vis the formal political sphere. The dilemmas experienced by the contemporary women's movement are in this regard remarkably similar to the choice the first wave of American feminists faced. Mobilized around the issue of suffrage for women, first-wave American feminists sought to open the electoral process to women's participation, at least as voters. Because it was closely linked to the progressive movement, however, the suffrage movement was influenced by the progressives' critique of the evils of "partyism" (Baer 1992). After winning the vote, some feminists sought to work for change inside the party system, while others resisted such action. American suffragist Carrie Chapman Catt declared in 1920 that "the only way to get things in this country is to find them on the inside of a political party ... You won't be so welcome there, but that is the place to be ... If you really want women's votes to count, make your way there" (in Ware 1987, 148). Other former suffragists disagreed. Anne Martin of Nevada, for example, argued that such a strategy would put women right where male political leaders wanted them: "Bound, gagged, divided and delivered to the Republican and Democratic parties" (ibid., 293).

The basic contours of the debate have not changed since the first-wave mobilization. The contemporary US women's movement has experienced a tension between feminists who advocate working for change by integrating women into established partisan elites and feminists who advocate eschewing mainstream politics in favour of strategies emphasizing social protest and cultural reform.[1] Since the early 1970s, the women's movement in the United States has devoted considerable resources to electoral and partisan politics, and particularly to the project of electing women to Congress. Over time, the emphasis of the movement's major national organizations on electoral politics has grown, and groups focused on electoral politics have become an integral and mainstream part of the women's movement. It should be noted that this account of the US women's movement is significantly different from that offered by Gelb (1989), who argues that the American movement is characterized by interest group lobbying rather than integration into political parties. This characterization ignores the complementary role that lobbying and electoral engagement (particularly through Political Action Committees) has taken for the American movement.

Various changes in the political opportunity structure from the 1960s on shaped the strategy of the women's movement vis-à-vis formal politics. Underlying this, however, were movement characteristics and fixed elements of the political opportunity structure that have facilitated or encouraged the movement's emphasis on electoral politics. Notably, ideology has played a role. The dominant, perhaps hegemonic, ideological strain in the American women's movement is liberal feminism. Although radical feminism is present in the US movement, it is not a strong force within major national women's organizations. Rather, radical feminists are more likely to be found in smaller local organizations, many of which concentrate on providing services, such as rape crisis centres and battered women's shelters. Liberal feminists are convinced that established institutions have a great capacity for evolution (Castro 1990, 49). A central component of the liberal feminist project is the integration of women into existing institutions, including political parties. Election of women to public office is a logical part of this project, both as an end in itself (equal opportunity for women in politics) and a means to an end (legislative implementation of the liberal feminist policy agenda). The ideological make-up of the women's movement in the United States does not offer a full explanation of its electoral strategy, however. Ideology cannot account for the steadily increasing focus of the US movement on electoral politics, as there is little evidence of ideological change within the movement between 1970 and 1993.

Fixed elements of the political opportunity structure have facilitated the women's movement's emphasis on electoral politics. First, the permeable character of American parties invited the movement's intervention in internal party affairs. Feminist organizations did not forge a new path into the internal politics of the Democrats, but rather they followed the path established by unions, civil rights activists, and even anti-war protesters who took their political activity inside the Democratic party. Second, certain aspects of the US congressional system encouraged the focus on electing women. Weak party discipline in Congress and the scope for individual representatives and senators to initiate legislation allowed women, once elected, to act as feminists. Compounding this, weak party discipline fosters transparency, allowing US feminists to gauge the extent to which the election of women did in fact further their policy agenda by examining the voting records on issues of importance to women.

Changes in political alliances and alignments have also affected the orientation of the women's movement. The internal politics of the Democratic party in the late 1960s and early 1970s created space for feminist activists to be drawn into the partisan political sphere. As the Republican party moved further to the right in the 1960s and then espoused a stern social conservatism in the 1980s, women's movement organizations were driven into the arms of the Democrats. The Republican party's shift to the right predates the mobilization of the women's movement. It began in 1964 with the nomination of Barry Goldwater as the party's presidential nominee. This wave of fiscally conservative, but socially libertarian, conservatism displaced established moderate Republicans, turning the party into a "virtually monolithic bastion of conservatism" (Miller and Jennings 1986, 12; Rae 1989, 5). A second wave of far more religiously motivated conservatism began in the 1970s and may not yet have crested. This social conservatism, espoused by evangelical Christians and pro-life activists, has transformed the Republican party into an anti-feminist political force inhospitable to even the most moderate liberal feminist. As a result, American feminists operating under the constraints of a fixed two-party system have had little alternative but to ally themselves with the Democrats.

Mobilization (1966-70)

The contemporary American women's movement has its roots in the cycle of protest that began in the early 1960s. A cycle of protest, according to Tarrow (1990, 253) is a "phase of heightened conflict and contention across the social system" involving a rapid diffusion of collective action, a quickened pace of innovation in the forms of contention, new or transformed collective action frames, and more intense interaction between challengers and authorities. The campaigns of civil disobedience in the streets and on university campuses, culminating in serious confrontations such as the riots outside the tumultuous 1968 Democratic National Convention and the Kent State shootings of 1970, certainly bear all the hallmarks of a cycle of protest. The "early riser" in the US cycle of protest in the 1960s was the civil rights movement, which began to challenge racial segregation laws and practices in southern states. Although the South was the locus of this activism, the movement attracted activists from northern states, thereby becoming national in scope. Later in the decade, the US government's military involvement in Vietnam and, more precisely, its use of the draft to recruit military personnel for its war effort, touched off massive protests on university campuses and elsewhere. From these roots blossomed a thriving social movement sector encompassing civil rights, anti-war, and new left groups.

One strand of contemporary US feminism has its roots directly in these overlapping social movements of the 1960s. Women involved in these movements experienced sexism from fellow activists and found their efforts to raise the issue were either trivialized or met with hostility. In response, activist women either replaced or supplemented their other involvements with feminist organizing (McGlen and O'Connor 1995, 11). Out of the movement sector emerged the "women's liberation" movement, composed initially of loose networks of consciousness-raising groups.

While younger women rebelled against sexism in the counterculture and applied the logic and ideologies of these radical movements to the condition of women, another stream of feminism was emerging out of the public sector and networks of mainstream women's organizations. In 1963, Betty Friedan's book *The Feminine Mystique* was published, and President Kennedy's Commission on the Status of Women reported. State commissions on the status of women were formed in all fifty states to issue reports on women's status. These developments laid the groundwork for the formation of the National Organization for Women (NOW) in 1966. Along with organizations like the Business and Professional Women's Clubs (BPW), American Association of University Women, and the Young Women's Christian Association (YWCA), NOW focused its attention on lobbying government for an end to discriminatory legislation and practice (Costain and Costain 1987, 198; Duerst-Lahti 1989).

Neither the radical nor the institutionalist strands of the emerging women's movement displayed any interest in parties or electoral politics in the mid-1960s. The radical or grass-roots stream focused its energies on protest actions, seeing political parties as barriers to change rather than a route to power. Consistent with its roots in the oppositional social movements of the era, the repertoire of collective action of the radical stream of the women's movement consisted mainly of the unconventional protest tactics that were a hallmark of the young radicals. For its part, the more moderate institutionalist stream concentrated on lobbying, particularly the executive branch (not a surprising focus given NOW's roots in the presidential and state commissions on the status of women, themselves initiated by the executive branch).

When it was formed, NOW was in the words of founder Betty Friedan "insistently non-political." By this, she meant the organization was not engaged in partisan politics. Its statement of purpose declared that "NOW will hold itself independent of any political party in order to mobilize the political power of all women and men intent on our goals" (in Friedan 1976, 91). This declaration of political autonomy did not mean that the organization planned to eschew electoral politics entirely. The statement also called on women to demand integration into political parties on an equal basis and envisaged the possibility of NOW becoming involved in mobilizing voters in support of women's equality (ibid.). In her first address as president of NOW, Friedan spoke about forming a "voting power bloc" and lobbying the platform committees of both parties to include women's rights issues in their policy platforms (ibid., 101). In the years immediately after it was founded, however, NOW did not develop relationships with either of the major political parties, nor did it involve itself significantly in electoral politics.

Different orientations towards established political structures were a source of conflict within NOW in its early years. As Castro (1990, 6) observes, "The philosophical positions were perhaps most clearly illustrated by Betty Friedan's statement that her goal was 'to get women into positions of power' and radical feminist Ti-Grace Atkinson's statement that she wanted 'to get rid of positions of power.'" Atkinson's statement is broadly reflective of the wholesale rejection by radical feminists of established political institutions and hierarchical relationships of power. For the radical stream of the movement, this stance appeared to rule out engagement with established political parties as a viable strategy.

Despite this apparent rejection of the strategy of working through political parties for social change, the Democratic party became a locus of activism in the late 1960s for most of the movements engaged in the cycle of protest. The party itself was profoundly divided during this era, with conservative southern Democrats who supported segregation in conflict with the more progressive bent of northern elements of the party. This division within the party presented an opportunity for activists. The civil rights movement had targeted the Democrats in 1964 with its "freedom summer" culminating in an effort to unseat the segregationist Mississippi delegation at the national convention that year. Anti-war and student movements brought their campaign to pull the United States out of Vietnam to the 1968 Democratic convention in Chicago, where their protests erupted into chaos in the streets. Even though most of the leadership of the peace caucus inside the Democratic party was male, many women involved in the anti-war movement were drawn into Democratic politics through George McGovern's campaign for the party's presidential nomination in 1968. This involvement paved the way for the entry of women activists into the party in the early 1970s (NWPC 1980, 22).

Politicization (1971-80)

By the early 1970s, the two streams of the women's movement were beginning to converge, largely under the auspices of NOW. Its momentum fuelled by considerable media attention in 1970, the movement united in a campaign for the Equal Rights Amendment (ERA). Despite this momentum, NOW president Betty Friedan (1976, 168) believed the movement had crested and would begin to decline if it did not become explicitly political, which is to say engaged in the partisan political arena. Friedan was by no means alone in her belief that the movement needed to enter the partisan political fray, as many activists had grown dissatisfied with their position as petitioners on the periphery of the political system (interview 07/02/95).

Before going on to discuss these events, however, it is important to locate the feminists' new-found interest in partisan politics in the context of social movement activity in the United States at the time. The divisions and shifting alliances within the Democratic party in the late 1960s drew activists into the party and made it a site of political contestation. In response to events at the 1968 convention, the Democrats embarked on a series of reforms designed to enhance internal democracy. This reform process created a window of opportunity for the newly mobilized movement to win a place for women inside the Democratic party. Although the growing involvement of feminist organizations in Democratic party politics can be understood as part of the broader strategy of social movements to use the party as a site of political contestation, feminist organizations departed from the other movements of the era by adopting an explicitly bipartisan approach and by establishing what would prove to be lasting ties with established partisans.

The first indication that the American women's movement was to become extensively involved in partisan and electoral politics was the founding of the National Women's Political Caucus (NWPC) in 1971. This represented a convergence of the two streams of the women's movement as well as feminists' growing interest in electoral politics. The bipartisan caucus brought together women already involved in Democratic and Republican party politics with feminist activists who sought to further their policy agenda by advocating the election and appointment of women, reforming party structures, and supporting feminist candidates across party lines (NWPC 1971).

Although the newly formed NWPC attracted a wide range of partisan and feminist activists, the growing interest in electoral politics was not uncontested. Robin Morgan's claim that "one more woman in the Congress is not going to change the basic lives of women" was representative of a minority view within the women's movement that saw the increasing emphasis on electoral politics as a potentially harmful distraction from the movement's more revolutionary mission. This is illustrated by Morgan's statement that she had "visions of women bleeding to death in the gutters while Betty Friedan has tea in the White House" (in Cohen 1988, 2). Morgan's rhetorical flourish notwithstanding, a French feminist historian has observed that the radical feminist critiques of the NWPC and the political engagement of liberal feminists were, from a non-American standpoint, "remarkable for their moderate tone" (Castro 1990, 121).

The idea of forming a feminist organization focused on electoral and partisan politics can be traced both to liberal feminist leader Betty Friedan and Democratic party activist Bella Abzug. Although the two women conceived of the idea more or less simultaneously, their visions for the caucus were not identical. Friedan envisioned an organization that would encompass women "representing all political elements" and extending beyond the membership of NOW or women's liberation groups to reach politically active women who had not yet identified themselves as feminist. In Friedan's view, the focus of the organization should be to unite women in caucuses within and across political lines to elect women and focus attention on women's issues (Friedan 1976, 168).

Abzug, along with Gloria Steinem and others, wanted to organize a coalition of the "outs" – the poor, Blacks, youth, women, and gays (Cohen 1988, 316). She believed the organization's primary objective should be to build a political movement of women for social change that would simultaneously help elect more women, minorities, and other underrepresented groups and build an electoral bloc strong enough to influence male politicians to support their programs (Abzug and Kelber 1984, 21). Abzug and her supporters explicitly rejected Friedan's conception of the caucus as supporting women for political office with fairly minimal guidelines, arguing that it would accomplish little to replace or supplement a White, male, middle-class elite with a White, female middle-class elite in the positions of power in the nation (Cohen 1988, 316).

The original character of the NWPC represented a compromise between the Friedan and Abzug camps. Delegates to the founding conference finally decided to form the NWPC in order "to help elect women and also men who declare themselves ready to fight for the needs and rights of women and all underrepresented groups" (in Cohen 1988, 318). The NWPC's statement of purpose pledged to oppose sexism, racism, institutional violence, and poverty through the election and appointment of women to political office, reform of political party structures to give women an equal voice in decision making and selection of candidates and support of women's issues and feminist candidates across party lines, and pledged to work in coalition with other oppressed groups (NWPC 1971).

During the 1972 primaries and elections, the two factions within the NWPC pursued different, and sometimes competing, strategies. Abzug's group immediately focused its attention on the internal structures of the Democratic and Republican parties in advance of the 1972 national conventions. It was successful in achieving significant guarantees of representation for women at the Democratic National Convention, but not at the Republican. At the Democratic convention, Abzug and her followers considered the nomination of a socially progressive candidate the highest priority, and supported George McGovern's ultimately successful bid for the Democratic presidential nomination. The Friedan camp, seeing the election of women as the primary objective of feminist activism, supported Shirley Chisholm's largely symbolic run for the same post. Abzug's faction controlled the NWPC, and refused to offer an endorsement of Chisholm's candidacy, causing Chisholm to resign from the caucus (Friedan 1976, 177). At the convention, Abzug and Gloria Steinem organized on behalf of Sissy Farenthold as the party's vice-presidential nominee. In the balloting, Farenthold placed second behind Thomas Eagleton, who was McGovern's vice-presidential choice. The activists who had put Farenthold's name forward considered this result to be an independent showing of women's political strength within the Democratic party (Abzug and Kelber 1984, 36).

Although the disagreements between Abzug and Friedan over the founding of the NWPC and its early actions can be interpreted partially as a rivalry between two strong-willed movement leaders, the substantive ideological and strategic differences between the two women should not be ignored. This tension between the project of electing women with a broad range of ideological positions and the project of mobilizing the women's movement as part of an ideologically coherent leftist-populist movement and a distinct constituency within Democratic politics became one of the persistent tensions within the women's movement in its dealings with the political process. There are both ideological and strategic elements to this conflict. In terms of ideology, Friedan's project of electing women with different political perspectives is reflective of the "circulation of elites" element of movement mobilization, which sees inherent value in placing women in positions of power, regardless of their politics.[2] In contrast to this, Abzug's efforts reflect an understanding of the women's movement as an ideologically coherent force that must distinguish between feminist and non-feminist women. This tension continues to manifest itself in debates within and between feminist organizations over the question of whether to support any woman over any man or any feminist running against a non-feminist of either sex.

In practical terms, Friedan's vision was clearly bipartisan, and involved less intensive links with either of the parties than Abzug's. The emphasis by Abzug on the "coalition of the outs" implied an effectively exclusive relationship with the Democratic party that would be more direct and intense than the relationship implicit in Friedan's notion. Abzug's strategy reflected her experience as a political operative: she saw little point in supporting the symbolic but futile candidacies that Friedan advocated. Instead, the Abzug faction chose to support a credible candidate – George McGovern – who appeared sympathetic to the women's movement and was the chosen candidate of the other progressive movements of the era.

The NWPC exercised a profound impact on the 1972 Democratic convention, winning representational guarantees for women within the party and securing the party's endorsement of much of the movement's policy agenda. The caucus was far less visible and effective at the 1972 Republican National Convention, where a small group of Republican women won approval of Rule 32, which established that state parties should endeavour to have equal representation for men and women in their delegations to future conventions. Unlike the gains made by Democratic women, this rule did not require gender parity among convention delegates.

While experiences at the 1972 conventions may have dampened the enthusiasm of the women involved, they did not abandon their efforts to influence the political parties from within and facilitate the participation of women at party conventions. The NWPC joined with the Black caucus in the Democratic party to oppose efforts to weaken the equal representation rules for convention delegates at a Democratic party mini-convention in 1974. This fight continued at the 1976 Democratic convention, where the NWPC's Democratic Task Force (DTF) and the women's caucus of the Democratic party formed a coalition to fight for language requiring equal division of delegate positions between men and women at future national conventions.[3] The coalition was unable to have its preferred language (requiring equal division) adopted, but compromised with President Jimmy Carter's organization to accept language that the party would "promote" equal division.

To the extent that Republican women were involved in the early feminist mobilization, it was in the movement's more moderate institutionalist stream. The formation of the NWPC in 1971 drew liberal Republican women into the women's movement. During the administration of

Richard Nixon, the idea of a feminist Republican was not nearly as problematic as it later became (interview 25/01/95). The NWPC's Republican Task Force (RTF) was formed in 1975 by Republican activists concerned that delegate gains for women would not be maintained at the 1976 convention. The RTF held a joint press conference with the Democratic Task Force (DTF) in May of 1976, attacking both parties' failure to approach gender parity among delegates. According to Feit (1979, 198), Republican women believed widespread press coverage made Republican state party chairmen balance delegations with more women. As a result, 31.5 percent of delegates to the 1976 Republican convention were women, a slight increase from 29.5 percent in 1972.

The NWPC's apparent success in working inside the two parties led the way for other organizations in the women's movement, and particularly NOW, to become involved inside the parties later in the decade (interview 02/02/95b). A pivotal year for NOW's involvement in electoral politics was 1975, in part because of an Internal Revenue Service (IRS) ruling that the organization could participate in electoral politics without losing its tax-exempt status, and also because NOW's national conference that year elected a national board oriented towards political engagement. From 1975 on, partisan and electoral engagement constituted a significant part of the organization's action repertoire (Barakso 1996).

At roughly the same time, changes in political rules taking the form of a new regulatory framework for political finance created the opportunity for the formation of women's political action committees (PACs), which later became significant parts of the infrastructure of the women's movement. Reforms to the US Federal Election Campaign Act in 1974 loosened restrictions on the formation of PACs, opening the door for them to proliferate. The act bans political contributions from organizations or corporations and allows only contributions from individuals, limited in size to $5,000 per candidate for each election. However, the law allows corporations, labour unions, and membership groups to create and fund the overhead expenses of PACs, which then solicit contributions from their members. The US legislation is substantially different from the Canadian, which limits the amount candidates and parties can spend but does not place limits on the source or the amount of contributions from individuals, corporations, and unions. The legislation also allows for the creation of "non-connected" PACs, which allow individuals to pool their contributions and pass them on to candidates. Since 1974, the total number of PACs registered with the Federal Elections Commission has expanded from just over 600 to almost 4,500 (see Alexander 1992).

Several feminist organizations formed PACs in the mid- to late-1970s. NOW formed its PAC in 1975 and Business and Professional Women

(BPW) followed in 1979. The NWPC formed two PACs: the Campaign Support Committee, which became active in the 1977-8 election cycle, and the Victory Fund, which became active in 1979-80. In addition to PACs formed by existing organizations, Democratic and Republican women activists created a non-connected PAC, the Women's Campaign Fund (WCF), in 1974. A bipartisan organization, the WCF funds only pro-choice women candidates. The WCF also contributes to candidates at the state level, and consequently it played a significant role in developing a pool of women who went on to run for national office. The resources commanded by these women's PACs in the 1970s were limited, so they exercised little influence. It was not until the early 1990s that the network of feminist PACs became powerful players in Washington.

The Reagan-Bush Era (1980-92)

From 1980 on, electoral and partisan politics became an increasingly central component of the political strategy of the American women's movement. An extensive network of organizations and political action committees emerged with the common purpose of electing more women. Moreover, feminist organizations continued to engage with the presidential parties, particularly the Democrats, in an effort to further their policy agenda.

Several factors combined to consolidate the growing emphasis in the women's movement on electoral politics and to shape the specifics of this strategy. At the macro-level, the characteristics of US political institutions fostered this. Specifically, the unsuccessful outcome of the campaign for the Equal Rights Amendment (ERA) left activists with a firm conviction that female legislators were their most reliable allies in the legislative sphere. Were it not for the transparency of legislative institutions and the limited party cohesion in legislatures, activists would not have been left with this lesson. At the meso-level, changes in control of political institutions, most notably the ascendance of the new religious right within the presidential wing of the Republican party and Reagan's subsequent capture of the presidency, had profound effects both on the strategy of the women's movement vis-à-vis political institutions and on the partisan orientation of the movement. Moreover, the erosion of the role of parties and candidate selection over this period created space for women's groups, among others, to step in and fill the candidate recruitment and support functions formerly the preserve of parties.

Electing Women to Congress

The campaign to ratify the Equal Rights Amendment preoccupied the US women's movement from the mid-1970s until 1982. The proposed constitutional amendment, which declared that "equality of rights under the law shall not be denied or abridged by the United States or any State on account of sex," won the necessary two-thirds support in the House of Representatives and Senate in 1972, thereby setting into motion the campaign for ratification, which required that thirty-eight state legislatures vote to ratify it. The state-by-state battle for ratification mobilized feminists across the country; it also prompted the formation of the first organized anti-feminist groups, most notably Phyllis Schlafly's STOP ERA. By the deadline for ratification in 1977, the amendment was three states short of ratification, and three other states had rescinded earlier ratification. In an unprecedented move, Congress voted to extend the deadline for ratification to 1982, but the campaign remained three states short.

A by-product of the intense ERA lobbying effort at the state level was a belief among activists that the election of women was essential if the movement was to achieve its policy objectives (interviews 02/02/95; 02/07/95; Carabillo et al. 1993, 103; Smeal 1984, 93-4). Activists had found the small band of women in state legislatures at the time more reliable allies than their male counterparts, even those who were supportive of the movement's objectives (interview 02/02/95). Moreover, this perception that women legislators were more committed to women's issues was supported by an emerging body of academic literature of which many movement leaders were aware.

Compounding the lessons learned during the battle for the ERA, the ascendance of the new right within the Republican party and the subsequent election of Ronald Reagan to the presidency in 1980 fuelled the movement's focus on the electoral arena. Among Reagan's staunchest supporters in his quest for the presidency were prominent anti-feminists, notably Schlafly of STOP ERA. Reagan was elected on a platform that disavowed his party's traditional support of the ERA and promised to use all of the tools available to the president – including the power of judicial nomination – to restrict women's access to abortion. Moreover, Reagan's economic policies favoured military spending at the expense of domestic spending that tended to benefit women and children.

With the Reagan Republicans in control of the executive branch and gradually transforming the judiciary, women's movement organizations increasingly came to focus their attentions on the legislative branch, most notably by working to elect pro-choice women to Congress. By 1988, Reagan had appointed three new conservative justices to the Supreme Court and promoted Justice Rehnquist to the position of Chief Justice, thereby shifting the Court's balance in a decidedly conservative direction. This program of judicial appointments substantially constrained the strategic options of the organized women's movement. In the words of one NOW activist: "If there was ever any doubt that a considerable amount of time, energy and resources of the women's movement should be directed at electing feminists to legislative and executive office, a glance at the state of the federal judiciary in America should put that doubt to rest ... It's time to rethink our strategy, sisters. The belief that 'we can always go to court' has been rendered a myth – at least for another generation" (NOW 1988c). Although movement organizations did continue to try to use the courts as an avenue for social change, their emphasis shifted away from the judicial branch towards the legislative branch through the 1980s. When feminist groups found themselves in court, it was as likely to be in a defensive action (often trying to prevent erosion or reversal of the abortion rights established in *Roe* v. *Wade*) as a proactive role.

The Republican domination of the White House was not the only notable change in the political opportunity structure during the 1980s. The declining role of political parties in candidate recruitment and support invited the involvement of women's groups and others in performing these functions, paving the way for PACs to assume these roles. This allowed women's PACs to gain stature and influence relatively quickly. Moreover, the increasing affluence and financial independence of middle-class American women facilitated the growth of PACs.

The organizational manifestation of the movement's growing focus on the legislative branch, and more precisely on the project of electing women, was the development of a network of relatively influential, permanent professionalized feminist organizations focused on electoral politics. The foundation for this network was provided by the existing feminist organizations – notably NOW and the NWPC, both of which became more engaged in electoral activity during this period. They were joined by several established women's organizations. For instance, the national federation of Business and Professional Women's Clubs formed a PAC in 1979 to contribute to candidates who support the organization's legislative platform, which included support for the ERA, economic equity, and civil rights for women, as well as reproductive choice (BPW 1994a). In addition, several new organizations focused primarily or exclusively on electoral politics were formed during the 1980s. In 1984, Democratic activists Delores Tucker, Shirley Chisholm, and several other African American women founded the National Political Congress of Black Women (NPCBW). Operating without paid staff or a national office, the coalition organized forty-two chapters across the country to press for the inclusion of more African American women in public office. The organization was formed because of frustration that neither African American nor White men included African American women when it came time for candidate selection. In addition, one of the founders – Shirley Chisholm – cites Walter Mondale's failure to reach out to African American women in his vice-presidential search in 1984 as an impetus for forming the organization (Kelber 1994, 187). In 1987, former NOW leader Eleanor Smeal formed the Fund for the Feminist Majority (FFM), an organization that is not a PAC but provides training and technical assistance to women considering running for office. The organization has worked with NOW in its efforts to influence party platforms and delegate selection procedures as well as on its voter registration drives (NOW 1988a; 1988b).

The most significant development during this period was the formation of several women's PACs. Of these, the largest and most prominent is EMILY's List, formed in 1985 by Ellen Malcolm, an independently wealthy Democrat and feminist. This organization contributes only to pro-choice Democratic women candidates at the gubernatorial and national levels and specializes in giving "seed" money well in advance of the primary election, thereby making the candidate appear more viable in the eyes of other potential contributors. While many other PACs will endorse or give token contributions to female candidates who have little chance of winning, EMILY's List screens candidates carefully to determine the viability of their candidacies. Once a candidate has received EMILY's List's endorsement, she is assured of early money to start her campaign and a continuous flow of contributions. The list engages in a practice known as "bundling," whereby its members write cheques not to the PAC, but rather to one of the candidates endorsed by the organization. The cheque is mailed to the PAC's Washington office, "bundled" together with other cheques, and then passed on to the candidate. This allows EMILY's List to circumvent rules limiting the amount that a PAC can contribute to one candidate. Funds from EMILY's List have made up as much as one-quarter of the total contributions to some women's campaigns. The organization claims to have bundled some $6.2 million in 1992, $8.4 million in 1994, and $6.6 million in 1996. This makes EMILY's List one of the largest PACs operating in the United States, and the magnitude of its resources has won the organization significant clout within the Democratic party.

The remarkable success of EMILY's List has prompted imitation.[4] In 1991, Republican activist Glenda Grunwald formed WISH List, which contributes to Republican pro-choice women and essentially imitates EMILY's List's practices. In an interesting case of bipartisan cooperation, Ellen Malcolm was extremely supportive of the formation of WISH List, and offered its founder considerable technical advice (Rimmerman 1994). WISH List claims to have contributed approximately $400,000 to pro-choice Republican women in 1992. The formation of WISH List prompted competition from within Republican circles. Worried that WISH List's pro-choice image would hurt the party, Republican leaders apparently sponsored the formation of the Women's Leadership Network, a PAC funding women Republicans regardless of their position on abortion. The organization's charter members have been described as "a who's who of [Bush administration] White House wives," including Vice President Dan Quayle's wife, Marilyn, and former RNC chair Lee Atwater's wife, Sally (Mundy 1992, 17). By 1994, the Women's Leadership Network was listed as terminated by the Federal Election Commission.

The total number of women's PACs operating at the national level varies depending on the definition of what constitutes a women's PAC. For the purpose of this analysis, three categories of women's PACs were defined:

- Type A: PACs that contribute money only to female candidates. The major PACs in this category are the WCF, the NWPC's two PACs, EMILY's List, and WISH List. Most, but not all, of the Type A PACs impose an ideological "litmus test" such as a pro-choice stance on abortion as a condition of funding.
- Type B: PACs that contribute to both female and male candidates using the candidate's record or position on feminist issues as the criterion for funding. Most or all of the contributors to these PACs are women. This category includes NOW's PAC, the Hollywood WCF, and the BPW's PAC.
- Type C: PACs that solicit contributions mainly from women, and contribute to both female and male candidates' positions on issues that are not necessarily feminist issues. These include the American Nurses' Association's PAC, the Women's Alliance for Israel, and Women's Action for Nuclear Disarmament. These are considered women's PACs because of their contributor base rather than their issue focus.

Clearly, Type A and B PACs more closely represent the involvement of the women's movement in electoral politics. Type C PACs, however, demonstrate the increasing power of women's political contributions. Moreover, to varying degrees, the PACs included in the third category – particularly the American Nurses' Association and Women's Action for Nuclear Disarmament – do consider candidates' sex and position on feminist issues in determining their contribution strategies.

There is, arguably, a fourth category of women's PAC that could be included: PACs that focus on one feminist issue (most notably abortion). Although these PACs do fund many of the same candidates as the women's PACs, they are not generally included in the category of women's PACs (see Nelson 1994). Two of the pro-choice PACs are major contributors. In the 1991-2 election cycle, NARAL PAC contributed a total of $493,201 to pro-choice candidates, and Voters for Choice contributed $264,950. The vast majority of the contributions made by these two PACs – 92 percent and 89 percent, respectively – went to Democrats.

Figure 2.1 illustrates the growing number of women's PACs active at the national level between 1978 and 1994. It shows an increase from five PACs in 1978 to a high of twenty-two in 1994. The largest increase came in 1984, when the number of PACs increased from eight to sixteen. The second largest increase came in 1992, the "year of the woman," when the number of active PACs increased from eighteen to twenty-two. It is not coincidental that both of these jumps came in presidential election years when women were highly visible in the campaign.

A similar pattern is evident in the total disbursements of women's PACs between 1977 and 1996. Figure 2.2 shows the total disbursements of women's PACs during this period in 1996 dollars.[5] The trend is a steady increase in the total contributions of women's PACs, with peaks in 1984 and 1992. EMILY's List, starting in 1986, and WISH List, starting in 1992, bundle contributions. Candidates report these contributions as coming from individuals rather than from the PAC, so there is no public record of the total amount of bundled contributions from the PAC. If these bundled contributions are included in the total disbursements to candidates, then

Figure 2.1

Number of active women's PACs by type, 1978-94

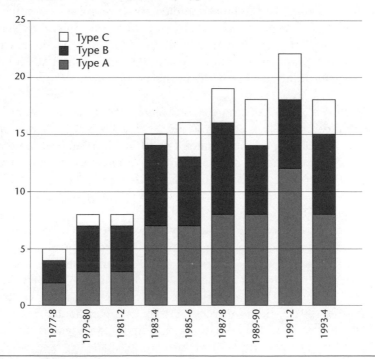

Source: Calculated from FEC data.

the total value of disbursements of women's PACs more than doubles between 1992 and 1994.

The pattern of contributions from women's PACs also demonstrates the increasing focus of the organizations in the women's movement on the election of women. First, Type A PACs (that give only to women) have come to account for a larger proportion of all women's PAC contributions. In 1980, Type A PACs accounted for only 17 percent of the total value of contributions from women's PACs, while Type B PACs accounted for 57 percent. By 1992, Type A PACs accounted for 31 percent of the total value of women's PAC contributions, and Type B PACs only 34 percent. This does not include EMILY's List's and WISH List's bundled contributions, which would significantly increase the proportion of total contributions coming from Type A PACs. Second, several Type B PACs have been giving increasing proportions of their contributions to women candidates. The most notable increase is NOW's PAC, which gave only 20 percent of the total value of its contributions to women candidates in 1980, but gave 94

Figure 2.2

Total PAC contributions, 1977-96

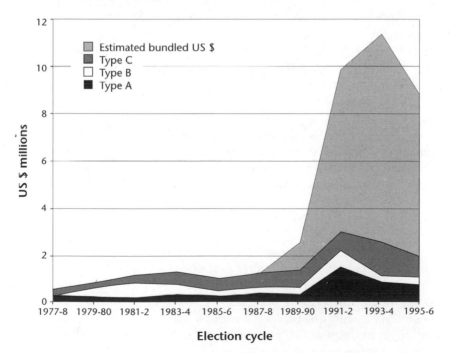

Source: Calculated from FEC data.

percent of the total value of its 1992 contributions to women (calculated from Federal Election Commission data).

Although raising funds to contribute to candidates is the primary function of PACs, several of the women's PACs have become active in other campaign-related activities. Both the NWPC and WCF are active in recruiting and training potential candidates, particularly at the local and state levels. EMILY's List provides extensive campaign advice to endorsed candidates and keeps a careful eye on the conduct and management of endorsed candidates' campaigns. It has also started to offer training for campaign workers in campaign management and fund-raising practices, thereby extending its influence inside the campaigns of endorsed candidates.

The net product of the growth and proliferation of these PACs and other organizations is a permanent, institutionalized network of national women's organizations focused on the electoral process. All of the major organizations and PACs maintain permanent offices with professional staffs in the Washington, DC, area. Several of the major players – EMILY's List, NOW, and the NWPC – meet regularly to share information regarding campaigns. Several of the organizations – including NOW, EMILY's List, and BPW – belong to Pro-Net, a Washington coalition that runs seminars dealing with strategy and funding and shares information regarding candidates for progressive PACs (Rimmerman 1994, 220). This forum extends the influence of the women's PACs into the broader community of "progressive" PACs. It gives PACs focused on reproductive choice, human rights, gay and lesbian rights, and environmental issues information about women candidates endorsed by these PACs (interview 02/24/95). The leadership role played by EMILY's List in this regard is particularly notable, as the PAC's criteria for judging a candidate's viability are generally considered to be quite stringent. In addition to Pro-Net, many of the groups – including the FFM, NOW, NWPC, and the National Political Congress of Black Women – are members of the Council of Presidents, the network of women's lobbying organizations in Washington (Council of Presidents 1993; Nelson 1994, 184).

Partisan Orientation

Reagan's election to the presidency in 1980 exercised a profound impact on the partisan orientation of organizations in the women's movement. Once the more cohesively conservative Republican party had captured the White House, the existing preference of women's organizations for the Democrats intensified, producing a closer affiliation with the party. As anti-feminist forces gained power within the Republican party, they were able to engineer the end of the party's traditional support for the ERA as well as a strong endorsement of pro-life stances on abortion, and they

Table 2.1

Major US women's organizations focusing on electoral and partisan politics

Organization	Formed	Partisanship	Activities	Status
NWPC	1971	Bipartisan	Funding (via PACs); recruitment and training; pressure on parties	Active
WCF	1974	Bipartisan	Funding (PAC); recruitment and training	Active
NOW/PAC	1975	Bipartisan	Funding (PAC); some pressure on parties	Active
EMILY's List	1985	Democratic	Funding (PAC); training	Active
FFM	1987	Bipartisan/ ties to new party	Training and technical assistance; some pressure on parties	Active
NPCBW	1987	Bipartisan	Voter registration; candidate training, endorsement, and support	Active
WISH List	1991	Republican	Funding (PAC); training	Active

made a fairly successful effort to purge liberal feminist women from the party (see Melich 1996; Freeman 1987). Thus, the 1980 Republican National Convention effectively marked the end of meaningful bipartisanship for the American women's movement.

As Table 2.1 shows, the majority of large national feminist organizations focused exclusively on partisan electoral politics and were formally bipartisan. In practice, however, most of these groups have closer ties to the Democrats than to the Republicans. Although it has made every effort to remain bipartisan, the NWPC has consistently played a more significant role in the Democratic party than in the Republican party, and its DTF has always been larger and more active than its Republican counterpart (Freeman 1987). The closer relations with the Democrats are also evident in the contribution patterns of the NWPC's two PACs. In every election cycle since 1977-8, over 60 percent of the total value of the NWPC PACs' contributions have gone to Democrats. In the 1985-6, 1987-8, and 1991-2 election cycles, over 90 percent of the total value has gone to Democratic candidates (calculated from Federal Election Commission records).

Figure 2.3

Women's PAC contributions by party, 1977-96

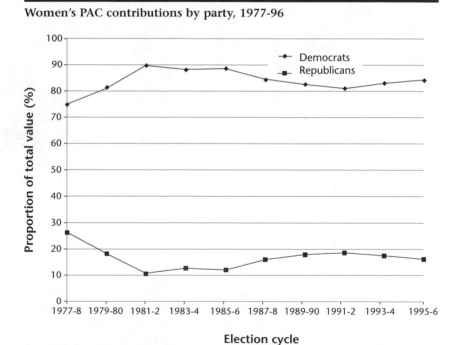

Election cycle

Source: Calculated from FEC data.

The distribution of women's PAC money illustrates the ties of the women's movement with the Democrats. As shown in Figure 2.3, over 70 percent of the total value of all women's PAC disbursements goes to Democrats. The figure is slightly lower for Type A PACs (that give only to women candidates), although the percentage would increase considerably from 1988 on if bundled contributions were included, since all of EMILY's List's bundled contributions go to Democratic candidates. From 1980 on, Type B PACs (that give to both men and women based on feminist policy issues) gave an overwhelming proportion of their total disbursements to Democrats, reflecting the Republicans' increasingly anti-feminist policy stances, particularly on abortion. When the proportion of total women's PAC money going to Democratic candidates is compared with that of other movements, however, it does not appear as high. In the 1989-90 election cycle, for example, 85 percent of women's PAC money went to Democrats, compared with between 90 percent and 98 percent of union PAC money and almost 95 percent of peace groups' contributions (Makinson 1992, 33). For the most part, bipartisan organizations like NWPC and the WCF strive to make their bipartisan label meaningful, but experience difficulties finding pro-choice Republican women who are willing to run (interviews, 03/05/94; 04/05/94).

As the Republicans became more overtly anti-feminist, NOW allied itself more closely with the Democrats. Throughout the 1970s and 1980s, NOW maintained a consistent presence at Democratic party conventions, joining with the NWPC and other women's organizations in their efforts to influence the content of the party's platform. At the 1980 convention, NOW joined the NWPC in its battle with the Carter campaign for a platform plank making party support for congressional candidates contingent on their endorsement of the ERA. Although the plank was a symbolic victory, the fight with the Carter camp marked a coming of age for NOW in Democratic party politics. Having demonstrated considerable clout within the party in 1980, NOW had become "members of the [Democratic] family" by the 1984 race (Freeman 1987, 234).

NOW's close ties to the Democrats, coupled with the emerging gender gap in public opinion and the anti-feminist stance of the Republican administration, pushed NOW in the direction of a more active and exclusive relationship with the party in 1984. Within NOW, the growing focus on electoral politics was not uncontested. At the 1982 national convention, Judy Goldsmith, the chosen candidate of NOW members committed to pursuing a pragmatic electoral strategy, only narrowly defeated a candidate advocating a return to more radical positions and unconventional political tactics (Ferree and Hess 1985, 118). With Goldsmith's victory, however, the organization was poised to become more directly involved in the 1984 election campaign. For the first time, NOW became explicitly involved in the Democratic party's nomination race as NOW's PAC formally endorsed Walter Mondale's candidacy for the party's nomination.[6] The leaders of NOW believed that endorsing Mondale would increase their bargaining power within the Democratic Party, thereby enhancing the organization's ability to have Mondale select a woman as his running mate (NOW 1984). The endorsement won NOW a place within the Mondale campaign and cemented the position of feminists as a key constituency within the party. NOW chapters were active in recruiting women to run on Mondale slates in the primaries and caucuses and NOW president Judy Goldsmith travelled with the Mondale campaign during the last weeks of the primaries (Frankovic 1988, 109, 119).

NOW was not the only organization in the women's movement to endorse the Democrats in 1984. The NWPC also gave the only presidential endorsement in its history to the Mondale-Ferraro ticket. This unprecedented move reflected both support for Ferraro's nomination and the disenchantment of Republican NWPC activists with the increasing social conservatism of their party in the aftermath of the 1980 convention. With Republican women on side, the decision to endorse a Democratic presidential candidate met very little resistance within the organization (interview 02/07/95).

Defeat of the Mondale-Ferraro ticket in 1984 forced a re-evaluation of NOW's relationship with the Democratic party. Claiming that during her presidency Judy Goldsmith had turned NOW into a wing of the Democratic party, and promising a return to more radical tactics, Eleanor Smeal contested and won the organization's presidency in 1985 (Buechler 1990, 68). Leaders of NOW were growing increasingly disillusioned with the Democratic party, complaining that "once again, our agenda is being relegated to the back burner and our votes are being taken for granted on the arrogant assumption that, come 1988, we won't have any other place to go and will be forced to accept whatever the Democrats choose to offer" (NOW 1987). Despite growing frustration with the Democrats, NOW did not have an alternative political route available to it, so the organization remained involved with the Democrats in 1988, lobbying for changes to the party's platform and rallying inside the party's convention (NOW 1988b).[7]

After the 1988 election, NOW leaders' disenchantment with the Democrats continued. They were particularly dissatisfied with the party's slow rate of improvement in the number of women and minorities elected (NOW 1992). Condemning the "failure of both major parties to address women's needs," delegates to the 1989 NOW national convention unanimously supported a resolution calling on the organization's leadership to investigate the feasibility of a new party. After a series of hearings across the country, NOW's commission for responsive democracy advocated the formation of a new political party, which was not to be exclusively a women's party, but rather a coalition of feminists, environmentalists, civil rights, and peace activists, as well as others (NOW 1992). Although leaders from NOW went on to establish the new party, it did not enjoy a high profile, nor did it receive the support of other major organizations in the women's movement. Perceiving NOW's decision as a serious defection from the movement's political strategy, leaders of other women's organizations distanced themselves from NOW on this matter.[8] The decision to sponsor the formation of a new political party also caused NOW to become even less involved in the Democratic party, as was demonstrated by the organization's decision to remain outside the Democratic national convention in 1992.

The ultimate legacy of the twelve-year Republican occupancy in the White House was to drive feminist organizations into the arms of the Democrats. Even the BPW was driven to endorse Bill Clinton's candidacy for the presidency in 1992. It is remarkable that the members of BPW would vote to endorse Clinton, given that the organization's membership includes as many Republicans as it does Democrats and that many of its members are small business owners who have some affinity with the Republicans on economic issues. Nonetheless, the prevailing sense of fatigue after twelve years of "anti-woman, anti-choice" Republican administration led the group to make its first presidential endorsement in its history. Moreover, over the same period BPW's PAC has gone from giving 69 percent of the total value of its contributions to the Democrats in 1980 to giving 93 percent in 1994 (calculated from FEC data). Thus, by the 1992 election, Democratic presidential nominee Bill Clinton had little difficulty winning the support of US feminists.

The Clinton Years (1992-6)

In the early 1990s, the opportunity structure facing the women's movement changed again. The confirmation hearings for Clarence Thomas, which sparked the "year of the woman" phenomenon in 1992, opened a window of opportunity for some well-positioned organizations in the women's movement. Changes in political alignments also altered the opportunity structure facing movement organizations in the 1990s. The election of Bill Clinton to the presidency in 1992 after twelve uninterrupted years of Republican rule offered at least a faint glimmer of hope for movement leaders. Only two years later, however, mid-term elections produced a decidedly conservative Republican-dominated Congress, supplanting the Democrats who had held a majority in Congress since 1982.

The Year of the Woman

In 1991, women across the United States were appalled by the televised spectacle of the all-White, all-male Senate Judiciary Committee grilling Anita Hill on her allegations of sexual harassment by Clarence Thomas, whom President Bush had nominated to fill a vacancy on the Supreme Court. Accompanying the outrage over the decision to ignore Hill's testimony and confirm Thomas's appointment was a huge expansion of interest in and support for the project of electing women. In the months following the hearings, contributions to women's PACs poured in from across the country. This vast increase in public support for women candidates came at a time when there was an infrastructure of women's PACs in place to channel the contributions to female candidates, and when a significant number of women had worked their way to local and state-level office and were poised to run for national office. The result of this confluence was the "year of the woman" in 1992, which saw significant increases in the number of women running, the media attention they received, the resources available to them, and, ultimately, the number of women in the House and the Senate. As can be seen in Figure 2.3 above, the "year of the woman" was actually the "year of the Democratic woman" since the main beneficiaries of this influx of cash were PACs that contributed only to Democrats, and the majority of the women first elected in 1992 were Democrats.

In essence, the stance of the women's movement in 1992 illustrated its dilemma vis-à-vis electoral politics. The Republican party was overtly hostile to the movement, and even the Democrats were not as open to the movement as activists would have liked. The one clear success for the movement, however, was the high profile of feminist PACs, most notably EMILY's List, at the Democratic convention and in the 1992 election.

The 1992 Republican convention, which served as a showcase for the Christian right's burgeoning influence within the party, was not a particularly hospitable place for feminists. Nonetheless, the NWPC formed an ad hoc coalition of pro-choice Republican and bipartisan groups including Republicans for Choice (RFC), National Republican Coalition for Choice (NRCC), WISH List, WCF, Planned Parenthood, BPW/USA, and the National Abortion Rights Action League (NARAL), in advance of the convention, and hosted a "showcase" for thirteen pro-choice Republican women at the convention (NWPC 1992, 1; Kelber 1994, 183). These efforts were overshadowed by the immense power of pro-life and Christian right groups within the party and on the platform committee.

Despite the emphasis on women's candidacies in 1992, feminist organizations played a remarkably muted role at the Democratic convention. Much of the attention was on the high-profile women candidates and their powerful financial backing from EMILY's List. NOW remained outside the convention, and many Democratic women in the NWPC and other feminist organizations muted their criticisms of party policy in order to appear united behind nominee Bill Clinton in hope of breaking the twelve-year Republican monopoly on the White House. Since women's caucus meetings at the 1992 convention were run by Democratic National Committee (DNC) women rather than by outside feminists, feminist issues did not attain the same profile as they had at earlier conventions (Kelber 1994; Freeman 1994). The primary reminder of the existence of the internal "femocratic" constituency came from the daily publication of the *Getting It Gazette,* which served as an outlet for more outspoken feminists (English 1992).

Feminists were, for the most part, disappointed by Clinton's record in office. On the positive side of the balance sheet, he did veto GOP legislation banning late-term abortion, passed legislation establishing family leave and addressing violence against women, and appointed women to high-profile posts. Despite this, his compromise "don't ask, don't tell" policy on lesbians and gays in the military, his failure to reform health care, his compromises on access to abortion for federal employees and women in the military, and his decision not to veto the GOP's far-reaching welfare reform bill lost Clinton a great deal of support among feminists.

As the 1996 presidential race approached, feminist groups faced a familiar dilemma: the incumbent Democratic president had not lived up to expectations, but his Republican opponent was an even less palatable choice. After Clinton signed the controversial Welfare Reform Act (which allowed state governments to curtail benefits for single mothers, among others), some prominent feminists proclaimed that they would abstain or vote for a minor party candidate rather than cast a ballot for Clinton. In an article in *Ms.,* for example, Barbara Ehrenreich (1996, 21) proclaimed her decision not to vote for Clinton, arguing that he had not only abandoned the activist liberal wing of the party, but had also stifled it: "Instead of recharging the left, the Clinton presidency had the unanticipated effect of gagging it ... Everyone made the same tragic error of imagining that because we had a Democrat in the White House, we had *access,* and because we had access, we finally had influence ... But an oppositional movement doesn't thrive because its leaders can lunch at the White House ... My unvote for Clinton (I wrote in Ralph Nader) was a vote against further quiescence, co-optation, and delusion." Others, like Gloria Steinem, urged feminists to "not only vote for Clinton, but work our asses off to get out the vote, regain leadership of congress and then do everything to repeal this ridiculous welfare bill," as this was the only course of action "that makes things better instead of worse" (*Getting It Gazette* 1996).

The election of a Republican-dominated House and Senate in the 1994 mid-term elections created a rallying point for feminist efforts in the 1996 elections. Although House Speaker Newt Gingrich's fiscally and socially conservative "Contract with America" had lost much of its momentum by 1996, the Republican Congress had already produced welfare and abortion legislation strongly opposed by feminist groups. Much of the feminist effort took the form of voter registration and get-out-the-vote campaigns, motivated by the belief that the 1994 Republican landslide had been aided considerably by low voter turnout among women, and particularly among women belonging to demographic groups that tended to vote Democrat. (In fact, the 1994 results had as much to do with male Democrats defecting to the Republicans as with a drop-off in women voting) (Seltzer et al. 1997, 3). To reverse this perceived trend, EMILY's List raised some $15 million for its "Women vote!" campaign, which banded together with other members of the Democratic coalition, notably the Service Employees International Union, to target potential female voters (EMILY's List 1995).

The 1996 NOW national conference passed a resolution making electoral politics a major focus for all levels of the organization through November. Following on this, NOW and its affiliated PAC engaged in aggressive field organizing in selected Senate and House campaigns, including those of Harvey Gantt, a Democrat running against arch-conservative Senator Jesse Helms in North Carolina. NOW's PAC also targeted its support on feminist incumbents affected by redistricting, alleging that the Republicans were trying to unseat these women through redistricting plans (NOW 1996). It is noteworthy that, in both 1994 and 1996, Type B PACs (such as NOW and BPW) gave 98 percent of the total value of their contributions to Democrats (see Figure 2.3 above). This reflects the ongoing support of organizations in the women's movement for the Democrats in the face of resolute Republican anti-feminism. Even the PAC affiliated with the Business and Professional Women's Clubs, which traditionally had distributed its contributions between Democrats and Republicans on approximately a 3:1 ratio, gave over 90 percent of the total value of its contributions to Democrats in the election cycles of 1989-90, 1991-2, and 1993-4.

With Congress controlled by Republicans, and the Republican party holding firm to its anti-feminist policy stances, feminist organizations had little choice but to remain loyal to the Democrats during Clinton's second term. This allegiance was strained not only by policy differences between movement organizations and the White House, but also by the scandal over the president's sexual relationship with a White House intern that consumed the administration for much of its second term. When Congress voted in 1998 to impeach President Clinton for having lied under oath about his relationship with Monica Lewinsky, feminist organizations rallied to his support. NOW, the FFM, the National Council of Negro Women, and the NWPC lobbied members of the House of Representatives to vote against impeachment (NOW 1999). Because of the polarization of the two political parties around feminist issues, these groups believed they had little choice but to support Clinton, no matter how offensive they considered his behaviour to have been. The Lewinsky incident and the impeachment trial served to demonstrate how limited the options are for the American women's movement in the US two-party system.

Conclusion

In comparative context, the ongoing engagement of the women's movement in the United States with partisan and electoral politics is remarkable. From the early 1970s to the present, electoral politics have been one of the core activities of American feminism, and there is little evidence suggesting that this is changing. Over this period, the extent of the movement's interest in electoral politics has waxed and waned in response to changing political circumstances. That said, the more stable elements of the political opportunity structure facing the movement – the two-party system and the congressional form of government – create a foundation for the movement's ongoing interest in electoral politics and alliance with the Democratic party. As we will see in Chapter 3, the Canadian women's movement faces a very different set of incentives in its dealings with parties and electoral politics, and its orientation towards the formal political arena has, consequently, been quite different.

3

Power Is Not Electoral: Canadian Feminists and Party Politics

While the American women's movement became progressively more engaged in electoral politics from 1970 on, the Canadian women's movement evolved in a very different direction. During the first fifteen years of feminist mobilization in Canada, the dominant ideological tendency within the movement at the national level was liberal, or reformist, feminism. Proponents of this tendency placed some emphasis on electoral politics and maintained a multipartisan stance, establishing ties with all three of the major political parties of the time. From 1985 until the present, however, changes in the movement and in the opportunity structure it faced engendered a growing conviction among activists that "power is not electoral." As a consequence, electoral politics came to play an even less significant role in the movement's repertoire of action, and its earlier multipartisanship evolved into an apartisan orientation. With the emergence of a new party system in 1993, the movement's orientation has changed again – returning to a closer alliance with the social democratic NDP, although still maintaining a distance from electoral politics.

The Canadian women's movement is more ideologically diverse than its predominantly liberal US counterpart. In English Canada, the women's movement has roots in both traditional women's organizations and the Canadian left, and parts of the Quebec women's movement have strong ties to Quebec nationalism. The US women's movement began as two streams, liberal and radical, that gradually merged into one predominantly liberal stream. The Canadian women's movement, by contrast, has since its mobilization encompassed substantial liberal, socialist, and radical elements. These three strands coexist under the aegis of the National Action Committee on the Status of Women (NAC), an umbrella organization that has emerged as the major Canadian women's group. Liberal feminism was the dominant ideological tendency in NAC until the mid-1980s, when socialist and radical feminists came to play a greater role in the organization. In the 1990s, NAC's organizational base has expanded to include immigrant and visible minority women's groups, and the organization has developed a deeply held commitment to anti-racist organizing and accommodation of ethno-cultural diversity.

NAC's umbrella structure has encouraged the diversity of Canadian feminism by providing an organizational form that allows NAC to operate as a loose coalition of various strands of feminism (Vickers et al. 1993). The absence of a large national membership-based group like NOW in the United States has, however, made it difficult to mobilize large campaigns on a national basis over a sustained period. There have, of course, been exceptions to this (most notably the fight for inclusion of equality rights in the Charter of Rights and Freedoms in 1981). Moreover, the policy agenda of Canadian feminism has tended to reflect the movement's internal diversity. Unlike the US movement, which was forced to engage in a lengthy and unsuccessful campaign for the Equal Rights Amendment and an even longer defensive campaign against anti-abortion activists, the Canadian movement has pursued a wider range of lower-profile issues including child care, pensions for homemakers, equal rights for Native women, and equal pay for work of equal value (Burt 1995). Moreover, since the mid-1980s, the movement's agenda has broadened to include issues that are not explicitly women's issues. This expansion of the agenda has brought movement organizations, especially NAC, to the forefront of campaigns opposing continental free trade agreements and cuts to social programs. Since the repatriation of the Canadian Constitution in 1982 (complete with the equality provisions women's groups fought for), NAC has been an outspoken critic of proposed constitutional amendments, once again going beyond simple status-of-women concerns.

The primary political cleavage within the province of Quebec falls between federalists and sovereigntists, and this is true among Québécois feminists as well. Liberal feminism in Quebec is associated with federalism and consequently with both the Liberal Party of Canada (LPC) and the Parti Libéral du Québec (PLQ). Maroney (1988, 415) argues that the predominantly liberal feminist Fédération des femmes du Québec (FFQ) and, to a lesser extent, the Association féminine d'éducation et d'action sociale (AFEAS), have been oriented to the PLQ not only as the ruling party, but as a reference group.[1] Radical feminism in Quebec has been associated with sovereigntism, claiming that there can be no liberation for women without liberation for Quebec, and vice versa. Radical feminist organizations such as the Front pour la libération des femmes refused to work with anglophone women either locally or nationally (Maroney 1988, 497), have focused their political efforts on the Quebec government and are allied with the sovereigntist Parti Québécois. English Canadian women's movement organizations, most notably NAC, have tried with varying degrees of success to accommodate francophone feminist organizations, but it is only the liberal stream of the Quebec women's movement that has engaged with English Canadian feminism (see Vickers et al. 1993).

The diverse and diffuse character of the Canadian women's movement means that it is sometimes difficult to make definitive statements regarding "the" orientation of the movement towards parties and electoral politics. It is possible to identify NAC's orientation, but even this is shaped in large part by the faction that holds power within NAC at any particular time. An illustration of these complexities is the curious situation in the mid-1980s wherein the women's organizations of the three major Canadian political parties were members of NAC, while NAC grew increasingly critical of political parties and severed its informal ties with party organizations. Even with these complexities, however, it is possible to note an evolution in the movement's orientation towards electoral and partisan politics between 1970 and the present.

In contrast to the American case, fixed elements of the opportunity structure for Canadian feminists have not created incentives to engage in the partisan political arena. The Canadian parliamentary system, with its strict party discipline, allows only limited autonomy for individual legislators. Moreover, the practice of caucus and Cabinet secrecy mean that if women in the political sphere are affecting policy, it is seldom public knowledge.

Less fixed elements of the political opportunity structure created different sets of opportunities and incentives for Canadian feminists at various times. The election of the neo-liberal government of Brian Mulroney in 1984 made the Canadian state less open to women's claims and thus constituted a disincentive for political activism, at least in the eyes of NAC leaders at the time.[2] The change in the Canadian party system in 1993 further decreased the Canadian state's openness to feminism, but this served to reinvigorate NAC's interest in electoral politics somewhat.

Throughout the 1980s and 1990s, Canada has been engaged in what one observer calls "mega constitutional change" (Russell 1993). In 1982, the country's constitution was repatriated from Britain (eliminating a colonial holdover) and the Charter of Rights and Freedoms was entrenched within it. The Charter was the first constitutional, as opposed to legislative, guarantee of individual rights and freedoms for Canadians. Because this was done without the assent of the government of Quebec, a second constitutional round was initiated in 1987, resulting in the Meech Lake Accord, which was not adopted because of the failure of two provincial legislatures to ratify it. In an effort to mend the resulting political damage (particularly in Quebec), the federal and provincial governments developed the Charlottetown Accord in 1992. When put to a national referendum, however, the accord was soundly defeated. This process has afforded the Canadian women's movement several opportunities to engage directly in the formal political arena in the 1980s and 1990s. These forays into the constitutional realm have, in turn, given organizations in the movement considerable resources in their dealings with political parties.

Suffrage and Beyond

The "first wave" of the women's movement in Canada centred on women's suffrage, and was part of the larger North American progressive movement that first emerged at the turn of the century (Phillips 1990, 40).[3] At the heart of the progressive movement was a critique of political parties and a suspicion of "partyism" that the suffragists shared (Bashevkin 1993, 6). Given, however, that the central demand of suffragists was to open the political system to the participation of women by expanding the franchise, the stance of the first wave vis-à-vis the partisan political arena was somewhat ambiguous. The suffragists who endorsed social or maternal feminism partially resolved this contradiction by arguing that women's participation would "purify" party politics by bringing to the partisan political arena the moral values women championed in the home. Bashevkin (1993, 7) argues that the suffragists' initial suspicion of the party system was proven correct when they and other progressive reformers entered the party-dominated system only to find that their broader structural objectives and their specific goals were marginalized by the very parliamentary system they had set out to reform.

The political marginalization of women by Canadian political parties persisted uncontested until the early 1970s. Women were active as party workers, but not as feminist agitators within the parties. When the second wave of the Canadian women's movement mobilized in the late 1960s, a new generation of feminists faced essentially the same dilemma as their suffragist forerunners. Bashevkin (1993) argues that this tension between independence and partisanship has shaped not only the development of contemporary English Canadian feminism but also the broader relationship between women and the party system. Vickers (1989) concurs, adding that this tension is internal not only to the movement, but to many individual feminists. The common theme that emerges from these accounts of the women's movement is the persistent tension between autonomous and integrative strategies. It is important to understand this as a tension, not as an either/or dichotomy, as the women's movement has pursued both autonomous and integrative strategies simultaneously (Vickers et al. 1993, 24; Bashevkin 1993, 3). In this vein, Briskin has suggested that, in the Canadian feminist experience, "mainstreaming" and "disengagement" are best understood as emphases rather than separate poles (Briskin 1991, 30). Without contesting this, one can argue that the nature of the coexistence of the two tendencies has changed over time.

Moderate Multipartisanship (1970-84)

From 1970 until 1984, the women's movement exhibited two discrete approaches to electoral and partisan politics. The more visible was the liberal feminist stream's moderate involvement in electoral and partisan politics. This took the form of encouraging political parties to nominate women candidates, monitoring party policies on status-of-women issues, and maintaining informal interpersonal ties between the movement organizations and the three political parties. At no time was NAC or any other organization directly involved with any of the political parties in a manner analogous to the NWPC's engagement with the Democrats in the early 1970s. The liberal and reformist stream of the Canadian women's movement was essentially multipartisan in orientation, maintaining ties to all three of the major parties. The closest connection was to the NDP, but there were also significant ties to the governing federal Liberal party.

Less visible was the radical feminist critique of this approach as an endorsement of a patriarchal political system. Radical feminists for the most part eschewed engagement with established political parties, and in some cases even rejected the idea of a feminist political party on the grounds that it would mean being co-opted by the patriarchal political establishment. Although radical feminists were a significant part of the women's movement, their objections to engaging with the political system were a minority voice dissenting from the liberal feminist majority that prevailed in national organizations at the time.[4]

The opportunity structure facing Canadian feminism during this period was relatively favourable to the engagement of women's movement organizations in the partisan electoral arena. The governing Liberal party was committed to fostering pan-Canadian citizen groups in an effort to bolster national unity, and the emerging women's movement was able to benefit from this in material ways. As the governing party between 1963 and 1984, the Liberals played a significant role in shaping the emerging movement, starting with the appointment of the Royal Commission on the Status of Women, whose report became the policy blueprint for liberal feminists in the early 1970s. It was a Liberal government that funded NAC's founding conference and instigated the practice of government funding for NAC and other women's organizations, including several of the organizations at the national and provincial levels that focused on electing women. There is some evidence to suggest that the federal government used its role as the emerging women's movement's major source of funding to direct the movement's development, albeit subtly.[5] After the

Strategy for Change Conference, for example, NAC's first president reported to the organization's steering committee that Bryce Mackasey, the minister responsible for the funding, wanted complete reports from the convention and was appalled that sixty radical women – some of whom were "known Trotskyites and Communists" – were admitted to the conference (NAC 1972b). The Secretary of State also funded the WPA's Women in Politics conference in 1973 and, in 1976, held a seminar on political action that brought together women's organizations and presidents of the established political parties (NAC 1976). Whether incidental or deliberate, this had the effect of steering the movement in the direction of moderate reform feminism in its first decade.

Vickers et al. (1993) argue that acceptance of the ordinary political process by Canadian feminists was closely linked to the statism of Canadian feminism. Women played a crucial role in establishing the Canadian welfare state (Andrew 1984), creating a certain sense of "ownership" that compounded the faith in state action that has characterized Canadian feminism from the outset. Moreover, as Findlay (1987, 31) argues convincingly, the willingness of Liberal governments in the 1970s and early 1980s to consult with women's organizations validated the faith of liberal feminists in the strategy of reform by the state. Although statism and engagement with established political parties do not necessarily go hand in hand, the former has certainly facilitated the latter.

The federal government's decision to repatriate the Canadian Constitution, complete with the Charter of Rights and Freedoms, created a remarkable opportunity for mobilization of Canadian feminists. Although this lobbying effort was focused largely on provincial governments, it drew women into the feminist movement and vastly increased the established political parties' respect for and attentiveness to the women's movement in the mid-1980s.

Reformist Feminism: Engaged with Party Politics

The contemporary Canadian women's movement began with calls for the establishment of a Royal Commission to study the status of women in Canada, and gained momentum after the *Report of the Royal Commission on the Status of Women* (RCSW) was released in 1970. The report identified the absence of women in public life as a significant obstacle to the achievement of equality for Canadian women. Noting that "the presence of a mere handful of women [in the government and Parliament of Canada] is no more than a token acknowledgement of their right to be there," the commission argued that "no country can make a claim to having equal status for its women so long as its government lies entirely in the hands of men" (RCSW 1970, 355). The report went on to advocate the appointment of women to the Senate and to other government boards and agencies, and urged political parties to nominate more female candidates. Seeing the separate women's organizations within political parties as "a group of volunteers dedicated to getting the party's male candidates elected" and a means of keeping women out of positions of authority within the parties, the commission recommended that women's associations within the political parties be amalgamated with the parties' main bodies (ibid., 344-8).

The RCSW's report can be seen as the blueprint for NAC's early interaction with the political system. It called on Canadian women to "show a greater determination to use their legal right to participate as citizens," and in NAC's early days activists rallied around this call. Vickers et al. (1993, 75) note that NAC was run during this period by a group of women who held fairly conventional ideas about organization and political process. In light of this, it is not surprising that the project of political integration envisioned by the RCSW was well received by activists in NAC at the time.

At the 1972 conference where NAC was founded, delegates devoted considerable attention to partisan political action, passing resolutions advocating that the new organization "seek out women candidates who will stress women's priority issues at all levels of government" (NAC 1972a). Envisioning women setting their own terms for participating in party politics and thereby transforming political parties, the political action workshop at the conference passed resolutions advocating the formation of women's caucuses within the political parties to press for the adoption of progressive women's policies. These caucuses were to criticize party leaders publicly if they took regressive stands on women's issues, an approach in sharp conflict with the established norms of Canadian political parties. Assuming that financial barriers stood in the way of women's candidacies, the delegates also passed several resolutions advocating reform of electoral finance regulations, including spending limits and public funding for candidates (ibid.).

After this initial burst of interest in party politics, NAC's focus shifted elsewhere. Rather than engaging directly with the three political parties as organizations, NAC leaders focused their efforts on lobbying the government to implement the recommendations of the RCSW report. This emphasis on lobbying government and bureaucratic officials was consistent with traditional lobby techniques employed by a wide range of organized interests at the time.[6]

A group that sustained a more consistent focus on electoral politics was Women for Political Action (WPA). In January of 1972, activists from the peace group Voice of Women (VOW), the Ontario Committee on the Status of Women, journalists Doris Anderson and June Callwood, and other like-minded women joined to form WPA. Their objective was to increase the number of women in all levels of politics. As with NAC, the formation of this group can be traced at least in part to activist women's desire to see the recommendations of the RCSW implemented. WPA diverged strategically from NAC in that it sought to implement the RCSW recommendations by working through the electoral process rather than concentrating on a lobbying strategy. WPA can best be understood as a minority stream within NAC at the time, as it was working for the same goals through somewhat different, yet complementary, channels.

In the federal election in fall of 1972, two WPA members (Aline Gregory and Kay Macpherson) ran as independent candidates in Toronto ridings. The decision to mount these candidacies was influenced by two factors. First, none of the three major political parties appeared committed to running women in ridings where they could win or to working on status-of-women issues. Second, WPA activists believed that women within the established parties were seriously constrained by party discipline and could therefore not work effectively for the advancement of women's issues (WPA 1972). The women involved were well aware that independent candidates seldom win seats in Canadian federal elections. Their purpose was to raise issues of concern to women and to push the established parties into running more women in subsequent elections. Although neither WPA nominee was elected, both ran credible campaigns and received some media attention. In the riding of Rosedale, Aline Gregory won 2.4 percent of the popular vote, while Kay Macpherson won 5.4 percent of the popular vote in the neighbouring riding of St. Paul's; see Canada (1973).

Following the 1972 election, however, WPA abandoned the strategy of running independent candidates in favour of working within the party system, calling this approach more "realistic and effective" (WPA 1972). The experience of mounting independent campaigns had shown WPA activists how difficult it was to run a competitive candidacy without the support of party organizations and party funds (interview 14/03/93). In addition, they believed that the political parties were beginning to be more open to female candidates and women's issues. Reconstituting their organization from a quasi-party (running candidates) to a multipartisan women's political caucus, WPA set out to work for the implementation of the recommendations of the RCSW politically, through the party system (WPA 1972). Towards this end, the organization focused on educating women about the political process and in political skills. In addition, it provided information about women contesting nominations within the three political parties, and encouraged women to join political parties. Despite this shift in emphasis, some women within the organization remained unwilling to become involved with the established political parties and chose instead to focus their energy on WPA itself.

In 1973, WPA (with the assistance of a $25,000 grant from the federal government) brought together 165 women from across Canada to discuss increasing the political participation of women. Of the delegates who indicated an organizational affiliation, about three-quarters were involved with WPA or status-of-women organizations, while the remaining quarter were divided evenly among the three established political parties.[7] Women at the conference discussed party platforms, deterrents to women in politics, and the mechanics of running a campaign. Among the resolutions passed were calls for reform of electoral laws to provide public funding and spending limits for campaigns (WPA 1973d). This supported the major provisions of Bill C-203, an electoral reform bill introduced into the House of Commons that same month and which became law one year later. Going beyond this, delegates also called on political parties to provide funds for candidates seeking nomination and to limit spending in nomination campaigns.

Through the 1970s and early 1980s, the liberal feminist commitment to the established political process remained the dominant, albeit contested, tendency within the institutionalized women's movement (Vickers et al. 1993, 37). NAC's primary focus was lobbying, not electoral politics, but its leaders remained supportive of women in the political parties.[8] One prominent NAC leader during this time saw taking feminist politics inside the established political parties as "an absolutely crucial part of the women's movement" (interview, 26/02/94). As discussed in Chapter 5, these efforts were facilitated considerably by the feminist mobilization taking place inside the political parties, particularly the NDP, at the time.

In 1980 and 1981, the federal government's initiative to repatriate the constitution from Britain and to introduce an entrenched Charter of Rights and Freedoms prompted an extensive and ultimately successful mobilization of Canadian feminists. In contrast to the US women's movement, which initiated a bitter and ultimately unsuccessful battle for an amendment to the US Constitution guaranteeing equal rights for women, Canadian feminists had never devoted a great deal of attention to the question of constitutional guarantees of equality. Once the federal government had placed the idea of an entrenched Charter on the constitutional agenda, however, many feminist activists were determined that sexual equality would be guaranteed in the document. Moreover, as Chaviva Hošek (1983, 284) observes, even though constitutional change had not been the first item on the women's agenda, energy and commitment were available as soon as the opportunity presented itself.

Support for an entrenched Charter was not universal among either feminists or women in general. Lynn McDonald, then president of NAC, was among those who were sceptical about the merits of a constitutionally entrenched guarantee of equality on the grounds that Canadian courts had shown little sympathy for feminist causes in the past, and the entrenchment of a Charter would only increase the power of the courts. Many francophone women were opposed to the constitutional deal that eventually emerged without the signature of the Premier of Quebec, and many women in the Western provinces shared their premiers' scepticism of an entrenched Charter. Nonetheless, there was remarkable support among women in English Canada for guarantees of equal rights in the new constitution. Moreover, once it became clear than an entrenched Charter would be part of the constitutional package, even those activists sceptical of the potential benefits of a Charter could be mobilized to try to improve the equality rights provisions contained in the document.

In the spring of 1980, following the first referendum on Quebec separation, the Trudeau government announced plans to "patriate" the Canadian constitution, replacing the British North America Act with a Canadian constitutional document. (This was intended to fulfil the federal government's promise of renewed federalism during the referendum campaign). The proposal included, among other things, an entrenched Charter of Rights and Freedoms that would establish guarantees of fundamental freedoms and empower the courts to provide remedies to citizens whose rights were infringed. Unlike the federal Human Rights Act of 1960, the Charter would apply to all levels of government, not merely the federal government, and would be entrenched in the Constitution rather than remaining a simple act of Parliament.

The proposed Charter included a section guaranteeing equal protection without discrimination based on sex, but this equal protection was subject to an override clause that allowed government to enact legislation "notwithstanding" the Charter. The override worried many feminist activists, as did the three-year moratorium before the equality provision would come into effect, as this measure was applied only to the sexual equality provisions. The efforts of feminist activists came to centre on the inclusion of section 28, an ERA-like statement of equality to which the override would not apply. In order to win these changes, feminists had to mount a two-stage mobilization, first to change the wording in the federal government's proposal and then to pressure the provincial premiers to include section 28.[9]

Because it took place so quickly and was ultimately successful, this campaign did not have as profound an impact on the strategic orientation of Canadian feminists as the fight for the ERA had on American feminists. It did, nonetheless, remind liberal feminists (who were the most vociferous advocates of an entrenched Charter) of the importance of having women in formal political elites. As Hošek (1983, 280) notes, the battle that

Canadian women had to mount to win meaningful equality provisions in the Charter revealed the marginal role of women in Canadian politics and the forcefulness they had to exert to avoid total exclusion. Canadian feminists were not, however, the only ones to learn something from the battle over equality provisions in the Charter. As one woman involved in the fight observed, political parties – and the Liberals in particular – were in awe of the political muscle of the women's movement after the Charter episode (interview 15/03/94).

Enjoying a higher public profile and greater respect from political parties in the aftermath of the Charter mobilization, Canadian feminists were poised to make their presence known during the 1984 federal election. Prior to the election, the NAC executive focused on the election of women as a high priority and, in one of a very few documented instances of NAC communicating directly with the extra-parliamentary wings of the political parties, the organization also wrote to the parties' national presidents urging them to strive for gender parity in candidate nominations (Hošek 1984). During the campaign, NAC sponsored a nationally televised debate on women's issues between the three party leaders. That NAC was able to get all three leaders to participate was a testament both to the movement's new-found clout in Ottawa and the high profile of Chaviva Hošek, NAC president at the time.

Between 1970 and 1984, the Canadian women's movement was essentially multipartisan in orientation. Informal interpersonal ties connected NAC to all three established national political parties at the time. A former president of NAC called interpersonal ties to the political parties "highly significant ... It was very important to have people from all parties and we actively sought them out" (interview 26/02/94). The closest ties were with the NDP, followed by the Liberals. Although their numbers were small, there were also a few "red tory" PC activists involved in feminist organizations. As Table 3.1 shows, almost all of the women who led NAC in its first decade had strong ties to one of the three major political parties. The first three presidents of NAC were affiliated with the PCs, the NDP, and the Liberals in turn.[10] Of NAC's first eight presidents (from 1972 until 1986), all but one were significantly involved in a political party before, during, or after their terms. Five of these women ran for office at the federal or provincial level for one of the major political parties, one held a senior party office while she was president of NAC and then went on to be appointed to the Senate, and one had strong ties to the NDP through her work with the union movement.

Although partisan differences were never the primary source of conflict among Canadian feminists, the movement's multipartisan stance did invite occasional conflicts along party lines. With the Liberal party forming the federal government and displaying considerable interest in the internal politics of the Canadian women's movement, women with ties to that party were sometimes looked on with suspicion by other feminist activists who saw them as furthering partisan interests within the movement. In the words of one activist, some of the Liberal women involved in the movement were perceived to be "hugely partisan. There is no other way to say it except that they were there for the party. And that was part of what they were doing. These things were not separable, so that became extremely contentious" (interview 13/04/94). The NDP and unaligned women sought to avoid having the Liberal government "direct" NAC through Liberal women involved in the organization. This distrust was heightened during the movement's battle with the Liberal government in 1981 over the Charter of Rights and Freedoms (Bashevkin 1993, 27).

For their part, Liberal women active in women's movement organizations resisted the efforts of socialist feminists to expand the movement's scope beyond status-of-women issues into a broader economic critique

Table 3.1

Political affiliations of NAC presidents

Years	Name	Party affiliation	Scope of involvement
1971-4	Laura Sabia	PC	Candidate (post-NAC presidency)
1974-5	Grace Hartman	NDP	Candidate (post-NAC presidency)
1975-7	Lorna Marsden	Liberal	National Policy Chair (during NAC presidency); appointed to Senate (post-NAC presidency)
1977-9	Kay Macpherson	NDP	Candidate (during and after NAC presidency)
1979-81	Lynn McDonald	NDP	Candidate/elected (post-NAC presidency)
1981-2	Jean Wood	Unknown	n/a
1982-4	Doris Anderson	Liberal	Candidate (pre-NAC presidency); appointed to CACSW (pre-NAC presidency)
1984-6	Chaviva Hošek	Liberal	Candidate/elected to Ontario legislature/appointed to Cabinet (post-NAC presidency); policy advisor to Prime Minister Chrétien (post-NAC presidency)

Source: Compiled from Vickers et al. (1993).

(interviews 26/02/94; 09/04/94; 13/04/94). Liberal women in NAC tried to prevent NDP "capture" of NAC, while at the same time trying to negotiate a place for feminism within the Liberal party (as will be discussed in greater detail in Chapter 5). The ongoing tension between NDP and Liberal women and the presence of substantial numbers of each within national organizations of the women's movement effectively precluded serious consideration of a semi-permanent or formal alliance between the movement and either of the political parties.[11] This can be contrasted to the American experience, where Democratic women vastly outnumbered Republican women in national movement organizations, thereby making possible the movement's close alliance with the Democrats.

Dissent from Radical Feminists

Throughout this period, radical and, to a lesser degree, socialist feminists contested the faith of liberal feminists in the political system's capacity for change. The RCSW's analysis of women's participation in public life did not meet with unquestioning approval from the entire feminist community. Its analyses threw into question the institutions of liberal democracy and the social and economic structures on which they rested. After the publication of the RCSW's report, radical feminists accused the commission of tokenism, singling out for criticism its recommendation that women be appointed to the Senate, an institution that was "a fossilized relic of feudal times" (Larkin 1971, 7). The integrative bent of the RCSW's recommendation that the political parties' women's organizations be amalgamated with mainstream party organizations also prompted criticism that stressed the importance of autonomous women's organizations. Larkin (ibid.) took the RCSW to task for failing to address the development of women's caucuses within the political parties (most notably the NDP and other leftist parties) which "have recognized that women must learn to work together to express collectively their demands if they are to achieve anything more than having a few more exceptional women assuming leadership positions within political groups." The radical feminist critique was voiced at NAC's founding convention when some sixty of the 500 delegates banded together to form a radical caucus, drawing together feminists who did not share the conference organizers' belief in the liberal democratic system (Adamson et al. 1988, 65). The caucus rejected the idea of working through established political parties and advocated formation of a feminist political party. These women were, however, very much in a minority at the conference and were not brought under the NAC umbrella until considerably later, so at that time the critique of the liberal feminist approach in NAC and WPA was merely a relatively muted dissenting voice.

In 1979, in an effort to reconcile the tension between the desire for a political voice and the unwillingness to engage with established political parties, a group of Toronto activists, most of whom could be described as radical feminists, formed the Feminist Party of Canada (FPC). The impetus for forming the FPC was a concern about the quantity and quality of women's representation in federal politics. The founders believed that a feminist political party was necessary to allow women to participate in the political arena while maintaining their feminist ideals. Their vision was for the party to act as a political voice for the women's liberation movement and to advocate a "politics of care and community" to replace the established parties' "politics of conquest and chaos" (FPC 1979; Zaborszky 1988, 258).

Like the political parties that have emerged out of social movements in Western Europe, the FPC rejected traditional forms of party organization, opting for non-hierarchical structures and voluntary committees instead of a leader. The party had neither a constitution nor an executive. These non-traditional arrangements did little to help the nascent party surmount the obstacles faced by new entrants to the political scene. Any "anti-party" party must come to terms with its inherent contradictions if it is to achieve any political success, and the FPC did not pass this test. FPC members were divided on the question of whether the organization should become a registered provincial political party in Ontario, with some members arguing that seeking this status meant being co-opted by the patriarchal establishment, and others contending that this was a necessary means to a political end (Zaborszky 1988, 259). The FPC did eventually set out to gain registered party status in Ontario, but became defunct before it could fulfil the requirements for registration. It never ran candidates in elections at either the federal or provincial level, and it had no impact on the other political parties.

Ultimately, the idea of a feminist political party was doomed by the single-member plurality electoral system employed in Canada, since in such a system it is virtually impossible for a political party without a regional base of support to elect candidates (Cairns 1968). Even if this were not the case, however, it is unlikely that the FPC would have experienced electoral success. The internal debates between activists who wanted to use the party as a vehicle to bring feminism into the formal political arena and activists who preferred the politics of protest were all-consuming, thereby rendering the party virtually immobile. In any case, radical feminist organizing was not the prominent stream of feminist organizing in Canada during the 1970s and early 1980s. After 1984, however, it gained prominence.

Diverging Strategies (1985-93)
After the 1984 federal election, the orientation of the women's movement towards electoral politics began to change subtly. Specifically, the tension

between liberal feminists favouring engagement with party politics and the radical feminists preferring more oppositional forms of political action became somewhat more pronounced. In part, the existing tension was more noticeable because radical and socialist feminists became a more powerful force within NAC, so the radical feminist critique of the strategy of engaging with established political parties became a more prominent voice within the national organization. As NAC became more radical and oppositional in stance, it also grew ever more critical of political parties in general and the three Canadian political parties in particular. Women engaged with political parties and the project of electing women became alienated from NAC and threw their energies into electoral work. These diverging tendencies in the women's movement did not result in overt conflict between proponents of the two points of view, but rather created a breakdown in communication whereby advocates of each strategy simply pursued their own course with little regard for the other approach.

Encouraged by the 1984 NAC-sponsored leaders' debate, liberal and reformist feminists in the mid-1980s became more active in the project of electing women. This renewed interest was reflected in the formation of several organizations focused on increasing the number of women holding elected office at both the provincial and national levels (Maillé 1990; see Table 3.2). Of these, the group that proved to be the most active and resilient is the Committee for '94. A small group of women involved in each of the three major political parties, as well as journalists and others, formed this committee in 1984. The founders perceived themselves – accurately – as women of considerable influence and accomplishment who could draw public attention to the numerical underrepresentation of women and push the established political parties to remedy this (interviews 04/06/94; 03/09/94). The committee's membership was limited to approximately thirty women, and membership was by invitation only, maintaining the group's elite character. Most, but not all, of the members were involved in party politics. The committee's focus was on raising public consciousness of women's underrepresentation, encouraging women to run, providing occasional training sessions, creating an informal network among partisan women, and encouraging the political parties to nominate more women. It did not endorse individual women's candidacies, nor did it contribute financially or otherwise to any campaigns. During the same period, the women's organizations in the three major political parties also came to focus greater attention on the election of women under their party's banner.[12]

As these movement and party organizations became more active in promoting the election of women, the rest of the women's movement was undergoing profound changes. Most notably, the ideological orientation of NAC's leadership changed as radical and socialist feminists came to control the organization's executive. The new leaders transformed NAC from a fairly conventional lobbying organization into a more oppositional protest-oriented group. This new oppositional stance involved a much less deferential attitude towards political elites, a growing emphasis on "unconventional" protest tactics as a part of the organization's action repertoire, and an expansion in focus from a narrower status-of-women approach to a broader economic and social critique (see Vickers et al. 1993, 293-5). As NAC's stance became more oppositional, electoral politics became an ever more marginal part of the organization's activities.

The new NAC leaders were sceptical of the potential impact and political importance of the integration of women into electoral and partisan politics. After the election of Kim Campbell as leader of the PC party, NAC president Judy Rebick (1993, 10) stated that "women like that are going to become our most bitter opponents." On another occasion, Rebick told a journalist that "the political system is so patriarchal and so hierarchical – it is such a male culture. What happens to women politicians is they either get sidelined within it or they get co-opted into it" (in Sharpe 1994, 213). Although NAC has maintained a rhetorical commitment to the election of women, its calls for measures to promote or guarantee the election of women are generally not couched in terms of the potential policy impact, but in terms of expanding public discourses about "representativeness" to include gendered dimensions (see, for example, Léger and Rebick 1993).

Table 3.2

Major Canadian women's organizations focusing on electoral and partisan politics

Organization	Formed	Partisanship	Activities	Status
Women for Political Action	1972	Multipartisan	Training; pressure on parties	Defunct (c. 1979)
Feminist Party of Canada	1979	Quasi-party	Act as political vehicle for women's liberation movement; possibly run candidates	Defunct (c. 1983)
Committee for '94	1984	Multipartisan	Training; recruitment; public education; pressure on parties	Defunct (c. 1996)
FRAPPE	1985	Multipartisan	Public pressure; support of candidates at nomination stage	Active
CWPR	1986	Multipartisan	Educate and motivate women to run; public pressure	Defunct (c. 1989)

This ambivalence is captured by grass-roots feminist Kike Roach's statement: "I'm equivocal about what party politics can do for disadvantaged people, since so much of it seems to be about kowtowing to a big-business agenda. But when I speak to women's groups, I say we should have 52 per cent representation in Parliament and in every level of government as a basic issue of fairness and democracy" (Rebick and Roach 1996, 165).

Compounding this scepticism, NAC leaders have grown increasingly critical of political parties as institutions, arguing that they privilege electoral success over the public interest and that women face substantial barriers within political parties. According to Rebick, "There's nothing more patriarchal than a political party. Some of our most effective women leaders have found it impossible to function in political parties" (Rebick and Roach 1996, 167-8).[13] This has also translated into a distrust of women who have partisan affiliations. The organization that in 1975 chose a vice-president of the Liberal party to lead it, in 1987 passed a resolution preventing a nominated party candidate or anyone holding a high-ranking elected or paid position in a political party from holding an executive position in the organization. In 1988, the NAC executive forced a woman who held the position of national advisor to the NDP on women's issues to resign her NAC executive position because of the perceived conflict of interest (NAC 1988a). This suggests a deep erosion of NAC's informal ties to the political parties. Although the parties' women's organizations remained members of NAC, they were seldom active within the organization. As discussed in greater detail below, this severing of ties signalled a marked change in NAC's partisan orientation.

As NAC's ties to the political parties eroded, the organization developed stronger links with social movement coalitions and the labour movement (Rebick 1992; Cohen 1992b; Gottlieb 1993). This began in 1985, when NAC joined the Family Allowance Coalition, established to oppose the Mulroney government's cuts to social programs. NAC's move towards participation in such coalitions stemmed in part from its search for a political vehicle other than a political party. The NAC executive's review of the 1988 election campaign discussed "the difficulty of not having a stance or party of our own" and concluded that the organization should work more in coalitions (NAC 1989). NAC went on to join the Action Canada Network, a social justice coalition of trade unions, women's, student, and farmer groups, teachers' and nurses' associations, and other public sector organizations (Rebick 1992, 48). It was largely through such coalitions that NAC mobilized in opposition to the Canada-United States Free Trade Agreement and the North American Free Trade Agreement (NAFTA).

As NAC became more oppositional in stance and disengaged from electoral and partisan politics, the distance between NAC and the women engaged in electoral politics grew. NAC's oppositional stance frustrated women working inside the political parties and in multipartisan organizations focused primarily on electoral politics, who saw it as counterproductive and ineffective. Over time, they have gradually disengaged from NAC. For their part, NAC leaders and activists did not perceive the strategy of working within existing political institutions to hold much potential for meaningful social or political change. The organizations focused on electoral politics are not well integrated into NAC, and thus are distanced from the organized women's movement. Most notably, the Committee for '94 did not have the close ties to NAC that earlier electorally focused organizations, particularly the WPA, enjoyed. The women involved in the committee considered themselves to be feminists, but their ties to political parties were generally stronger than their links to other women's movement organizations. While remaining a member of NAC, the committee did not send a representative to NAC's annual meetings, and some members of the committee were critical of NAC's increasingly oppositional political stance (interviews 09/03/94, 10/03/94). When NAC took a controversial stand against the Charlottetown Accord (which all three major parties had endorsed), there was some discussion among members of the Committee for '94 about pulling out of NAC, but no such decision was made. There is evidence of a similar rift between women in the political parties and NAC. In the words of one partisan woman who was extensively involved with NAC in the 1970s, "Inside each of the political parties now you have a women's movement almost on its own. And the links to NAC have broken down ... it's no longer important to go to the NAC annual meeting in order to be a feminist activist in the parties" (interview 26/02/94). The net result of these diverging tendencies has been a growing gulf within the women's movement. This had profound implications for the content of feminist activism within the political parties, as is discussed in Chapter 5.

Partisan Orientation
As NAC grew critical of electoral politics and political parties, its ties to the three major political parties eroded. The group's earlier multipartisanship was replaced by an apartisan orientation, which is to say that it emphasized competing with political parties as an intermediary between society and the state.

NAC's ties to the Progressive Conservative party, never strong, were the first to be cut. As neo-conservatives displaced more moderate elements in the party during the early 1980s, it became less open to the claims of liberal feminism than it had been under the leadership of Joe Clark. The relationship between NAC and the Conservatives deteriorated even further after the party formed the federal government in 1984 (Cohen 1992b, 220). The election of the first Mulroney government in 1984 coincided roughly with the emergence of a backlash against the women's movement. Feminist leaders were alarmed by the emergence of the anti-feminist organization Realistic Equal and Active for Life Women (REAL Women) and the apparent sympathy it had won from elements within the Conservative party. In 1985, while REAL Women was lobbying to receive public funding through the Secretary of State's Women's Program, approximately thirty members of the PC caucus met representatives of the organization (Pal 1993, 147). In response to this pressure, the government extended public funding previously earmarked for feminist organizations to the anti-feminist organization to hold a conference. Moreover, as the Mulroney government pursued its neo-liberal agenda of deficit reduction, cutbacks to social programs, and free trade with the United States, feminist activists increasingly found themselves in profound opposition to government policy. Cohen (1992b) notes that the absence of women affiliated to the PCs within NAC in the mid-1980s meant that there was little resistance within the organization to adopting a more oppositional stance towards the government. This can be contrasted to the previous era, when Liberal women within NAC stood in the way of more harsh criticisms of federal policy.

Relations between NAC and the Conservatives deteriorated even further in the aftermath of the 1988 election, during which NAC was an outspoken opponent of the Canada-United States Free Trade Agreement. The Mulroney government responded harshly to this. In 1989, Cabinet ministers refused to attend NAC's annual parliamentary lobby for the first time since it began in 1976. In the same year, the federal government froze the budget of the Secretary of State's Women's Program (including NAC's funding) and then reduced it in 1990 (Pal 1993, 147). Through the rest of the Mulroney mandate, NAC was a thorn in the government's side, opposing vociferously the government's constitutional initiatives, its pursuit of a broader North American Free Trade Agreement, and its efforts to reduce or eliminate various social programs.[14]

While NAC severed any remaining ties it had to the PCs in the mid-1980s, its connections to the Liberals were not so much severed as allowed to wither slowly. The Liberals faced a daunting task of rebuilding after its defeat in 1984 and had little to offer women's movement organizations. At the same time, the changing character of NAC did not encourage Liberal women to remain involved in the organization during this time. Several Liberal women chose to become involved with the Women's Legal Education and Action Fund (LEAF) rather than NAC during this period.

The most surprising development in the period from 1985 to 1993 was the breakdown of cordial relations between NAC and the NDP. As noted

above, the NDP has always come closer than the other major political parties to adopting a feminist policy agenda as its own and, as discussed in
Chapter 6, there was a significant feminist mobilization within the party
in the early 1970s. Given that radical and socialist feminists came to play
a more prominent role in NAC in the mid-1980s and that NAC developed
closer links with the labour movement during this period, it would be reasonable to expect that NAC might have become more closely allied with
the NDP. This did not prove to be the case, however.

Prior to the 1988 federal election, Judy Rebick, then the high-profile
leader of NAC, ran for an NDP nomination in a Toronto riding, but was
defeated by a male candidate. Rebick said of this, "If I'd taken the nomination, the women's movement would have been mobilized ... Since then,
I've gotten so disillusioned with the NDP that I wouldn't run for them" (in
Sharpe 1994, 170). During the 1988 campaign, the NDP sought NAC's
endorsement, but NAC refused and even made its participation in social
movement coalitions contingent on the coalitions' non-partisanship
(interview 13/04/94). Many feminists supported the NDP but doubted the
party's commitment to the movement's agenda and were consequently
reluctant to enter into any formal alliance (interview 13/04/94). After the
1988 election, NAC leaders joined union leaders and others in criticizing
the NDP for ceding the leadership of the anti-free trade campaign to the
Liberals. Ironically, NAC's opposition to the Canada-United States Free
Trade Agreement created the mistaken impression that NAC endorsed the
NDP in 1988 (see, for example, Pal 1993, 145, 147). This is curious on two
grounds: first, because NAC explicitly refused the NDP's request for an
endorsement in that year, and second, because, much to the NDP's cha-
grin, it was the Liberals rather than the NDP that led the fight against free
trade in the 1988 election.

NAC's relationship with the NDP became even more strained in 1992,
when NAC opposed the Charlottetown Accord, a constitutional package
endorsed by all three political parties. NAC's decision to oppose the accord
marked a coming of age of a new politics of diversity within the organization. In an interview with a feminist newspaper, Rebick attributed the decision to strong opposition from women activists at the grass-roots level,
women of colour, Aboriginal women, and trade union women. NAC's decision to oppose the Charlottetown Accord was influenced by the Native
Women's Association of Canada (NWAC), which opposed the accord and
which had failed in its bid to gain a seat at the constitutional negotiating
table. NWAC did not represent the views of all Aboriginal women, many of
whom supported the Charlottetown Accord and its recognition of an inherent right to native self-government. Rebick later stated that the decision
"was a transformative moment for me because I knew this organization

had really changed. That's what gave us the strength to do it ... We said, ultimately, if we make a decision based on saving NAC rather than on what is in the best interests of women, we are doing the same thing we criticize political parties of" (Huang and Jaffer 1993, 10).

By deciding to oppose the accord, NAC knowingly alienated its traditional allies in the political parties, particularly the NDP (Gottleib 1993, 371). This alienation was made all the more profound during the 1993 campaign when the new NAC president, Sunera Thobani, told reporters that the NDP ignored the concerns of women just as the Liberals and Conservatives did (McLeod 1994, 124). This statement reflected NAC's disappointment that the NDP under the leadership of Audrey McLaughlin had failed to make women's issues the centrepiece of its political strategy (ibid.).

As NAC grew distant from the political parties, its stance became effectively apartisan. NAC leaders claimed that the failure of political parties to provide adequate representation for the public forced the organization to transform itself into "the extra-parliamentary opposition" (Gottleib 1993, 380-1). In the words of former NAC president Judy Rebick, "People see us as one of the only progressive voices that has any power. And they want us to do everything, not just focus on women's issues. *They want us to act like a political party*" (in Gottleib 1993, 381, emphasis added). This idea that NAC could link society and the state more effectively than political parties lies at the heart of its apartisan orientation. The organization's stance was not non-partisan, in the sense that its focus remained very much in the formal political arena, yet rejected political parties' monopoly of the arena.

NAC's ability to perform the functions of a political party had limits. The organization was certainly capable of aggregating and articulating interests, two of the crucial functions of political parties. Even if NAC cannot or did not aggregate the interests of men, it has demonstrated a capacity to speak for a diverse range of women. Preoccupation with internal questions of representation and inclusiveness contributed to NAC's ability to act as an aggregator and articulator of interests – notably those of First Nations women, immigrant women, visible minority women, and lesbians – that have heretofore not had champions in the political arena. What NAC could not do is break the political parties' monopoly on electoral competition. NAC did not contest elections nor could it form a government. In this sense, its apartisan stance falls short of competing with political parties. Moreover, having severed its ties to political parties, NAC no longer acts as a source of personnel for parties to recruit.

Two sets of factors – one internal to the women's movement and the other external – explain the changes in NAC's orientation towards electoral politics and the party system. The first, and most significant, internal factor is the changing composition of NAC. Because NAC is an umbrella organization within which a diverse range of feminisms coexist, it has always been host to a range of opinions regarding strategic orientation. NAC's executive has always included women who reject the strategy of working through political parties or the electoral route as "naive" or as compromising the integrity of the women's movement (interviews 26/02/94; 09/04/94; 13/04/94). Between 1984 and 1987, NAC's membership expanded rapidly to include more women's service and advocacy groups (such as women's centres and shelters), women's caucuses of labour unions, and organizations representing more marginal segments of the female population such as immigrant women, visible minority women, women with disabilities, and lesbians (Vickers et al. 1993, 142-4). This rapid expansion in the membership and in the diversity of feminisms within NAC resulted in the election of socialist and radical feminists to leadership positions within the organization. As NAC's membership expanded, the rejection of party politics gained currency within the organization. Moreover, many of the liberal feminists who advocated working through political parties and emphasized the importance of interpersonal ties with the political parties moved on to other endeavours (several running for office) and, in some cases, became alienated from NAC (interviews 26/02/94; 25/03/94; 06/04/94).

Compounding this, many activists became disillusioned with the strategy of working inside established political parties because the results were so much less than had originally been expected. Rosemary Brown (1988, 106), who ran for the leadership of the NDP in 1975 in an effort to bring feminism into the formal political arena, has noted that attempts to bring women's issues onto the public agenda by increasing the representation of women in electoral politics have had "disappointing" results. She argues that her own experience suggests the existence of "very real limits to using electoral politics as a tool to attack discriminatory barriers and ... [to] end women's oppression. The reality is less than the promise" (ibid.). Brown is by no means alone in her changing perception of the potential benefits of electoral politics for feminists. In the words of one long-time activist, the women's movement has "lost a great deal of [its] confidence that the government can change much ... Women are questioning the power of the individual Member of Parliament and the parties ... to effect any adequate changes. So many of the questions are sort of supraparliamentary" (interview 14/03/94). Former NAC president Judy Rebick expressed this very clearly when she observed that even though she had lost an NDP nomination by a mere twenty-two votes, her political influence was greater as NAC president: "Where would I have been more effective from 1989 to 1993 –

as an NDP backbencher or as president of NAC? There's no question I was more effective as president of NAC" (Rebick and Roach 1996, 168).

A third internal factor, integrally related to the changing composition of NAC, is the evolution in the ideological character of the women's movement. Prior to 1984, the dominant ideological tendency within the Canadian women's movement and within NAC was what Vickers et al. (1993, 37) term "radical liberalism." The core elements of radical liberalism were a commitment to working within the political process and a belief in the efficacy of state action, particularly of welfare state programs. Given that the roots of the contemporary Canadian movement lie in traditional women's organizations, the commitment to the established political process was not at all surprising. The project of integrating women into established political parties and electoral politics constituted an integral component of this acceptance of the existing political process. Although some activists did seek to circumvent political parties by running independent candidates, their activity remained within the confines of electoral politics and, in the case of the WPA, was rapidly absorbed into traditional partisan folds.

After the mid-1980s, however, NAC's earlier commitment to working through established institutions waned. NAC's critique of the unrepresentativeness of Canadian political institutions extended beyond concerns regarding the demographic composition of political institutions to include a fundamental questioning of the presuppositions of representative democracy. Some NAC leaders rejected the idea that one person can "speak for" another and consequently question the very idea of representative democracy (see Day 1993).

A key element in any explanation of the shift away from engagement with established political parties must look to the faith of the women's movement in the capacity of the state to effect change. To come to terms with this, however, it is necessary to look at external factors – the changing political opportunity structure. In the words of one NAC activist, "The things going on inside the organization [through the mid-1980s] relate to the things going on outside of the organization as well" (interview 13/04/94). More specifically, both the change in government in 1984 and the apparently declining capacity of the Canadian state contributed to this change in the ideological character of the movement.

The election of the Progressive Conservative government led by Brian Mulroney marked an end to the federal government's willingness to consult with and provide substantial financial resources to feminist organizations. As already noted, the Mulroney government slashed funding to feminist groups, decreased these groups' access to the policy process, and on occasion appeared to ally itself with the anti-feminist organization REAL Women.

Although the Conservatives never adopted the blatant anti-feminism of the American Republicans, their neo-liberal agenda was anathematic to the socialist feminism prevalent in NAC during this period. The election of this less responsive federal government, then, forced NAC to rethink its lobby strategy and contributed to a radicalization of the organization.

The second element is an apparent decline in the capacity of the Canadian state to effect change. Entry into the Canada-United States Free Trade Agreement in 1989 and NAFTA in 1993, coupled with the broader phenomenon of globalization, limited the Canadian state's ability to intervene in certain policy areas. These same factors may have exacerbated pressures for harmonization with US regulations and standards in a range of policy areas including taxation, labour legislation, and social policy.[15] An even more important, and related, source of constraint was the perceived fiscal crisis of the state. The pervasive belief among political actors and international investors that the Canadian government's level of indebtedness was nearing critical proportions acted as a profound limit on policy options. Moreover, it prompted a significant trend towards decentralization through the 1980s and early 1990s, as the federal government reduced its role in providing funding to provincial governments for social programs, education, and health care (see Maslove 1992). These constraints on the capacity of the Canadian federal state made it a less promising focus for feminist intervention and contributed to a scepticism among some feminist activists that real change could be achieved though traditional political channels. This stands in contrast to the expanding interventionist state of the 1970s that provided relatively fertile ground for the policy agenda of the emerging women's movement (Vickers et al. 1993, 52).

Clearly, in light of the election of the Mulroney government and the declining capacity of the Canadian state, NAC's move away from its earlier multipartisan strategy was reasonable. This raises the question, however, of why other Canadian feminists grew more interested in the project of electing women during the same period. In large part, this can be attributed to a growing gulf in the social location of activists. On the one hand, many of the activists who had led the movement in its first decade benefited from the movement's success and used it as a springboard into the Canadian political elite. Their own successes reinforced the perception that integration into partisan and electoral politics was an essential means of achieving power for women and implementing the movement's policy agenda. As these women were drawn into the partisan fold, their links with organized feminism outside the political parties in many cases weakened. At the same time, the increasing diversity and scope of the women's movement meant that a growing proportion of activists were "outsiders" suspicious of established political parties and institutions. Where the first generation of activists saw open doors, the next generation sees potential traps and the looming threat of co-optation. It is not surprising, then, that the two elements of the women's movement embarked on different paths.

The Chrétien Years (1993-2000)
The results of the 1993 federal election profoundly changed the opportunity structure facing the Canadian women's movement. Given NAC's high-profile role in fighting the Charlottetown Accord and its acrimonious relationship with the Mulroney government, one might have expected that the organization was poised to assume a higher profile and a less confrontational relationship with a newly elected Liberal government. As it turned out, however, this was not to be. Rather, the shattering of the old Canadian party system and the ascendance of the right-wing Reform party as the major opposition party in English Canada profoundly limited the opportunities available to feminist activists within the formal political arena. Compounding this, NAC president Judy Rebick stepped down from her post and was replaced by Sunera Thobani. Thobani provided strong leadership within the organization, but was unable to replicate Rebick's extraordinary success in gaining public and media attention for the organization. As a consequence of these factors, NAC found itself all but shut out of the formal political arena. During the 1997 federal election, the organization struggled to have women's issues addressed at all in the campaign.

The 1993 federal election decimated the three-party system that had been in place since the 1960s. The Liberal party was elected with a majority, but the NDP and the PCs won so few seats that both lost their status as official parties in the House of Commons.[16] Replacing them were the right-wing, socially conservative Reform party and the separatist Bloc Québécois (BQ). Although the BQ formed the official Opposition, its separatist stance meant that its interventions into broader Canadian debates were limited in scope and number. As a consequence, the major opposition party within English Canada was the Reform party. With its agenda of deficit reduction, fiscal responsibility, and a brand of social conservatism, the Reform party effectively pulled the political centre of gravity in English Canada to the right. Facing Reform as a political opponent and a fiscal situation that was perceived to be spiralling out of control, the Liberal government pursued a policy agenda that centred around cutbacks to government programs and transfers. It reformed the system of fiscal federalism radically, effectively offloading many of its budgetary difficulties onto provincial governments and significantly reducing the federal presence in the fields of social services, health, and education.

These developments had profound consequences for feminist activism in Canada. First, the change in the party system significantly reduced feminist access into the formal political arena. The Reform party was hardly disposed towards cooperation with feminists. In fact Reform refused to meet with NAC during its annual lobbies. The Liberals, more concerned with competition from the right than from the left, had little incentive to engage with feminists. Moreover, having set out on a course of deficit reduction and program cutbacks, the Liberal government's policy agenda had become far less ideologically congruent with that of the women's movement than had been the case for earlier Liberal administrations. With the NDP reduced to a rump and all but one of the party's female MPs defeated, feminist activists found themselves without many influential allies within the partisan political arena. Partially as a consequence of this, feminist issues had limited profile from 1993 to 1997.

The same was true in the 1997 federal election. Despite NAC's renewed efforts to put gender issues on the national political agenda, they received virtually no discussion during the campaign, much to NAC's dismay (Rinehart 1997). NAC tried to repeat its success from 1984 and sponsored a debate for the party leaders on women's issues. With the exception of the NDP's new leader Alexa McDonough, however, none of the major party leaders attended. The Liberal minister responsible for the status of women, Hedy Fry, was scheduled to attend to represent the government, but she cancelled with short notice. Instead of having the debate televised on the national networks as it was in 1984, NAC was able only to have the debate televised on CPAC, a cable channel catering to political junkies. Not even Newsworld (the Canadian CNN) televised the debate. In short, NAC was making valiant efforts to re-enter the national partisan political debate, but found the political parties far less willing than they had previously been to address feminist issues explicitly.

NAC's partisan leanings became fairly clear in its press releases during and after the election. The morning after the election, under the headline "Canada Sends a Wake-Up Call to the Liberals," the group's press release claimed that "with the NDP and Bloc in the House, women's groups can at least be assured that social justice issues will be given attention and keep the Liberals from continuing to slip into the abyss of right-wing rhetoric. The successful campaign run by Alexa McDonough, Leader of the NDP, is a victory for women's groups across Canada as there will be more voices in Parliament speaking about the bread and butter issues such as: social programs, medicare, funding to women's groups, etc." The press release went on to attribute the increased number of women in the House of Commons (fifty-eight, up slightly from fifty-three) to the NDP, claiming that "the party's policy on gender equality ... provided the leadership which the Liberals have tried to emulate with the appointment of a number of women." The number of women elected, NAC claimed, was "indicative of the strong role the NDP undertook in this election" (NAC 1997).

The language in this press release went far beyond the careful non-partisan rhetoric that NAC had used in earlier years. In part, this reflects a reduction in the constraints that previously prevented the group from engaging more directly in the partisan political arena. As federal funding to the organization has declined and ties to the union movement have been strengthened, NAC has become somewhat less constrained in its ability to enter the partisan arena more directly. Moreover, as NAC's internal composition has changed, its interpersonal ties to the Liberal party have been significantly diminished, so there is no longer an internal pressure not to engage more directly with the NDP. Not only have the constraints to NAC's partisan engagement been diminished, but the incentives for partisan engagement also increased substantially after the 1993 election. In short, the virtual absence of the NDP from the federal political arena after 1993 meant that NAC and other left-leaning and progressive groups had no political voice, and consequently could only protest the Chrétien government's hard-line stance on deficit reduction from the outside. With the Canadian party system in flux in 1997, it was imperative that the NDP be returned to Parliament with enough seats to ensure its survival. It is also noteworthy that as NAC's policy focus has shifted over time to focus primarily on economic issues such as free trade, support for social programs, child care and child poverty, and issues concerning immigrant and visible minority women, its agenda has become all the more congruent with that of the NDP.

During the Chrétien government's second term, NAC faced profound difficulties. The federal government once again cut the organization's funding, bringing it to the brink of bankruptcy. Although the Liberals, NDP, and BQ continued to meet with the organization during its annual parliamentary lobby, by 1999 the Conservatives had joined Reform in refusing to meet with the group. In total, only twenty-eight of 301 MPs attended the lobby. During the 1999 lobby, the group maintained its confrontational approach, booing Cabinet ministers and refusing to let them finish answering questions (Alberts 1999). In short, NAC's apartisan stance meant that the organization found itself firmly on the outside of the formal political arena at the national level.

Conclusion

Relative to the US women's movement, the Canadian movement has not focused particularly intensely on electoral politics. Over time, in fact, its interest in the electoral arena has diminished. This in large part reflects the incentives embedded in the political opportunity structure facing the

Canadian women's movement. The combination of parliamentary government, highly disciplined and cohesive political parties, and a state increasingly constrained by fiscal and global pressures has limited the efforts of the Canadian women's movement within the partisan political arena. Ironically, even though the Canadian women's movement has focused less attention on electoral politics than its American counterpart, Canadian political parties have been as responsive, if not more responsive, to organized feminism than their US counterparts. It is to the question of partisan responsiveness that we now turn.

4

Polarization: American Parties Respond

The story of American political parties' responsiveness to the contemporary women's movement begins in the early 1970s, when both the Democrats and the Republicans started to grapple with the question of how to appeal to women as a newly politicized group. Although the Democrats went considerably further than the Republicans in their efforts to forge alliances with feminist organizations, both parties initially sought to win the allegiance of "women voters" through appeals based in moderate feminism.

The Democrats continued on this path through the 1980s. Feminist organizations advocated and won representational guarantees for women at the party's conventions, thereby creating a feminist presence working on behalf of a feminist policy agenda within the party. In 1984, women's movement organizations were instrumental in the party's decision to pursue a "gender gap" strategy and in presidential nominee Walter Mondale's selection of Geraldine Ferraro as his running mate. Subsequently, however, the movement-party alliance weakened as movement organizations focused less on presidential politics and as a neo-liberal faction determined to moderate the party's ideological stance gained influence within the party and displaced internal constituencies, including feminists.

The Republican party, since 1980, has been overtly anti-feminist in stance. It has created the appearance of responsiveness to the women's movement by encouraging the inclusion of women in high-profile elite positions in the party, but has defined its policy stance in direct opposition to the feminist policy agenda. There are some attitudinal feminists included in party elites, but their numbers are small and their influence apparently limited. This situation has been fostered by the captive relationship between the anti-feminist religious right and the Republican party since the early 1980s.

As a consequence of these diverging trajectories, the US party system has effectively polarized in its response to feminism. The Democrats became the party of feminists, and the GOP the party of anti-feminism. This dynamic is self-reinforcing: once polarization has taken place and each party is entrenched in its stance, there is little potential for alliances to shift or stances to soften until some external event disrupts the equilibrium. Thus, even though both parties have moderated their stances somewhat since the 1980s, the polarized pattern persists to the present.

The American Party System

American politics is characterized by a two-party system with heterogeneous parties organized through confederal principles. What this means is that the two national parties are alliances, sometimes uneasy, of distinctive state parties. Complicating matters further, the national political parties are organized into three discrete branches: the presidential, congressional, and senatorial parties. The two latter wings of each party centre on the caucus in the respective legislative chamber. In addition to the caucus organization and the leadership it elects, both parties have congressional and senatorial campaign committees that raise money and, to a degree, coordinate electoral activities. The presidential wings of the two parties are centred on the national committees: the Republican National Committee (RNC) and Democratic National Committee (DNC). The national committees are the closest American equivalents of national party organization as understood elsewhere. The committees themselves are composed of representatives of the state parties, as well as representatives of the senatorial and congressional wings of the parties; they maintain permanent offices in Washington, DC, and focus on election preparedness. When the party holds the White House, or once a presidential candidate has been nominated, the national committees are effectively controlled by the presidential campaign organization. Since the 1980s, both national committees have become more prominent, professionalized organizations. This has particularly been the case for the RNC, which outstripped the DNC considerably throughout the 1980s and early 1990s in its professionalization and ability to raise funds (Aldrich 1995, 257).[1]

Another significant change in the US party system in recent decades has been the increasing ideological homogeneity of the parties. Although by comparative standards American political parties remain loose conglomerations of various ideas and interests, the trend in recent decades has been towards greater ideological homogeneity, with the Republicans becoming a more ideologically cohesive conservative party, and the Democrats becoming more liberal. As with the professionalization of the national committee, this trend has been more pronounced in the Republican party than in the Democratic.

The conservative transformation of the Republican party took place in two waves. The first was a growing support for a secular, libertarian brand of conservatism typified by Barry Goldwater, the party's presidential nominee in 1964. This wave of conservatism displaced liberal Republicans, turning the party into a "virtually monolithic bastion of conservatism" (Miller and Jennings 1986, 12; Rae 1989, 5). The second wave of conservatism came in the 1970s and may not yet have crested. It has washed away what was left of the liberal presence in the party, and has come into conflict with the party's secular conservatives. This second wave is a social conservatism espoused by evangelical Christians and pro-life activists. The religious right has been a significant presence in the Republican party since the 1970s, but the formation of the Christian Coalition in 1990 has formalized and intensified the Christian presence in the party. Although not distinct in ethnic or confessional terms, the ideological bent and social agenda of the Christian right, as well as the grass-roots support it commands, have presented a profound challenge to the GOP, leaving party regulars plaintively calling for a "big tent" with room for all. The conflict between the Christian right, the "Goldwater Republicans," and the last vestiges of the liberal Republicans provides the backdrop for the examination of the Republican party's response to the women's movement.

Since 1968, the Democrats have struggled to maintain their crumbling "new deal" coalition while accommodating new social groups – including the women's movement – that saw the party as their own. The "new deal" coalition of the South, the cities, immigrants, Blacks, the working class, and unions eroded through the 1960s and 1970s. As the party lost support in the South and among blue collar workers (the "Reagan Democrats"), ideological liberals, Blacks, Hispanics, women, gays and lesbians, and environmentalists have become key internal constituencies. Thus, as the influence of old-school southern Democrats has waned, the party as a whole has become somewhat more liberal.

As a result of the entry of these groups into party affairs, the party is heterogeneous in composition, and its activists' primary political referents are interest groups (Klinkner 1994a, 206). The culture of this heterogeneous party is characterized by a bottom-up understanding of power, a penchant for conflictual intra-party debates, and a reliance on procedural, rather than organizational reforms (Freeman 1987; Klinkner 1994a). The internal tension between old and new coalition members has been manifested in conflicts within the party over the advisability of procedural reforms designed to enhance internal democracy and inclusiveness, as well as conflicts over the party's ideological stance and image.

Rae (1994, 20) notes that by the late 1980s, four distinct factions within the party could be identified: the new left and minorities faction, the party regulars, the neo-liberals, and the South. He argues, however, that there are clear indications of a long-term erosion in the influence of regulars at the party's elite level and a much slower erosion of the southern Democrats. The neo-liberal faction, which is associated with the Democratic leadership council, and which is generally supportive of the new left position on the rights of women and minorities, is coming to dominate the Democratic party. The conflicts among new politics groups and the "party regulars" provided the backdrop for the emergence of feminism as a constituency within the party in the 1970s and early 1980s; the ascendance of the neo-liberal faction and its efforts to moderate the party's policy stance and image provides the backdrop for feminists' efforts to retain their place in the party in the late 1980s and 1990s.

Pre-Mobilization (Suffrage to 1970)

Had they been given a glimpse into the late twentieth century, American suffragists might have been surprised to learn that the Democrats would become champions of feminism and the Republicans its opponent. At the time of the battle to win the vote for women, the situation was the reverse. The Republican National Committee endorsed woman suffrage at its 1916 convention (although the platform plank left the matter up to the states to implement as they saw fit). The powerful southern wing of the Democratic party staunchly opposed woman suffrage (Graham 1996, 84, 114). Even though this gave the Republicans an advantage among newly enfranchised female voters, party leaders feared women voters would create a "petticoat hierarchy which may at will upset all orderly slates and commit undreamed of executions at the polls" (in Chafe 1991, 25). Both political parties viewed the expansion of the franchise and the formation of the non-partisan League of Women Voters (LWV) as threatening and possibly disruptive developments. Although the league refrained from pressuring the parties to include women in party bodies, both parties undertook to create roles for women in a pre-emptive effort to win the allegiance of newly enfranchised voters.

To solidify support among women, the Republicans established a women's division of the RNC in 1919 and in 1924 adopted a rule requiring that the RNC be composed of one committeeman and one committee-woman from each state and territory. From 1924 on, the post of vice-chair was held by a woman who acted as the national head of Republican women (LWV 1927b). The Democrats took similar actions. To gain votes in the eleven western states where women had already been enfranchised, the party established the women's division of the DNC in 1916. The 1920 national convention passed a resolution mandating election of a national committeewoman from every state by the same method as that of the national committeeman from that state (NWPC 1980, 3). From 1920 on, the post of party vice-chair was reserved for a woman.

The parties' enthusiasm for these internal reorganizations faded rapidly. The 1920 and 1924 elections demonstrated that women – when they did vote – did not vote as a bloc, nor did they punish candidates who had failed to defer to women's organizations on key issues (Cott 1990, 158-9). Although the DNC retained the fifty/fifty representational structure it had put in place in the early 1920s, it went no further. Moreover, the fifty/fifty principle, although mandated by law in several states, was enforced at the state level only sporadically (LWV 1927b). The superficiality of the fifty/fifty measure soon became apparent to feminist activists, who noted its minimal effectiveness and dismissed it as a "gesture to placate" women (LWV 1927a).

In 1932, the Democrats took a first step towards what would be their 1972 rendezvous with the women's movement. Franklin Delano Roosevelt's New Deal administration was an activist, interventionist effort to alleviate suffering caused by the Great Depression. This shift towards interventionist government prompted a realignment of the US electorate, as the beneficiaries of the federal government's new activism were drawn together into the New Deal coalition (McSweeney and Zvesper 1991, 31). This coalition was composed of the party's stalwart supporters in the South, residents of northern cities, immigrants, Blacks, the working class, and unions.

The New Deal administration was important to the relationship that eventually emerged between the party and the women's movement in two ways. First, the party's espousal of activist government and identification with disadvantaged groups during the New Deal made it the logical political home for the second wave of the women's movement once it emerged. Second, the role that women played in the New Deal administration and in building the Democratic party into a national organization during this era established a feminist presence in the party that, although it waned in the 1950s, nonetheless offered the basis for a revitalization in the early 1970s.

The New Deal administration drew women to the Democrats, both as voters and administrators. Activist women, many of whom were colleagues and friends of the First Lady, went to Washington in unprecedented numbers to assume positions in the Roosevelt administration. One of these women was Mary (Molly) Dewson, a prominent social activist and close ally of Eleanor Roosevelt. FDR appointed Dewson director of the DNC women's division in 1932, and she transformed the division into a powerful force within the party. With Eleanor Roosevelt's support, Dewson convinced FDR to make the women's division a full-time operation and then proceeded to use it as a base for her successful efforts to have women appointed to positions in the administration (Ware 1987, 168-84).

Dewson was also instrumental in pushing the party to accept equal representation for women on the platform committee in 1940 (ibid., 218). The women's division in the DNC grew less influential after Dewson retired as director, and subsequently varied according to the ability and influence of the woman holding the director's post. It regained some of its earlier clout when India Edwards served as director during the early 1950s.

This success in revitalizing the women's division within the DNC and in attracting women to the Democratic party prompted the formation in 1938 of the National Federation of Republican Women (NFRW), a federation of state and local Republican women's clubs. The initiative for the federation came from the chair of the RNC at the time, who was concerned that local Republican women's clubs were campaigning for FDR (interview 01/02/95). He sent Marion Martin – then RNC assistant chair and head of the women's division – to form the federation. Its primary function was to be national party building, by forging links between local and national party organizations. Until 1948, the women's division of the RNC exercised effective control over the NFRW (Baer 1991b). The organization gradually gained independence from the RNC as its financial and organizational base grew.

After the Second World War, traditional gender roles were more strictly enforced at the social level, and women in the parties were expected to conform to societal norms. In 1951, President Truman offered the post of DNC chair to India Edwards, who refused it because she did not believe that men in the party were ready to accept a woman in the post (Edwards 1977). In 1953, the chair of the DNC dissolved the women's division in the name of integrating women into the party. Edwards, who was the DNC vice-chair and director of the women's division at the time, said this of the decision: "Theoretically, it was a good idea, but I knew that actually it meant women would no longer be planning and activating the committee's educational work. It meant that the women would not have their own budget and not be able to make decisions about anything of importance" (ibid., 203). When Edwards resigned from her position as the DNC's vice-chair shortly after the decision to disband the women's division, she was replaced by Katie Loucheim. According to then DNC chair Steve Mitchell, Loucheim's qualifications for the post were her lovely Georgetown house, her ability to entertain beautifully, and her wealthy husband (ibid., 258). With this appointment, the role of women in the Democratic party settled into more traditional patterns consistent with the prevailing ethos of the era.

This should not, however, be taken to mean that women were not involved in party activities during the postwar period. In fact, women who were not employed outside the home played a substantial role in running the day-to-day affairs of local party organizations. Their role was so impor-tant that the large-scale entry of women into the paid labour force in the 1960s and beyond played a significant role in the decline of the "amateur democrat" and the rise of professionalized partisans in the late 1960s and early 1970s (Ware 1985, 77-8). Despite their crucial contributions to main-taining local party organizations, women for the most part did not play leadership roles, and their participation was not politicized along gender lines.

Initial Party Responses (1970-2)
All of this changed in the early 1970s with the mobilization of the con-temporary women's movement and the apparent politicization of women as an electoral force to be reckoned with. As discussed in Chapter 2, the American women's movement first turned its attention to partisan politics in the months leading up to the 1972 party conventions. The newly formed National Women's Political Caucus (NWPC) began to pressure both parties to increase the representation of women at their national conven-tions to be held later that year. While the NWPC's interventions had little effect on the representation of women at the Republican convention in 1972, its influence on the Democratic National Convention was profound.

Examining both parties' responses to feminism in 1972, it is clear that party strategists perceived the emerging women's movement as a poten-tially powerful source of change in the behaviour of the US electorate. In a sense, this is analogous with the parties' expectations of profound change after the enfranchisement of women. As in the period just after suffrage was extended to women, both political parties made significant efforts to appeal to what they perceived would be the interest of "women voters" in the early 1970s.

The Democrats
After the 1968 convention vividly demonstrated the conflicts between party regulars and "new politics" groups within the party, the DNC estab-lished a party reform commission to consider measures to democratize its presidential nomination process and thereby hopefully restore legitimacy to party leaders. Responding to reformist forces within the party, the McGovern-Fraser Commission included in its 1971 report a recommenda-tion that racial minorities, youth, and women be represented in state del-egations "in reasonable relationship to their presence in the population of the state." A footnote clarified that "this is not to be accomplished by the mandatory imposition of quotas" (in Shafer 1983, 465).

Having decided to focus on delegate selection at the 1972 conventions, NWPC leaders wrote to the chairs of both the Democratic and Republican national committees. The letter to the DNC interpreted the "reasonable representation" rule to mean that women should be represented in each state delegation in the same proportion as in the state's population (that is, a majority). The letter also threatened state-by-state credentials challenges from the NWPC's national network of feminist lawyers if this were not the case. The letter was little more than a bold negotiating stance. The leaders of the NWPC did not expect that the party would agree to anything close to 50 percent representation for women, and the nation-wide network of feminist lawyers was an empty threat, as the new organization had almost no local or state organization in place at the time (Shafer 1983, 479).

The NWPC's efforts were supported by other reform forces in the party, including the Center for Political Reform, Americans for Democratic Action, and, most significantly, the reform commission co-chair Don Fraser, who was married to one of the leading NWPC activists. Fraser intervened forcefully with Democratic leaders to advocate an interpretation of the rules that would guarantee 50 percent representation for women. This support, along with Democratic leaders' belief that the NWPC's threatened credentials challenges were credible, led the party's rules committee to adopt an interpretation of the reasonable representation rule that guaranteed women close to 50 percent representation at the 1972 convention.

This outcome far exceeded the expectations of caucus leaders, and the unanticipated success in part reflects the momentum of the women's movement in the early 1970s. Even though NWPC leaders knew that they lacked the state-by-state organization that would have allowed credentials challenges, party leaders apparently perceived the movement's strength as posing a credible threat. Kirkpatrick (1976, 381-2) reports that McGovern strategists believed that the political mobilization of women constituted an important new resource for their candidate. Recalling NWPC co-founder Bella Abzug's support for McGovern, and her vision of the caucus as a coalition of progressive forces, this was a reasonable belief, at least in terms of campaign workers.

Many feminist activists calling for reform were new to Democratic politics, so they were able to confront the party without fear of personal consequences. In a statement that may overestimate the significance of NOW relative to the NWPC, former NOW president Eleanor Smeal noted that "NOW did a hell of a job. Women inside the party helped too, but they had a lot to lose. We were obnoxious, because we had nothing to lose" (in English 1992).

It is significant that women's movement activists and organizations played such a crucial precipitating role in the campaign to introduce guarantees of equal representation at the Democratic National Convention. Unlike the postsuffrage era, when the political parties pre-emptively introduced organizational guarantees for women, party leaders in the early 1970s acquiesced to direct feminist demands. This had the dual effect of giving movement activists a sense of "ownership" of the reforms and giving movement organizations credibility within party circles. Without in any way underestimating the significance of movement activists in securing this provision, it must be noted that the women's movement probably would not have won so decisive a victory had the Democratic party not already been engaged in an extensive process of reform. This was not merely fortuitous coincidence; the reform process had been set in motion by the social movements that contributed to the mobilization of the women's movement.[2] The Democrats' extensive new reform standards, coupled with the prominent role reform-minded Democrats played within the NWPC, greatly increased the new organization's chances of winning significant concessions from the Democrats (Shafer 1983).

Even given that the feminist mobilization within the Democratic party coincided with an existing reform process, party leaders were strangely acquiescent to the NWPC's demands, lending some credibility to the suggestion that these reserved positions for women in various Democratic party organizations (both temporary and permanent) were primarily intended to deflect them from a more serious organizational challenge to the male leaders (Baer and Bositis 1993, 145). While organizational reforms did displace male party activists from delegate positions, thereby robbing them of some prestige and the opportunity to attend the convention, they did not cause a profound shift in the Democratic party's internal power structure. To the extent that the organizational reforms yielded results, they were modest. Looking at events at the 1972 convention, it is clear that the women's movement had a small short-term impact on the numerical representation of women within the party, on party policy, and on the attitudinal composition of convention delegates.

The most immediate and direct effect of the organizational guarantees was a substantial increase in the number of women at the 1972 Democratic National Convention. While only 13 percent of delegates to the 1968 convention were women, 40 percent of delegates were women in 1972. In order for the representational guarantees to be a political resource for the women's movement, it was necessary that women active in or sympathetic to the movement be mobilized to fill the delegate spots reserved for women. Towards this end, the NWPC in 1972 established a project called the Women's Education for Delegate Selection that gave women information on how to run as delegates to party conventions (Abzug and Kelber 1984, 32). This effort was relatively successful, since approximately 10 percent of women at the 1972 convention were active in the caucus. Two years later, at the party's 1974 mid-term convention, more than half of the female delegates said they participated in either the NWPC or NOW (Appendix, data set: Party Elite 1974).

Seeking to extend their influence in the party further, feminist activists launched two bids for power at the 1972 Democratic convention. The first was the presidential candidacy of Shirley Chisholm, the first Black woman elected to the House of Representatives. As discussed in Chapter 2, Chisholm's largely symbolic candidacy had the backing of several prominent feminists such as Betty Friedan, but not the endorsement of the NWPC. Other NWPC activists, perceiving the vice-presidential nomination to be a more attainable objective, placed Sissy Farenthold's name on the vice-presidential ballot. With backing from leaders of the NWPC, the Black caucus, the Spanish-speaking caucus, and the anti-war Americans for Democratic Action, Farenthold won 420 votes, placing second after McGovern's chosen candidate (Frappollo 1973, 74). Although neither of these efforts yielded any material gains, they did signal the potential political clout of the women's movement.

The inroads feminist organizations made in 1972 had a limited impact on the DNC. Women had equal representation on the DNC since 1920, but national committeewomen were appointed by the state parties, which were, for the most part, still controlled by party regulars. Because the impact of the women's movement had been on the national party, its ability to use the representational guarantees for women on the DNC was decidedly limited. The one notable, if short-lived, gain for women on the DNC came with McGovern's appointment of Jean Westwood as chair. She is the only woman ever to have held the position.

The women's movement also exercised direct influence on party policy in 1972. The NWPC presented a set of issue recommendations to both parties, and actively promoted them at the Democratic convention (Abzug and Kelber 1984, 34). The close ties between the NWPC leadership and the McGovern campaign, coupled with the perception of party strategists that feminist issues might win electoral support, meant that all but one of the key items of the movement's agenda were included in the party's 1972 platform document.[3] Among the items included in the platform were commitments to engage in a priority effort to ratify the Equal Rights Amendment; to eliminate discrimination against women in employment, education, housing, credit, and social security; to extend the Equal Pay Act to cover women; to guarantee equal pay for comparable work; and to amend the Internal Revenue Code to permit working families to deduct child care and housekeeping as a business expense. Taken as a whole, these platform planks represented an ambitious program of legislative reform designed to facilitate women's participation in the workforce on equal terms, and to do away with the myriad of discriminatory practices permitted, either implicitly or explicitly, by law.[4]

The only issue on which the party balked was abortion. Reproductive freedom had not yet become the source of controversy that it would be after the 1973 Supreme Court decision in *Roe* v. *Wade,* but feminist activists had joined with organizations such as Planned Parenthood to bring abortion onto the public agenda and to begin challenges to the constitutionality of existing laws. Mindful of the Democratic party's traditional support among Roman Catholics, however, McGovern was unwilling to enter the campaign with a plank advocating a woman's right to reproductive freedom. Feminist activists at the convention forced a floor vote on the issue, which they lost by a margin of three to two (Freeman 1987, 224). The platform did, however, include a plank promising women access to family planning services.

In addition to its effect on party policy, feminism had a direct effect on the attitudes of convention delegates. Specifically, the influx of women into Democratic politics in 1972 increased attitudinal support for key feminist issues among Democratic party elites. By changing the demographic and political profile of the convention, the women's movement ensured greater support among delegates for its policy agenda than would otherwise have been the case. Because the 1972 convention delegate survey was the first of its kind, it is impossible to compare the attitudes of delegates in 1968 and 1972.[5] It is, however, possible to identify attitudinal differences between men and women at the 1972 convention, from which the effect of the reforms on the attitudes of delegates in the aggregate can be extrapolated.

The 1972 delegate survey found women more likely than men to approve of women's liberation and to advocate feminist stances on the key policy issues of abortion and child care. When asked to rate the women's liberation movement on a "thermometer" scale of 1 to 100, the mean score among women was 66 degrees and, among men, 54 degrees. Delegates apparently held the NWPC in higher esteem than the women's liberation movement as a whole, probably because they perceived the caucus to be more moderate. When asked to give thermometer ratings to the NWPC, female delegates gave it 76 degrees on average, while male delegates awarded it 63 degrees.[6] There were also sexual differences among delegates on policy issues raised by the women's movement. On the issue of abortion, 47 percent of women and 29 percent of men approved of granting access to abortion "if the woman wants it" (the least restrictive option). Delegates were considerably more supportive of a national child care program, with 70 percent of women and 56 percent of men "very much in favor" (Kirkpatrick 1976, 443). Clearly, the influx of women into convention politics made the party elite more favourably disposed towards feminism as well as the key policy issues raised by the movement.

The direct impact of the women's movement on the Democratic party becomes even more evident when female respondents to the delegate survey are disaggregated according to candidate preference. As discussed above, most women active in the feminist movement were drawn into the party through the McGovern campaign. Consequently, the new feminist presence in the party was concentrated among women who supported McGovern. Of the women who identified themselves as McGovern supporters, 56 percent advocated the least restrictive alternative on abortion, as compared with 47 percent of all Democratic women and 37 percent of men supporting McGovern. Similarly, 82 percent of women supporting McGovern were "very much in favor" of public day care, as compared with 70 percent of all Democratic women and 75 percent of men supporting McGovern (Kirkpatrick 1976, 443).

Although the influx of women into the ranks of the party elite shaped the aggregate attitudinal composition of the national convention, it did not lead to a decline in party loyalty among delegates. There is no survey evidence suggesting that neophyte activists privileged their allegiance to the women's movement over their partisan activism. In fact, women were slightly more likely than men to identify their party activity as a higher priority than their interest group activism. Moreover, women who belonged to feminist groups were slightly more likely than other women to rank their party involvement as more important than interest group activism (Appendix, data set: Convention Delegate Study 1972).[7] A 1980 panel study of Democratic convention delegates found that female delegates to the 1972 convention who were liberal in orientation were as likely to remain engaged in party politics until at least 1980 as were their male counterparts (Miller and Jennings 1986, 71). The significance of these findings is twofold. First, they demonstrate that in the minds of most feminist activists engaged with the party, feminism was compatible with partisan engagement. Second, they throw into question the arguments of party scholars, notably Shafer (1983), who assert that the influx of women's movement activists into the Democratic party contributed directly to a decline of the party because the new activists were representatives of "special interests" rather than loyal partisans. Given the degree of loyalty to the Democratic party these women express, it is difficult to accept the claim that they have contributed significantly to a decline in party organization; rather, they appear to have been part of a significant evolution in party organization and patterns of activism.

The Republicans
Although the National Women's Political Caucus (NWPC) explicitly constituted itself as a bipartisan organization and sought to improve the

numerical representation of women at the national conventions of both parties, its impact on the Republicans was far less than on the Democrats. The relatively small number of Republican women involved in the NWPC, the absence of procedural footholds in the Republican rules such as those created by the McGovern-Fraser Commission, and opposition in principle to quotas meant that the Republicans were far less receptive to the NWPC's efforts to have the parties increase women's representation at their conventions (Shafer 1983). Although the Republican party did adopt resolutions encouraging equal representation of women in the early 1970s, no mandatory measures were passed.

In 1972, a small group of Republican women affiliated with the NWPC won approval of Rule 32, which established that state parties should endeavour to have equal representation for men and women in their delegations to future conventions. Unlike the gains made by Democratic women, this rule did not require gender parity among convention delegates. Nonetheless, the pressure placed on the party apparently resulted in an increased presence for women. As Table 4.1 shows, the representation of women at the 1972 convention (where they were 30 percent of delegates) was a substantial increase from 1968 (where women were only 17 percent of delegates).

Although slow to respond to the representational agenda of the newly mobilized feminist movement, the Republicans' 1972 platform showed clear signs of an effort to appeal to women with feminist leanings. As party insider Tanya Melich recalls, Republican feminists in Washington "had convinced Nixon's campaign team that supporting opportunities for women was a plus" (Melich 1996, 30). In addition to retaining its support for the Equal Rights Amendment, the party pledged support for federally funded day care and vigorous action on behalf of women's equality and in opposition to discrimination in the workplace, the educational system, and

Table 4.1

Women's representation at national party conventions, 1968-92

Year	Democrats (%)	Republicans (%)
1968	13	17
1972	40	30
1976	34	31
1980	49	29
1984	50	44
1988	49	35
1992	49	41

Sources: CAWP (1988); Baer (1993, 560); Katz and Mair (1992, 911).

the field of credit. It is not a coincidence that the NWPC had pressured the Republican party on all of these issues. The platform also committed the party to work towards appointment of women to high-level positions in the federal government, including the Cabinet and the Supreme Court. Consistent with this moderate endorsement of feminist issues, the Nixon administration was relatively positive in its treatment of women, and many "status of women" activists considered this era reasonably productive in terms of policy gains (interview 01/25/95). Most notably, the presidential wing of the party was solidly in support of the ERA, which had by then become a priority item for the women's movement. The one issue Republicans were unwilling to address in 1972 was reproductive freedom. Feminist Republicans at the convention had enough seats on the platform committee to force a floor fight on abortion but chose not to create a confrontation, so the platform remained silent on the issue.

Backlash (1973-9)

After their extraordinary success in 1972, feminists were confronted with a backlash in both parties. For the Democrats, this centred on a tension between McGovernite "new politics" forces and party regulars. For the Republicans, the backlash was the first intimation of the imminent ascendance of the anti-feminist new right within the party. For feminist activists in both parties, the essential task was defending the gains they had already made, rather than trying to move forward.

The Democrats

George McGovern's loss to Richard Nixon in the 1972 election marked the end of the brief "new politics" ascendancy in the Democratic party, as party regulars resurfaced to claim their place at the helm of the party organization. Soon after the election, they successfully challenged Jean Westwood's hold on the position of DNC chair. This challenge was mounted, in the words of Alabama Governor George Wallace, to "give the party back to the average man" (in Klinkner 1994a, 108). Within this context, feminists in the party made defending and consolidating their gains a top priority. This defensive effort was for the most part successful, and the relationship between women's movement organizations and the Democratic party remained fairly close, if sometimes adversarial, during this era.

The 1972 reforms became a major point of conflict between "new politics" Democrats and party regulars. Party regulars held these reforms responsible for the nomination of a presidential candidate unable to appeal to a broad enough portion of the electorate to win the presidency. The reforms also represented a significant erosion of the role of state parties and a concomitant increase in the national party's strength. Despite this, all but the most extreme of the party's more traditional elements were willing to acknowledge the basic legitimacy of the procedural reforms (ibid., 113). This at least partially explains why the party did not entirely abandon the reforms after 1972.

Shortly after the election, the DNC appointed Baltimore city council member Barbara Mikulski to chair a commission revisiting the reforms, particularly those mandating representational quotas.[8] The Mikulski Commission's report advocated abandoning strict quotas in favour of a less rigid "affirmative action" approach. This did not apply to the representation of women, as the equal division of all delegations between men and women was to remain in the party rules. The new rules did, however, shift the burden of proof from the state parties to the challengers to show that there had been discriminatory intent, making it more difficult to mount a successful credentials challenge (ibid., 117).

Even though women fared better than other groups in the revisited reforms, women's movement organizations and feminists in the party worked to oppose any attempt to roll back the reforms won in 1972. At a party mini-convention in 1974, the NWPC joined with the Democratic Black caucus to oppose efforts to weaken the equal representation rules for convention delegates. This fight continued at the 1976 Democratic convention, where the NWPC Democratic Task Force (DTF) and the women's caucus of the Democratic party formed a coalition to advocate equal division of delegate positions between men and women at future national conventions. The coalition was unable to win its preferred language (requiring equal division), but compromised with the Carter organization on language to the effect that the party would "promote" equal division. This was apparently adequate, as women were 49 percent of delegates at the 1980 convention, and have maintained representation roughly equal to that of men at all subsequent national conventions (see Table 4.1 above).

In contrast to the inclusion of most of the policy stances advocated by the movement in the 1972 platform, feminist issues were given considerably less attention in 1976. This can be attributed to the interaction of several factors. First, the electoral impact of feminism was minimal in 1972, so party strategists lacked the incentive to endorse a feminist policy agenda. Second, women's movement activists were far less prominent in the Carter campaign organization than they had been in McGovern's organization in 1972, so they were less able to affect the content of the party platform. Third, the Carter campaign sought to project a moderate image, and consequently opposed separate platform planks on issues of concern to constituencies in the party.

In the 1976 platform, the Democrats retained their commitment to the ERA and to the elimination of discrimination in federal programs and in housing, but the commitments were less extensive and less specific than in 1972. The Carter campaign took issue with two of the items advocated by NWPC activists: gay rights and abortion. Although efforts to obtain recognition of the civil rights of gays and lesbians were unsuccessful, feminist activists won a major victory on the abortion issue (Abzug and Kelber 1984, 46). In the years between the 1972 and 1976 conventions, pro-choice activists won a victory on abortion through constitutional challenge; the Supreme Court's 1973 decision in *Roe* v. *Wade* effectively enshrined American women's right to abortion. Under pressure from the NWPC, the Democratic Women's Caucus (DWC), NOW, the National Abortion Rights Action Committee, and Planned Parenthood, the Carter campaign eventually agreed to include a plank in the platform indicating that the party did not advocate a constitutional amendment to overturn *Roe* v. *Wade.*

The Republicans
The representational gains Republican women had won in 1972 were maintained in 1976, in large part as a result of efforts of the NWPC's newly formed Republican Task Force, which held a joint press conference with its Democratic counterpart attacking both parties' failure to approach gender parity among delegates. Republican women believed widespread press coverage made state party chairmen balance delegations with more women (Feit 1979, 198). As a result, 31.5 percent of delegates to the 1976 convention were women, a slight increase from 1972. Although their numbers were small, several women held senior party posts during this period, most notably Mary Louise Smith, who served as RNC chair under President Gerald Ford. What is noteworthy about Smith and others (such as Mary Dent Crisp, who served as party co-chair) is that they were sympathetic to or active in Republican feminist circles and served as a conduit between the social movement and party (see Melich 1996). The Nixon administration was relatively positive in its treatment of women's issues, and many "status of women" activists considered this era positive in policy terms (interview 01/25/95). Most notably, the official party was solidly behind the ERA, which had by then become a priority item for the women's movement.

By the 1976 convention, however, the Republican party was devastated by the Watergate scandal, new right forces were becoming an ever more important internal constituency, and anti-ERA groups had begun to mobilize within the party. These developments set the stage for conflicts over the ERA and reproductive freedom. Freeman (1987, 227) notes that all of the Republican NWPC activists were connected to the Ford campaign, so the contest between Ford and Reagan at the convention provided the backdrop for conflicts over key policy items in the platform debate. In setting their strategy, the Republican NWPC activists decided not to "contaminate" the ERA by linking it with the abortion issue, so they formally worked only on the ERA issue. They would, however, work unofficially to keep an anti-abortion plank out of the platform (ibid., 227). The battle to retain the party's support for the ERA was hard-fought, with Phyllis Schlafly's STOP ERA organization, along with other new right pro-Reagan forces, contesting the question. The pro-ERA language was retained in the platform by a vote of fifty-one to forty-seven in the platform committee. The Republican feminists' unofficial efforts to keep the anti-abortion plank out of the platform were not successful, however. The anti-abortion platform language introduced by Reagan supporters on the platform committee was approved overwhelmingly in the sub-committee dealing with the issue, and was not contested in the full committee. Feminists were able to bring the question to a floor vote, but the anti-abortion plank was sustained by a substantial margin in the floor vote (ibid., 227). The platform, consequently, indicated that the Republican party's response to the Supreme Court's 1973 decision in *Roe* v. *Wade* was contrary to the response by the women's movement. The platform indicated the party's support for "those who seek enactment of a constitutional amendment to restore protection of the right to life for unborn children." In addition to including the anti-abortion plank in its 1976 platform, the Republican party dropped many of the pledges to work for women's equality that it had included in its 1972 platform. Even in the areas where the party's commitments were retained – employment, child care, housing, and social security – the language was lukewarm and the pledges far less specific than they had been in the 1972 platform.

The Reagan-Bush Era (1980-92)

The US party system's polarization around feminism can be traced to the 1980 election campaign. In his bid for the Republican nomination, Ronald Reagan assembled a coalition of fiscal and social conservatives, including well-organized anti-feminist groups that had mobilized to oppose ratification of the ERA. At the 1980 convention, the Republicans dropped their long-standing platform commitment to the ERA and adopted strong pro-life rhetoric, thereby establishing the anti-feminist stance the party has since maintained. In response to the Republicans' anti-feminist stance, and in an effort to benefit from the GOP's apparent electoral "woman problem," the Democrats entered into a close alliance with feminist groups in advance of the 1984 election. When this gender gap strategy failed to win back the White House for the party, the Democrats' enthusiasm for alliance with organized feminism faded somewhat. Despite this, however, the Democratic party maintained feminist stances on most of the issues raised by the women's movement.

The Reagan Election, 1980

The 1980 election marked a turning-point in the Republican response to feminism. The party dropped its moderate, conciliatory stance and began to define itself in opposition to the women's movement and feminist issues, in essence declaring what Melich (1996) has termed "the Republican war on women." Although foreshadowed in the 1976 platform, the anti-feminism of the contemporary Republican party became abundantly clear in the 1980 platform document. Most notably, the platform committee voted to drop the pro-ERA plank from the platform, replacing it with hollow reaffirmations of the party's "historic commitment to equal rights and equality for women" and rejecting compromise language acknowledging Republicans who had different views on the ERA (Cohodas 1984, 2088). Even vague statements promising to meet working women's need for child care were followed by protestations of the importance of mothers and homemakers in maintaining the country's values. Moreover, the language of the anti-abortion plank was strengthened to voice support for congressional efforts to restrict the use of tax dollars for abortion.

The Democrats essentially held the line on feminist issues in 1980, reflecting a stalemate between feminists within the party and the Carter campaign organization. Movement organizations could not count on ties to the presidential nominee's campaign to further their policy agenda. Rather, they had developed sufficient organizational momentum and allies within the party to win victories on selected issues. Had the women's movement not developed these skills and resources, it is unlikely that key issues such as reproductive freedom would have been included in the party's platform in 1980. The two policy issues on which feminist activists and the Carter campaign came into conflict were the ERA and abortion. The presidents of NOW and the NWPC had decided that their priority platform issue at the convention would be a plank committing the party to withholding financial support and technical campaign assistance from candidates who did not support the ERA. The Carter campaign opposed the idea of imposing an ideological "litmus test" on candidates in a pluralist party, but eventually acquiesced to the measure when the National Education Association, which had the largest single block of Carter delegates at the convention, announced its support (Freeman 1987, 231). On the abortion issue, with NARAL leading the fight, pro-choice activists proposed an amendment to the platform endorsing government funding of abortions for poor women. Despite Carter's personal opposition to abortion, this plank was adopted with little debate (ibid.). The 1980 platform also included planks on less controversial feminist issues. It committed the party to the principle of equal pay for work of comparable value, expanded child care programs, elimination of discrimination in educational programs, and the use of affirmative action to remedy patterns of discrimination.

Electoral defeat in 1980 once again altered the relationship between the Democratic party and the women's movement. When Carter lost to Reagan, the internal balance of power in the Democratic party shifted. At the same time, the women's movement had come to focus more attention on party politics, and in particular on the Democrats. Compounding the influence they had already won within the Democratic presidential party, women's movement organizations had an additional resource available to them in their dealings with the party in the early 1980s – the emergence of a "gender gap" in political preferences. The women's movement was able to capitalize on growing gender differences in party identification and voting intentions and, as a result, the movement-party relationship grew closer during the year prior to the 1984 election as the party adopted the gender gap strategy that leaders of the women's movement were advocating.

Figure 4.1

Gender gap in party identification, 1952-92

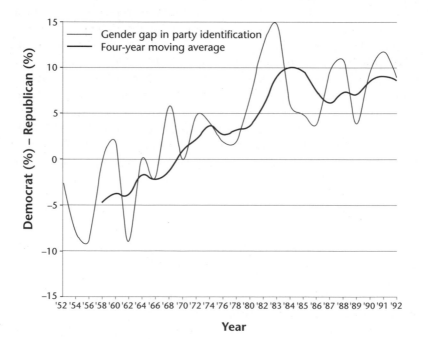

Source: Calculated from Kirschten (1984) and McGlen and O'Connor (1995).

The Gender Gap Strategy, 1984

The gender gap strategy was possible because of the emergence of a widen-ing difference in the party identification and voting patterns of US women and men. As Figure 4.1 shows, since 1972 American women increasingly identified with the Democratic party and men with the Republicans.[9] The gender gap is not merely a difference in party identification, since gender differences have been found in voting behaviour in presidential and con-gressional elections. Democratic presidential candidates received more support from women than men in every election year since 1972, with the exception of 1976.

Leaders of feminist organizations became aware of this gender gap in the early 1980s, and they set out to use it as a political resource in their deal-ings with the Democratic party. After the 1980 election, NOW staff mem-bers began assembling survey data on these emerging gender differences and released them to the media on a regular basis (Witt et al. 1994, 160-1). The press coverage of this new phenomenon attracted the attention of party strategists, who came to see the party's constituencies (including women, Blacks, and Hispanics) as a potential source of electoral strength, particularly if they could be mobilized to vote in greater numbers. The low rate of voter turnout in US elections makes voter registration a potentially effective means of achieving electoral success. In the 1980 presidential elec-tion, only 54 percent of people eligible to vote actually cast ballots. The rate of voter turnout tends to be even lower among the economically disad-vantaged and minority groups, both of which tend to vote for Democrats.

Gender gaps in party identification can be formed by an aggregate shift among either women or men, or a combination of the two. In this light, the gender gap that emerged in the early 1980s could have been inter-preted not so much as the Republicans' "woman problem" but as the Democrats' "man problem." The strategic success of women's movement leaders lay in convincing the Democrats in 1984 to understand the gender gap as a political strength waiting to be exploited, rather than as a weak-ness needing to be remedied.

The perception that a gender gap constituted a potential resource for electoral success contributed to the DNC's decision to pursue a gender gap strategy in 1984. In that election, party strategists set out to mobilize core con-stituencies – including women – to vote. The key to this plan was voter regis-tration. Even before the vice-presidential nomination of Geraldine Ferraro, the Democrats and dozens of women's groups had started a voter sign-up and "get out the vote" campaign aimed at women (Granat 1984, 1722). Between 1980 and 1984, DNC chair Charles Mannatt allocated substantial support to the DNC's women's caucus in the hope that additional resources would trans-late into increased support among women (Klinkner 1994a, 172).

As the 1984 primary season began, NOW made it clear that the nomination of a woman vice-presidential candidate was its top priority. As discussed in Chapter 2, the movement's unsuccessful campaign for ERA ratification, coupled with the anti-feminist ethos of the Reagan administration, had focused the attention of women's movement organizations on the project of electing more women to public office. In this sense, the effort to nominate a woman for the vice-presidency was the centrepiece of the movement's broader effort to elect women to public office.

Women's movement organizations had won considerable influence in the presidential wing of the party and were ready to use their clout. Enough women had been elected to national-level office that there were "qualified" women available to suggest as potential nominees. These factors, combined with the prospect of a female electorate that appeared ready to oust Ronald Reagan, laid the groundwork for the nomination of New York Congresswoman Geraldine Ferraro as the Democratic vice-presidential candidate.

During the primaries, women's movement leaders and women inside the party began to pressure the candidates for the presidential nomination to select a woman as their running mate. NOW made it clear to candidates seeking the nomination that the price of NOW's endorsement was a firm commitment to putting a woman on the ticket. Within party circles, a group of prominent activists with solid Democratic credentials began to plan a strategy centred around publicizing the potential power of the women's vote and the idea of a woman on the ticket (Witt et al. 1994, 162). Under pressure from women inside the party and women's organizations outside the party, Walter Mondale selected Geraldine Ferraro as his running mate.

Having endorsed Mondale in the primaries, NOW won a place within the Mondale campaign and cemented the movement's position as a key constituency within the party. NOW chapters recruited Mondale delegates and NOW president Judy Goldsmith travelled with the Mondale campaign during the last weeks of the primaries (Frankovic 1988, 109, 119). Because of the widely held belief that Ferraro's nomination would yield electoral benefit for the party ticket, it met little resistance within party circles. Key strategists thought that Ferraro's name on the ballot would be an important asset in the campaign to register women (Granat 1984, 1722). More than three-quarters of delegates and party office-holders surveyed prior to the election believed that having a woman on the ticket would help the party. Women were somewhat more likely than men to anticipate that a female vice-presidential candidate would improve the party's electoral fortunes: of those surveyed, 81 percent of women and 73 percent of men agreed or strongly agreed that a female vice-presidential candidate would help the campaign (Appendix, data set: Party Elite 1984).[10] A survey taken after the election found that many delegates later changed their views on this, although women still tended to view Ferraro's candidacy in a more positive light than men. Over half the women surveyed believed Ferraro's candidacy had helped the party and most delegates of either sex thought Ferraro's nomination helped, rather than hurt, the cause of women seeking public office (Appendix, data set: Convention Delegate Study 1984).

The Democrats' gender gap strategy did not yield the anticipated electoral benefit in the 1984 presidential election. Mondale and Ferraro lost to incumbent Ronald Reagan by an 18 percent margin, the party's worst showing in a presidential election since 1972. Even though the ten-point gender gap in the 1984 election was the largest on record, Reagan's popularity and the Republicans' more effective voter registration efforts overwhelmed the Mondale-Ferraro campaign, rendering the gender gap strategy a failure.

In retrospect, NOW's decision to make the vice-presidency a top priority may seem naive, or even misguided. Although the US vice-president is only a heartbeat (or an impeachment proceeding) away from the presidency, the position itself holds little power. Vice-presidents spend much of their time standing in for the president at ceremonial occasions in distant capitals and usually have only limited influence over policy.[11] As a strategy for achieving policy change, then, NOW's campaign fell far short. Even so, the election of a woman to the position may well have furthered the goal of electing a woman to the highly symbolic and powerful position of president. Certainly, many successful bids for the White House have been launched from the vice-presidential residence. NOW's decision to pursue this strategy is even more understandable if one assumes – as many feminist activists and party strategists did in 1984 – that the presence of a woman on the ticket would make a certain number of women either switch their votes from the Republicans or else vote when they would not have otherwise. It was not until the 1984 election results proved this assumption untrue that the vice-presidential strategy was set aside.

Even though women's movement organizations and the Democratic party were as closely allied in 1984 as they had been in 1972, the party was not nearly as responsive to the women's movement in policy terms. By citing Judy Goldsmith's testimony before the platform committee, the 1984 platform acknowledged the close relationship between Democrats and women's movement organizations. Beyond this, however, there was little change from 1980. The only notable addition to the 1984 platform was a commitment to increase the number of visible minorities and women in Congress and in government, to spend "maximum" resources to elect women and minority candidates, and to target the bulk of the party's voter registration funds on efforts to register minorities and women.

The 1984 platform reaffirmed the party's support of the ERA, although it dropped a controversial provision withholding financial support and technical assistance from Democratic candidates who did not support the amendment. As in 1980, the platform articulated a pro-choice stance on abortion and opposed government limits on the reproductive freedom of poor Americans, a thinly veiled attack on the Reagan administration's "gag rule" that prevented federally funded agencies from identifying abortion as an alternative when counselling pregnant women. The platform also made commitments on equal pay for work of comparable worth, universally available day care with federal or business funding, and improved civil rights protection. There were no commitments on education, small business, or social security, all subjects that had been addressed in the 1980 platform.

Despite the platform's weak commitment on issues of particular importance to women, female delegates were more satisfied with the content of the platform than were their male counterparts. Of delegates surveyed after the convention, 18 percent of men and 27 percent of women indicated that the 1984 platform document reflected their views "very well." Women who belonged to political women's groups were even more likely to approve of the platform, with 30 percent saying the document reflected their views "very well."[12] Given that feminist leaders had made the vice-presidency, not policy, their focus in 1984, this sense of satisfaction with the platform document presumably had more to do with a perception that feminist groups had achieved their political objectives at the convention than with a careful reading of the platform document.

It was in the realm of representational responsiveness that women's movement organizations won their most notable victories in 1984. In addition to the high-profile nomination of Geraldine Ferraro as the Democrats' vice-presidential candidate, women played a highly visible role at the party's convention. Because of the representational guarantees in place, almost half the delegates to the 1984 Democratic National Convention were women. The majority of these women (68 percent) attributed their selection as delegates to representational guarantees (Appendix, data set: Convention Delegate Study 1984). Some evidence suggests women's movement organizations were more successful in having their members selected as delegates to the 1984 convention than in the past. Of the female delegates surveyed in a postconvention study, 59 percent reported being active or inactive members of a "politically related women's group" (ibid.). This figure represents a slight increase from 1980, when 54 percent of women delegates reported political women's group activity (Convention Delegate Study 1980).

Moreover, the Democrats' use of the gender gap strategy caused the Republicans to promote women. In an effort to combat their electoral "woman problem," Reagan campaign officials pressured state parties to ensure that their delegations to the national convention approached gender parity (Baer 1993, 560; Kirschten 1984, 1084). An unprecedented 44 percent of delegates to the 1984 convention were women. (In 1988, the proportion dropped back to one-third.) Similarly, Reagan's campaign recruited high-profile women to organize Women for Reagan-Bush, the Republican Senatorial Campaign Committee (RSCC) pledged money for any Republican woman running for the Senate, and women were profiled at the 1984 convention (Kirschten 1984). In both 1984 and 1988, moreover, the party's platform made strong commitments to the appointment of women to senior positions in the administration and to the promotion of women's candidacies for all levels of public office.

Feminist Republicans, however, were shut out of the 1984 convention entirely. A few testified before the platform committee in favour of the Equal Rights Amendment, but committee members grilled them on Democratic vice-presidential candidate Geraldine Ferraro's finances rather than the ERA (Freeman 1987, 233). The content of the platform on women's issues was determined in large part by Phyllis Schlafly (ibid., 232), resulting in blatantly anti-feminist policy stances. The ERA was conspicuous in its absence from the platform, and, although the platform endorsed the principle of equal pay for equal work, it explicitly opposed the concept of comparable worth on the grounds that "the free market system can determine the value of jobs better than any government authority." The language on abortion became even more confrontational, applauding President Reagan's fine record of judicial appointments "who respect traditional family values and the sanctity of innocent human life." The platform language also included the curious endorsement of "legislation to make clear that the 14th amendment's protections apply to unborn children." Although not made explicit, this promise to entitle the fetus to equal protection of the laws would mean that abortion was not only forbidden, but to be treated as murder. In other words, doctors performing abortions would have to be charged as murderers under such a law and would, in some states, be subject to the death penalty (Kinsley 1992).

In short, 1984 was the year when the US party system was most polarized around feminism. The Republicans were clearly allied with anti-feminist forces, and the Democrats with organized feminism. Although this basic pattern persists to the present, it has never again assumed so marked a form as it did in 1984.

Moderation, 1988

Although this polarization did not disappear after 1984, both parties moderated their stances somewhat in the subsequent years. The Democrats introduced reforms designed to temper the influence of the party's internal constituencies, including women, while the Republicans tried to cope with their electoral "woman problem" by making some appeals to working women, notably on child care policy.

After the Democrats' devastating loss in the 1984 presidential election, a sense of mutual disenchantment set in between the women's movement and the presidential wing of the party. As in 1973, the defeated presidential party turned away from its internal constituencies in an effort to regain the political centre. In response to this, feminist organizations shifted their focus towards the congressional party and started to pursue a PAC strategy more vigorously. The relationship between women's movement organizations and the presidential party consequently became more distant from 1985 onwards. Despite this decay in the alliance between movement organizations and the party, feminists had made their mark on the Democrats. The representational guarantees they had won were not abandoned, and partisan elites continued to display attitudinal support for the women's movement's key policy issues.

In the aftermath of the 1984 election, the Democratic National Committee (DNC) elected as its new chair Paul Kirk, who pledged to restrict the influence of the "special interests" that he saw as agents of Mondale's demise. Kirk reversed his predecessor's policy of giving organizational support to internal constituencies and removed official recognition and organizational support from party caucuses, although the women's, Black, and Hispanic caucuses each retained one seat on the DNC executive committee (Klinkner 1994a, 184). Kirk's internal reorganization also abolished the office of women's activities and other constituency-based offices, replacing them with a system of regional desks (Baer and Bositis 1993; NFDW n.d.).[13] There was considerable support for this move among partisans. A majority of party office-holders and delegates to the 1988 national convention surveyed agreed that "caucuses overrepresent special interests." Women were, however, less likely to agree with this statement – only 50 percent of women surveyed agreed, compared with 62 percent of men.[14]

With their hard-won position in the presidential wing of the party eroding in the mid-1980s, feminist organizations and activists increasingly turned their attention to the congressional wing, where the project of electing women was starting to gain some momentum. This shift was not solely in response to changes in the presidential party; it also reflected the disappointment of movement leaders over the failure of the gender gap strategy and their conviction, in the aftermath of the ERA ratification campaign, that it was essential that more women be elected.

It must be noted that the congressional wing of the party is even less centralized and cohesive than the presidential wing. It consists, essentially, of current Democratic members of Congress and Democratic congressional candidates, and their campaign organizations and staffs. The only coordinating bodies are the House and Senate caucuses and the congressional and senatorial campaign committees, which are committees of the respective caucuses. To assert that feminist organizations focused more attention on the congressional wing of the party, then, is merely to say that they focused resources on encouraging and facilitating women's campaigns.

This strategy yielded modest results. Although progress was slow, the numbers of women running as candidates for the party and the numbers of Democratic women in Congress increased considerably between 1984 and 1993. Through the late 1980s, there were steady gains in the number of women running in Democratic primaries. This translated into an increase in the number of women candidates and, finally, into rising numbers of Democratic women in both the House of Representatives and the Senate (see Table 4.2).

Progress on women's representation was not matched by progress on the policy front. The Democrats' 1988 platform was written by a party establishment that believed its less moderate internal constituencies were responsible in part for the party's loss in 1984. DNC chair Paul Kirk made it clear that the platform document was to be "brief, bland and bullet-proof, free of the special interest snags that have embarrassed Democratic candidates in the past" (in Reid 1988). Although the party did not back away from its commitments on key women's issues, the platform language seemed designed to soften these commitments. Instead of promising "comparable worth" as it had in the past, the platform endorsed "pay equity for working women." Similarly, the platform retained its commitment to "freedom of reproductive choice" without mentioning the word "abortion" (ibid.). Even more indicative of the waning fortunes of feminists within the Democratic party, the first draft of the platform stated that "equal rights, regardless of gender, should be guaranteed in the Constitution" but did not specifically mention the ERA (Balz 1988). Subsequent drafts explicitly endorsed the ERA, maintaining the party's existing commitment to the amendment.

Just as the Democrats' support for feminism was moderated in 1988, the GOP's anti-feminism was also tempered slightly that year. As there was no incumbent presidential candidate, the potential for conflict was greater than at the 1984 convention. Moreover, Bush was perceived by many feminists to be less harshly opposed to feminism than his predecessor. Feminist Republican women came to the 1988 convention with the modest goal of forcing a debate on the party's abortion stance for the first time in eight years. In this, they were successful, but they were soundly defeated by conservative forces on the platform committee when the matter was raised

Table 4.2

Women candidates and women elected, 1970-92

Year	Candidates (% of all Democratic candidates)		Elected (% of all Democrats elected that year)		Candidates (% of all Republican candidates)		Elected (% of all Republicans elected that year)	
	House	Senate	House	Senate	House	Senate	House	Senate
1970	4	0	4	0	3	3	2	0
1972	6	0	5	0	2	6	1	0
1974	7	6	5	0	4	3	3	0
1976	8	3	5	0	5	0	4	0
1978	7	3	4	0	5	3	3	5
1980	7	6	4	0	6	9	5	5
1982	6	6	5	0	7	6	5	0
1984	7	18	4	0	9	13	6	6
1986	7	9	5	5	9	9	6	0
1988	8	5	5	0	7	6	6	0
1990	10	9	8	0	8	15	6	0
1992	16	20	14	25	8	6	7	7

Sources: Katz and Mair (1992, 912); Biersack and Herrnson (1994, 167-8).

(Simpson 1988, 92). When the abortion issue was discussed in the platform committee, Bush workers lobbied delegates, telling them that this vote was a test of their loyalty to the nominee (ibid., 94).

Moderate Republican women such as Representatives Lynn Martin and Nancy Johnson, and former RNC chair Mary Louise Smith, having chosen to work inside the Bush campaign, were less confrontational in their approaches, and were successful in having a promise for a child care program included in their party's platform (ibid., 93). Even this plank bore marks of compromise, affirming that "the family's most important function is to raise the next generation of Americans, handing on to them the Judaeo-Christian values of Western civilization" and that "the best care for most children, especially in their early years, is parental." Moreover, in keeping with the party's emphasis on limited government, the platform called for "a reform of the tort liability system to prevent excessive litigation that discourages child care by groups who stand ready to meet the needs of working parents."

The Bush campaign did not perceive the party's stance on abortion and the ERA as electoral liabilities. In their view, the "activist-type" women who held strong opinions on these issues were likely to be staunch Democrats in any case. The gender gap strategy they adopted emphasized recognizing women's increased participation in the workforce. Bush's chief policy advisor on gender gap issues believed that Bush and other GOP candidates should stress that their policies, by creating a booming private sector, generated opportunities for women to meet their responsibility for their families' well-being (Blustein 1988).

Despite the party's open opposition to the feminist policy agenda, rhetorical platform commitments have tended to be softened somewhat once the conventions ended. The conservatism of GOP activists has created a dynamic whereby potential nominees must establish their conservative bona fides during the race for the nomination, but then try to repair the damage with more moderate voters during the presidential campaign itself. This was demonstrated clearly in 1988, when none of the candidates for the Republicans' presidential nomination would accept invitations to speak at the Women's Agenda Conference, which brought together forty women's groups, including the moderate Business and Professional Women (BPW) USA and the American Association of University Women, both of which have memberships that are roughly half Republican ("A Convention Bush Won't Pass Up" 1988). Having won the nomination but trailing Democratic nominee Michael Dukakis by fifteen to twenty-five points among women, Bush addressed the national convention of the BPW and used the occasion to introduce his comprehensive $2.2 billion child care strategy (ibid.; Blustein 1988).

Significant numbers of women entered the upper echelons of the party in the late 1980s and early 1990s. A prime example is Mary Matalin, who rose from a junior post at the RNC through a series of progressively more senior jobs until she was appointed chief of staff. In 1992, she went on to manage George Bush's presidential campaign. Unlike their predecessors in the 1970s, however, these women have not acted as a conduit between women's movement and political party. A *Washington Post* profile of the unprecedented number of women working in campaign management positions on George Bush's 1988 campaign found that these women rejected the idea that they would have a special insight or dedication to women's issues. "Pressed to talk about themselves as a class, they summon up heavy irony and describe themselves as 'chicks'" (Williams 1988).

Comparison: Attitudinal Responsiveness

The polarization of the US political parties around feminism during the 1980s was not merely a product of party leaders and strategists. Rather, this polarization was reflected in the attitudes of partisan activists (represented by delegates to the two parties' national conventions during the decade). On the major issues raised by the women's movement, delegates to Democratic conventions were, on the whole, supportive, while Republicans were opposed. While gender differences on these issues tended to be sizeable among delegates to Democratic conventions, they were small or non-existent among Republican delegates. Examining the patterns of intra-party cleavage more carefully, it becomes clear that the influx of women, particularly women active in feminist organizations outside the party, into the Democratic party in the 1970s and 1980s created a strong internal feminist constituency. The key event for the Republican party was an influx of socially conservative evangelical Christians who, regardless of their gender, stood in firm opposition to the feminist agenda.

On abortion and the ERA – the two feminist issues that have had the highest profile in the American public arena – delegates to the two parties' conventions were as polarized in their attitudes as their parties were in their platform stances. Democrats were solidly in support of the ERA, with over 80 percent of delegates endorsing the amendment at each convention throughout the decade. Republicans, in contrast, were considerably less supportive of the amendment, with less than one-third of delegates to the 1980, 1984, and 1988 conventions endorsing it (see Figure 4.2). On this issue, convention delegates were out of synch with the party's supporters. A poll taken a month before the party's 1988 convention found that 58 percent of Republican-identified men and 55 percent of Republican-identified women supported passage of the Equal Rights Amendment (Peterson and Hill 1988).

On the controversial abortion question, the gulf between Democratic and Republican delegates was almost as large. As Figure 4.3 shows, over half of the delegates to Democratic conventions supported a pro-choice stance on abortion. It should be noted, moreover, that the question wordings used define a pro-choice stance quite strictly as unrestricted access to abortion and exclude those delegates who advocated conditional access to abortion. Republican delegates were, not surprisingly, considerably less likely to support unrestricted access to abortion. Through the 1980s, approximately 20 percent of GOP delegates advocated such options. Although by no means pro-choice, Republican delegates' attitudes on the abortion issue were less radically anti-abortion than might be expected given the party's pro-life image and the inclusion of a plank in the party's platform throughout the 1980s advocating such an amendment. When asked if they supported a constitutional amendment banning abortion, only 40 percent of delegates to the 1988 convention and one-third of delegates to the 1992 convention advocated such a measure.

Almost as different as the two parties' delegates' reactions to feminist issues are the patterns of cleavage within each party on these issues. Within the Democratic party, there was a pronounced difference between male and female delegates, and an even more pronounced difference between female delegates who belonged to women's organizations outside the party and all

Figure 4.2

Support of US party convention delegates for ERA, 1980-8

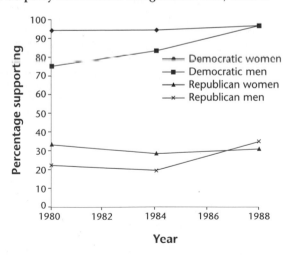

Note: Support in 1980 and 1984 was expressed as "pro-ERA." Support in 1988 was specifically for "ratification."
Sources: Party Elite 1980; Party Elite 1984; ABC 1988.

other delegates. Male and female delegates differed in their evaluation of the women's movement. A survey of delegates to the party's 1984 convention found that on a thermometer scale from 1 to 100, the mean evaluation of the women's movement was 68 degrees for men and 81 degrees for women (calculated from Appendix, data set: Convention Delegate Study 1984).[15] As Figures 4.2 and 4.3 clearly illustrate, men and women in the Democratic party differed profoundly in their attitudes on abortion and differed considerably in their support for the ERA. Breaking this down even further, we find that women who belonged to a political women's organization outside the party were even more supportive than other women of the women's movement's positions on these two issues. As Table 4.3 demonstrates, differences among women on these issues were even larger than the differences between men and women.

Gender differences among Republican delegates tended to be smaller, and were in some cases non-existent. In contrast to the role women entering Democratic party politics have played, there is little evidence suggesting that women entering Republican politics have brought feminist ideas with them and injected them into party life.

Republican women were somewhat more supportive than men of a pro-choice position on abortion, but the differences were small in magnitude

Figure 4.3

Support of US party convention delegates for pro-choice stance, 1972-92

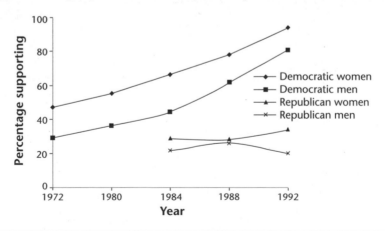

Note: Wording of support varied: 1972 ("if woman wants it"); 1980 ("never be forbidden"); 1984 ("woman's choice"); 1988 ("no restrictions" according to party elite and "legal as now" according to *New York Times*); and 1992 ("always permitted"). See Appendix, Scale construction.
Sources: Kirkpatrick (1976, 446). See also Appendix, data sets: Convention Delegate Study 1980; Party Elite 1984, 1988; *Washington Post* 1992 (Democrat and Republican); *New York Times* 1988 (Democrat and Republican).

Table 4.3

Democratic women delegates' attitudes towards abortion and the ERA, 1980 and 1984

	1980		1984	
	Abortion "never forbid" % (n)	ERA "strongly approve"/"approve" % (n)	Abortion "never forbid" % (n)	ERA "strongly approve"/"approve" % (n)
Member of women's group	66 (296)	98 (451)	72 (318)	90 (412)
Non-member	43 (142)	86 (285)	54 (166)	70 (216)
Member – non-member	23	12	18	20
χ^2 significance	***	***	***	***

*** $p < .001$

Sources: Appendix, calculated from data sets: Party Elite 1980 and 1984.

and statistically insignificant. This is consistent with the pattern found in the general public, where gender is found to have a negligible impact on attitudes towards abortion (Cook et al. 1992). As was the case with other items measuring Republicans' attitudes towards abortion, the gender difference on the question of a constitutional amendment banning abortion was small and statistically insignificant. GOP delegates were split along gender lines on the question of the ERA. As Figure 4.2 shows, Republican women were significantly more supportive of the ERA than were Republican men in 1980 and 1984. In 1988, however, Republican men were slightly more supportive of the amendment than were women. It is noteworthy that gender differences on the ERA emerged among convention delegates in 1980 and 1984 when there were no comparable differences in public opinion. This does suggest a degree of gender consciousness among female Republicans. Employment outside the home affected Republican women's attitudes towards the ERA substantially. In 1984, only 15 percent of housewives were ERA supporters, as compared with 32 percent of women employed outside the home. These differences notwithstanding, even the employed Republican women were far less supportive of the amendment than were women in the general public.

A more substantial cleavage among Republican delegates was based in religion. Support for a constitutional amendment banning abortion came mainly from born-again Christians. At the 1988 convention, 61 percent of born-again men and 85 percent of born-again women favoured the amendment, compared with only 21 percent of men and 20 percent of women who did not identify themselves as born-again Christians. Similarly, born-again Christians were substantially less supportive of the ERA than were other delegates. In 1988, only 12 percent of born-again Christian delegates supported the amendment, as compared with 38 percent of other delegates (calculated from Appendix, data set: *Washington Post,* Democrats, 1988).

The pattern of gender differences that emerged among Democratic and Republican delegates on feminist issues is similar to that on general ideological orientation. While male and female Republicans differed little in their ideological orientation, female Democrats tended to be substantially more liberal than their male counterparts. What this means, in essence, is that the influx of women into party politics in the 1970s and 1980s had a substantial effect on the ideological composition of the Democratic party but little on the Republicans.

Women activists in the Democratic party were consistently more liberal in their ideological self-placement than their male counterparts. As Figure 4.4 illustrates, there have been persistent gender-based differences in ideology throughout the twenty-year period. The magnitude of these differences grew in the 1980s, as male Democrats became slightly more conservative but female Democrats did not. It is noteworthy that the largest difference came in 1984, when NOW was extensively involved in the presidential nominee's campaign organization and at which a female vice-presidential nominee was elected. These differences in ideological self-placement are small, yet persistent. This suggests that the representational guarantees ensuring women's inclusion in elite party bodies have made the Democratic party slightly more liberal in orientation than it would otherwise have been.

In contrast to this, there were only minor ideological distinctions between men and women at Republican conventions in the 1980s. As with the Democrats, Republican women were slightly more liberal, on average, than Republican men. The Republican gender gaps were, however, small in magnitude and statistically insignificant. This is partly because of the decline in activism in the party of liberal Republican women. A panel study of delegates to Republican conventions found that women who dropped out of the Republican party elite between 1972 and 1980 were quite clearly less conservative than their male counterparts, and also less conservative than the women who remained active (Miller and Jennings 1986, 71). It is also noteworthy that, in both 1980 and 1984, no significant gender

Figure 4.4

Ideological self-placement of US party convention delegates, 1980-92

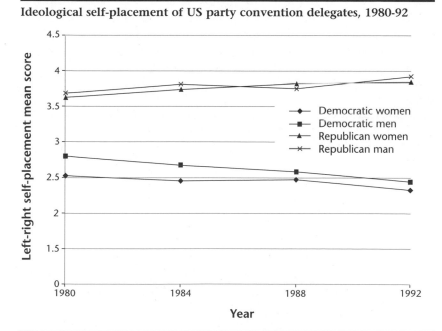

Sources: See Appendix for Party Elite 1980; Party Elite 1984; *New York Times* 1988; Party Elite 1992.

differences emerged in response to items tapping into the increasing conservatism of the party. When delegates to the 1980 convention were asked
whether the party should become more conservative, women were only
slightly more likely to disagree than were men (see Table 4.4). Similarly,
there were no significant gender differences in delegates' evaluation of the
conservatism of the 1984 platform, which excluded the ERA and adopted
an extreme anti-abortion stance. Republican women responding to the
1984 survey of the party elite were slightly, but not significantly, more
likely than men to think that the party's 1984 platform was too conservative. The absence of statistically significant gender differences on these
items lends further support to the contention that women within the
Republican party do not constitute an ideologically distinct group.

Comparison: Women's Organizations in the Parties

To understand the polarization of the US party system in the 1980s, it is
useful to examine the roles played by women's organizations in the two
political parties over this period. Women's organizations in the Democratic
party played only a minor role, effectively ceding any potential leadership
role to outside women's organizations. This, in effect, facilitated the close
relationship between autonomous organizations in the women's movement and the party through much of the decade. In contrast to this, the
Republican women's organization is an important presence within that
party. To the extent that any autonomous feminist organization had ties
with the GOP during the 1980s, its influence was easily offset by the power
of the anti-feminist groups affiliated with the party.

Table 4.4

**Additional measures of conservatism among Republican delegates, by
gender, 1980 and 1984**

	1980 Party should become more conservative: "disagree" or "strongly disagree" % (n)	1984 GOP platform too conservative: "agree" or "strongly agree" % (n)
Male	26 (218)	29 (198)
Female	30 (86)	34 (140)
Female – male	4	5
χ^2 significance	No	No

Source: Appendix, calculated from data sets: Party Elite 1980 and 1984.

The DNC recognizes the National Federation of Democratic Women (NFDW) as the constituent group of Democratic women. The organization was formed in 1971 as a federation of state Democratic women's organizations. The organization's status as the recognized constituent group means that it has three seats on the DNC, and its president sits on the executive committee of the DNC. The NFDW is not clearly feminist in orientation. Its stated objectives are to unite the women of the Democratic party, promote the party's cause, and to encourage full participation by women in every level of the party's structure. The state organizations that constitute the NFDW fulfil a traditional "ladies' auxiliary" function, taking on tasks such as staffing the state party's booth at the state fair, fundraising for the state party, and operating membership drives (NFDW 1994). Despite its status as the party's recognized constituent group, the NFDW has never achieved an influential position within the national party. It has no permanent office and lacks financial resources. According to Baer (1991a), the NFDW has little influence or presence in the DNC. The only evidence that the NFDW has taken on a feminist role is its meagre efforts to fund women candidates in recent years.

The second major women's organization within the party is the women's caucus (DWC) of the DNC, which is composed of all of the women on the national committee. These women elect a chair for the women's caucus, who sits on the DNC executive committee. At party conventions, the caucus unofficially expands to include all female delegates. The caucus is of limited significance in party affairs, but its chair does have some power within the party. Baer notes that the caucus has no access to any organization that links the national party to state and local Democratic women. At party conventions since 1984, the meetings of the caucus have been subsidized by outside women's groups.

Using data from the 1988 Party Elite Survey, it is possible to compare the women active in these two party organizations. Of the female DNC members, county chairs and national convention delegates surveyed, 24 percent reported being active in the NFDW and 56 percent in the DWC. Women active in the NFDW were more likely than other women to be White, married, over forty, and involved in the party for more than ten years; women active in the DWC were also more likely to be in their forties, and were significantly more likely to have been involved in the party for over ten years. Unlike NFDW activists, DWC activists were more likely than other Democratic women to have postgraduate education and professional jobs. What this suggests is that the women involved in the two organizations were of the same generation, but from substantially different backgrounds. Sharper contrasts appear when these women's attitudes are examined. DWC activists were significantly more likely to be members of feminist and pro-choice groups outside the party and were more likely to advocate a pro-choice stance on abortion; NFDW activists were less likely than other women in the party to hold such memberships or advocate reproductive choice. DWC activists were slightly more liberal than non-activists in their ideological self-placement, and scored substantially higher on a scale measuring attitudinal feminism; NFDW activists were slightly more conservative and scored somewhat lower on a scale measuring attitudinal feminism (see Table 4.5). In short, the NFDW resembles a more traditional ladies' auxiliary, while the DWC appears to be a feminist organization within the party.

Notwithstanding the role of the DWC, feminist Democrats have ceded their potential leadership role within the party to outside women's groups (Kelber 1994, 209). As discussed in Chapter 2, it is the Democratic Task Force (DTF) of the NWPC, along with other groups such as NOW, NARAL, and the Fund for the Feminist Majority (FFM) that have played the most prominent role in advocating feminist policy stances – including calls for equal representation for women and greater numbers of women candidates – within the party. The NWPC spearheaded the drive for representational guarantees in the 1970s; the NWPC and NOW were at the forefront of battles to have the party platform reflect the key policy items of the women's movement;

Table 4.5

NFDW activist, DWC activist, and non-activist women compared (selected attitudinal measures)

	Abortion: no restrictions	Ideological self-placement[a] (mean score)	Feminism scale[b]
NFDW active	69%	2.5085	2.2203
	(38)	(59)	(59)
Not active	71%	2.3149	2.1720
	(128)	(181)	(186)
Significance	No	No	No
DWC active	79%	2.2932	2.4044
	(103)	(133)	(136)
Not active	60%	2.4486	1.9083
	(63)	(107)	(107)
Significance	**	No	***

Notes:
a   1 = very Liberal; 5 = very Conservative
b   0 = not feminist; 3 = most feminist. For details regarding the construction and reliability of the feminism scale, see Appendix.
*** $p < .001$
** $p < .01$
Source: Appendix, calculated from data set: Party Elite 1988.

NOW led the campaign for a female vice-presidential nominee in 1984; EMILY's List and other women's PACs have provided most of the impetus for the campaign to elect more Democratic women. The DWC has participated in many of these efforts, and has in some cases been the organizational locus for such efforts during party conventions. On these occasions, however, the DWC has been essentially an "empty shell" that women's movement organizations fill and animate.

The leadership role occupied by autonomous movement organizations has profound implications for party responsiveness to the women's movement. The close movement-party alliance in the early 1980s left an apparently permanent legacy with the Democratic party. This legacy consisted of representational guarantees for women, attitudinal adherence to core feminist policy issues, and a pro-choice, pro-ERA policy stance. It did not include a strong feminist women's organization within the Democratic party. This has meant that the movement-party relationship has taken the form of direct organization-to-organization contacts, so feminist policy stances are not sifted through and reinterpreted by partisan women acting as intermediaries between women's movement organizations and political parties. In this sense, the women's movement was able to achieve a high level of party responsiveness in the 1970s and early 1980s. However, it also means that the Democratic party's responsiveness has declined when movement organizations disengaged from party politics.

Although the Republican party can boast a far more active and influential women's organization than the Democrats, there is little evidence to suggest that this or other women's organizations in the party are a channel through which feminist ideas come to the party. The party's official women's organization, the National Federation of Republican Women, shies away from affiliation with either feminist or anti-feminist camps. Pro-choice organizations in the party are, to some extent, feminist but their ties to the women's movement are tenuous at best. Offsetting any influence the pro-choice organizations might have on the party are two powerful anti-feminist organizations with close ties to party leaders: Eagle Forum and Concerned Women for America.

Since it was formed in 1938, the National Federation of Republican Women (NFRW) has been the organization representing Republican women within the party. Although it has in some sense responded to the emergence of the contemporary women's movement, the NFRW does not act as a feminist force within the party. Rather, it defines itself in terms of service to the party and promotes women in only the most cautious and non-controversial way.

The NFRW was initially a "ladies' auxiliary" that mobilized women to work on behalf of (male) Republican candidates and to strengthen the party's organizational base. It was formed at the behest of the RNC and, for a considerable time, remained financially dependent upon and politically subservient to the regular party.

From the mid-1970s on, the NFRW achieved financial independence from the RNC and gained effective control of the women's division of the party, establishing itself as the one organization representing elected Republican female public and party officials and volunteer activists (Baer 1991b). The NFRW has become a financially independent, professionalized force within the party with an annual budget of over $1 million and its own headquarters. Although the women's division of the party no longer exists, the NFRW maintains strong ties with the office of the RNC co-chair, who is responsible for liaison with the party's auxiliaries. The NFRW is, moreover, an important locus of involvement for women in the party. A survey of party leaders and delegates to the 1988 national convention found that 78 percent of Republican women surveyed had been involved in some way with the NFRW (Appendix, data set: Party Elite 1988).

Although the NFRW's focus on providing campaign support for Republican candidates has remained constant since its formation, it has become considerably more professionalized over time. The NFRW since 1979 has sponsored schools for learning campaign management for its members and offers training in polling techniques so that members can provide low-cost polling to candidates (Baer 1991b). Women in the NFRW see themselves as competent, seasoned campaigners loyal to the party. Local and state chapters of the NFRW will adopt a campaign or a precinct organization, sometimes in order to "save" an organization that is experiencing difficulties (interview 02/01/95).

The one objective that the NFRW and the contemporary women's movement share is the election of women. As early as 1976, the NFRW was publishing a booklet entitled *Consider Yourself for Public Office: Guidelines for Women Candidates* (NFRW 1981). The organization continues to run seminars for women Republican candidates. Despite this apparent commitment to the project of electing women, there are some generational tensions within the NFRW over whether the organization's resources should go to support "the best" candidate, or only female candidates. Where the NFRW departs most significantly from the women's movement is in its rejection of ideological litmus tests for female candidates.

The NFRW occupies an ambivalent position on the political terrain that has been shaped by contemporary feminism. As a voice for women in the Republican party, the organization has taken party leaders to task for their records on women's issues when the party's electoral fortunes appear to be at stake. For example, NFRW leaders chided President Reagan for his administration's record on women's issues which, they claimed, "fell somewhere between apathetic and anti-woman" in the eyes of the average woman (Kirschten 1984, 1083).

Otherwise, the NFRW has carefully avoided the political pitfalls of the feminist terrain. Its leaders have carefully avoided taking a position on the ERA and the abortion issue, both of which have been the source of considerable acrimony within the party. While claiming that the GOP has traditionally been the champion of women's rights, the federation's publicity materials carefully avoid mention of the party's earlier support for the ERA (NFRW 1987).[16] The NFRW's ability to remain outside the fray of intra-party disputes over these issues is interesting. It has never been captured or even influenced by feminist Republicans, but it has also rebuffed advances by anti-feminists, most notably Phyllis Schlafly.

Although it has avoided becoming explicitly anti-feminist, the NFRW defines itself in opposition to the women's movement. In its official history, the NFRW explicitly distanced itself from the movement, asking, "What distinguishes a successful, enduring cause from the movements, the short-lived crusades, and the ebb and flow of public opinion? For the [NFRW] ... the key to success lies in a devotion to purpose, a dedication to the principles of common sense government and most importantly the tireless efforts of thousands of outstanding Republican women" (NFRW 1987, 5). The history goes on to note that because of these tireless efforts, "Republican women today do not have to spend their time 'hitting the streets' as the so-called feminists have done, to get an equal voice. Our voices are heard – from city hall to the halls of Congress" (ibid., 25). This voice, the history claims, has been "earned" by Republican women working within the party, as distinct from a role that is "given" to women elsewhere – referring presumably to the quotas and affirmative action measures used more extensively in the Democratic party and advocated by women's movement organizations.

Some idea of the demographic and attitudinal characteristics of the women active in the NFRW can be gleaned from the 1988 Party Elite Study.[17] The women who reported being active within the NFRW were more likely than other Republican women to be White, housewives, in their forties or fifties, and involved in the party for over ten years. They were also more likely to belong to a pro-life group, and were less likely to support a pro-choice stance on abortion (see Table 4.6). Although the difference was not statistically significant, NFRW women scored lower, on average, on a feminism scale, and they were significantly more conservative, than other Republican women. In short, there is no evidence to suggest a radical potential lurking behind the NFRW's loyalist façade.

In the absence of any overtly feminist organizations within the Republican party, one might look to the two major pro-choice groups as potentially feminist pockets within it. Although both Republicans for

Choice (RFC) and the National Republican Coalition for Choice (NRCC) maintain ties to the women's movement through their occasional cooperative alliances with Planned Parenthood (and, less frequently, NARAL), neither can be described as feminist organizations per se.

The group that comes closer to being feminist is the NRCC, led by former RNC co-chair Mary Dent Crisp, who alienated herself from the GOP hierarchy when she publicly denounced the party's decision to remove support for the ERA from its 1980 platform. The NRCC was formed in the aftermath of the Supreme Court's decision in *Webster* v. *Reproductive Services* partially reversing *Roe* v. *Wade*. The majority of the NRCC's members are women, and it is located firmly in the moderate Republican camp, maintaining ties with the Republican mainstream committee, the Ripon Society, and the Log Cabin Republicans, among others. It is connected, through Crisp, to the Republican Task Force (RTF) of the NWPC and also NARAL. Although Crisp and many of the other women involved in the NRCC do understand abortion as a women's issue, their efforts do not extend to other questions of concern to women. The abortion issue is so contentious within the Republican party that the NRCC's seemingly modest objective of keeping abortion out of the Republican platform is an all-consuming (and probably hopeless) task.

Despite the Christian Coalition's characterization of Republicans for Choice leader Ann Stone as a "radical feminist" (Christian Coalition 1992), there is little reason to characterize either Stone or her organization as feminist. The only evidence that would suggest that RFC is feminist are the group's tenuous connections to Planned Parenthood (but not NARAL) and Ann Stone's involvement in the 1988 Women's Agenda Conference (Taylor 1988).

Table 4.6

NFRW activists and non-activist women compared (selected attitudinal measures)

	Abortion: no restrictions	Ideological self-placement[a] (mean score)	Feminism scale[b]
NFRW Active	16%	3.8142	0.3894
	(17)	(113)	(113)
Not active	29%	3.5000	0.5313
	(9)	(32)	(32)
Significance	No	*	No

a   1 = very Liberal; 5 = very Conservative
b   0 = not feminist; 3 = most feminist. For details regarding the construction and reliability of the feminism scale, see Appendix.
* p < .05
Source: Appendix, calculated from data set: Party Elite 1988.

The 25,000 members/contributors to Republicans for Choice are mixed equally in terms of gender and are, for the most part, "Goldwater Republicans" concerned about the Christian right moving in to "take over our party." Stone claims that she was inspired to form the organization by former RNC chair Lee Atwater, who suggested that the pro-choice banner had to be carried by a conservative woman like Stone with solid party credentials. In fact, Stone's conservative credentials are so solid that other established pro-choice Republicans are sceptical of her organization. They have expressed doubt that anyone who has worked on campaigns for ultra-conservative Senator Jesse Helms, and who worked in Reagan's presidential campaigns in 1976 and 1980 is genuinely pro-choice, and have raised the possibility that Stone was anointed by the party establishment to siphon off money from genuine pro-choice organizations, and that Stone's direct-mail company (which did all of RFC's fund-raising) has made considerable profit without handing out much money to pro-choice Republican candidates (Sherill 1992; Matlack 1991).

Whether legitimate or not, the RFC's literature does not construct the abortion issue in gendered terms, except to argue that the party's pro-life stance threatens the party's ability to win votes from women (RFC n.d.b). In keeping with its libertarian progenitors, the organization constructs state regulation of abortion as an unconscionable (and un-Republican) government intrusion into the private realm. The dual focus of RFC's efforts are keeping abortion out of the party's platform and electing pro-choice Republicans of either sex. There is, however, a sense in which the RFC's emphasis on the choice issue is really a proxy for a debate over which group of conservatives owns the Republican party. Abortion has become a focal point of conflict within the Republican party, but the conflict is less about feminism than it is about a battle for control of the party between "old" libertarian conservatives and "new" Christian fundamentalist social conservatives. In fact, RFC's statement of purpose says that it will "face down Robertson, Buchanan and Schlafly and take the party back to its roots" (RFC n.d.d).

The clout of anti-feminist organizations associated with the Republicans far outweighs that of the pro-choice organizations. The two most prominent anti-feminist organizations are Phyllis Schlafly's Eagle Forum and Beverly LaHaye's Concerned Women for America (CWA). Both organizations exist independently of the Republican party, and are connected to it only informally.

Eagle Forum gained prominence in Republican circles through Schlafly's leading role as an ERA opponent. The organization emphasizes the importance of traditional family values and the merits of women remaining in the home. Although the group's financial clout is limited (its PAC raised only $148,000 for candidates in the 1992 election), its influence on the party comes from Schlafly's personal stature and the important role Eagle Forum members play as campaign volunteers. When Schlafly pulled Eagle Forum members from Reagan campaign offices during the 1980 campaign, several of the campaign offices found themselves unable to answer their telephones (Freeman 1987, 230). Schlafly was closely affiliated with Reagan, and his eight years in the White House were the height of her influence within the party. In recent years, Schlafly has developed some ties with the Christian Coalition, for example, speaking on "defending the pro-life plank in the Republican platform" at the Christian Coalition's 1991 "Road to Victory" Conference.

Concerned Women for America was formed in 1979 by Beverly LaHaye, wife of televangelist Tim LaHaye. The CWA was a strong proponent of the Reagan-Bush policy agenda, lobbying against comparable worth, in favour of Robert Bork's appointment to the Supreme Court, and on behalf of the Nicaraguan Contras (Diamond 1989). The organization's contacts with the Republican party have been via other Christian right organizations. Although CWA does not endorse candidates, LaHaye will give personal endorsements to those candidates whom she believes are sufficiently conservative. In 1988, LaHaye made it clear to group members that she considered Pat Robertson and Jack Kemp "good conservatives," although she later withdrew her backing of Kemp after his campaign chose "to compromise conservative principles ... for the purposes of broadening support for [his] presidential bid" ("Kemp Loses Endorsement" 1988.).

The patterns of women's organizing within the Democratic and Republican parties underline the contrast between them in terms of responsiveness to feminism. Although holdovers of the ladies' auxiliary model of women's involvement in party affairs remain within the Democratic party, the more prominent form of women's organizing is explicitly feminist and has cultivated, even relied upon, ties with autonomous feminist groups. Women's organizing within the GOP, in contrast to this, has defined itself in opposition to the women's movement and creates no base from which feminist activism could emerge.

The Clinton Era (1992-2000)

With Democrat Bill Clinton's election to the White House in 1992 – the so-called year of the woman in US politics – there appeared every reason to believe that a new era of political responsiveness to organized feminism was dawning. The reality, in fact, has been far less rosy than the prospect. Clinton's campaign organization avoided strong programmatic commitments to the women's movement in an effort to ensure the party's electability. Once in office, Clinton was only an occasional ally of organized feminism. With "angry White men" electing a solidly Republican Congress and Senate in the 1994 mid-term elections, the Clinton White House distanced itself even further from the women's movement, and the president infuriated feminist leaders by signing the controversial Welfare Reform Bill in 1996. Nonetheless, the strong presence of the Christian right within the Republican party meant that feminists had no alternative but to continue to ally themselves with the Clinton Democrats in an effort to prevent another period of social conservative domination of the White House. Thus, the pattern of polarization has continued, albeit in moderated form.

The Democrats
In the 1990s, ties between organized feminism and the presidential wing of the Democratic party have weakened somewhat, and women's organizations within the party have proved unable to assume the leadership role on feminist issues that movement organizations once played. Although feminist in orientation, the Democratic Women's Caucus effectively ceded its leadership role in the party to women's groups external to the party (Kelber 1994). Having relinquished this leadership role, women in the party found themselves without necessary internal resources when women's movement organizations turned their attention elsewhere. In her testimony to the 1992 platform hearings, Bella Abzug pointed to the caucus's low-profile role, noted that it received no formal assistance from the DNC and made few demands on policy issues, and concluded that it failed to exert sufficient pressure on the DNC chair (ibid., 209). One observer asserted that at the 1992 convention the DNC's women's caucus was "under the control of the DNC" and did not diverge from the party's pragmatic strategy for winning the White House (ibid., 188).

Although several ad hoc women's organizations sprang up in the party in the early 1990s, none appears poised to take the lead on feminist issues. The National Women's Democratic Network (NWDN) grew out of the campaign organization Women for Clinton/Gore. A grass-roots communication network of approximately 1,000 women with directors in twenty-five states, the NWDN works on local organizing, fund-raising, and voter turnout activities as well as lobbying Democratic legislators on issues of importance to women. Members receive monthly action alerts from the director of Women's Outreach at the DNC and act on them through phone banks and letter-writing campaigns, essentially functioning as a grass-roots lobby supporting the president's legislative agenda (interview 02/02/95a).

Another addition to the constellation of women's organizations within the party is the DNC's Women's Leadership Forum, which is essentially a club of major female donors. An offshoot of the Business Leadership Forum, the organization has about 500 well-heeled members, all of whom have contributed over $1,000 to the party. The $1.5 million that this organization has raised for the DNC goes directly into the party's general revenues and is not earmarked in any way. The elite group holds bimonthly meetings, has an annual conference, holds workshops on networking, and issues a quarterly bulletin.

The emergence of these new ad hoc organizations demonstrates the ongoing feminist consciousness of Democratic women. Even though their insistence on being separate from regular party organizations and their preoccupation with networking reflects a sort of feminist consciousness (insofar as it demands gender-based organizations), their primary purpose is to integrate women into the regular party. It is not coincidental that these organizations are emerging as women's movement organizations external to the party are turning their attention to candidacy and away from internal party affairs.

The one feminist organization that became a much more visible and influential organization in the Democratic party in the 1990s is the political action committee EMILY's List. Because of its financial clout and campaign expertise, EMILY's List has come to wield considerable power within Democratic circles. Even though its funds represent only a small fraction of the total money going to Democratic candidates, they can represent as much as a quarter of the funds going to female candidates. Both the Democratic Senatorial Campaign Committee (DSCC) and the Democratic Congressional Campaign Committee (DCCC) look to EMILY's List for advice on which women to back, and sometimes defer to the PAC's staff on strategic advice for funded campaigns (interview 02/24/95).

It was in the realm of representational responsiveness that feminists made their greatest advances in the 1990s. Of particular importance are the gains in the numbers of Democratic women elected to Congress in 1992, the "year of the woman." This phenomenon can be attributed to the coincidence of several factors. As discussed in Chapter 2, the most immediately apparent is the Clarence Thomas nomination hearings, which featured the all-male Senate Judiciary Committee interrogating Anita Hill after she came forward with allegations of sexual harassment. Even without this catalyst and the consequent infusion of cash from women's PACs, Democratic women were poised to make substantial gains in 1992. An unusually high number of House seats were open, offering women the opportunity to enter in greater numbers. In addition, the pool of potential candidates (most notably women who had held state-level office) had grown substantially, so there were women who could mount credible House and Senate campaigns. In addition, on the initiative of Senator Barbara Mikulski, the DSCC formed a women's council in 1992 that raised approximately $1.5 million for Democratic women running for the

Senate. Finally, the electorate's apparent desire for change gave women candidates – perceived as political "outsiders" – an advantage in some races (Wilcox 1994b, 3). The net result was the election of an unprecedented number of women, who made up 14 percent of the Democratic caucus in the House of Representatives and 25 percent of the Democratic Senators elected in 1992.

As the numbers of Democratic women in Congress increased in the early 1990s, women were finally able to break the glass ceiling of party leadership. Until 1994, no Democratic woman had ever held a leadership position or even chaired a committee in either house, despite the Democrats' majority in both houses over most of the past thirty years. In 1994, Barbara Mikulski was elected conference secretary in the Senate, and in the House, Barbara Kennelly was elected caucus vice-chair (Congressional Quarterly 1995).

While Democratic women were making significant representational gains, they were less successful in terms of policy responsiveness. The Democrats' 1992 platform was even less forthcoming on women's issues than the 1988 platform. As had been the case in 1984, it was women's candidacies rather than women's issues that formed the focus of attention at the convention. As Jo Freeman (1994, 74) put it, "Showcasing candidates and raising money took up more time than talking about the right to choose." Having embarked on a campaign to create a new political party, NOW departed from earlier practice and remained outside the convention. Other women's movement organizations did not enjoy high visibility, nor did they play a significant role in platform development. Freeman (ibid., 77) observed that whereas previously organizations like NARAL, NWPC, BPW, the YWCA, and others "have joined together to negotiate specific language with the platform committee or the campaign [and] occasionally individuals representing feminist organizations have been appointed to the platform committee," in 1992 "neither happened ... The [Clinton] campaign had an especially close working relationship with NARAL and was particularly concerned with health issues. Consequently, the women on the committee ... made a special effort to put in planks on women's health issues such as breast cancer, while more traditional feminist issues, such as the ERA and pay equity, barely got an honorable mention."

The party retained its pro-ERA, pro-choice stance, yet the tone of the rhetoric in the platform appeared to distance the party from its past association with the women's movement. The Democratic party's commitment to quality and affordable child care was prefaced with the statement: "Governments don't raise children, people do. People who bring children into this world have a responsibility to care for them and give them values, discipline and motivation." Even more notable in light of the party's efforts to highlight "choice" at the convention was the statement that followed the abortion plank: "The goal of our nation must be to make abortion less necessary, not more difficult or dangerous. We pledge to support contraceptive research, family planning, comprehensive family life education, and policies that support healthy childbearing and enable parents to care most effectively for their children" (Appendix, data set: ABC News/*Washington Post*, Democrats, 1992). The tone of the 1992 platform was not lost on feminist activists. The *Getting It Gazette*, a publication distributed by feminist Democrats at the convention, characterized the platform in this way: "Designed to appeal to a broad spectrum of American voters, the platform avoids addressing women, as though we were a fractious special interest group." Long-time feminist leader Pat Reuss wrote in the *Gazette* about her search for the word "women" in the platform: "We thought it might be under 'violence' as in 'against women.' Nope. Rape? Nope. Battered women? Nope. What we had was efforts being directed to preserving the family unit. That's nice. And when the violence gets really bad, we can put our children in shelters ... Certainly women would be under the ERA. But guess what. The ERA was – oops, we forgot to put that in, said the men. Called it a technical error" (in Kelber 1994, 189). Clearly, by 1992, the influence that feminist organizations and activists had once exercised over the Democratic party's platform document had all but disappeared.

The same was true of the 1996 platform document. With regard to the welfare reform legislation opposed by most feminist groups, the platform spoke about the "historic chance ... to break the cycle of dependency for millions of Americans." The document hinted at some of the feminist and other advocacy organizations' objections to the legislation, calling for measures to ensure that children are protected and challenging states to exempt battered women from time limits and other restrictions. On abortion, the document restated the party's pro-choice stance and pointed to Clinton's record on ending the gag rule and ensuring safety at family planning and women's health clinics. As in 1992, this statement was tempered with a commitment to reduce the abortion rate by providing support for family planning. The platform document also highlighted Clinton's national campaign to reduce the teen pregnancy rate, noting that the president "expanded support for community-based prevention programs that teach abstinence and demand responsibility." The plank went on to read: "We must send the strongest possible signal to young people that it is wrong to get pregnant or father a child until they are married and ready to support that child and raise that child." Although this language in no way eroded the party's pro-choice stance, it certainly did suggest an effort to co-opt at least part of the Republicans' "family values" agenda. When Republican Vice President Dan Quayle criticized the television character

Murphy Brown for having a child out of wedlock in the early 1990s, Democrats were among those who attacked him for imposing his values on women. A few short years later, the party had moved to a stance not that different from Quayle's – insisting that marriage was a prerequisite for child-bearing. One issue on which the platform did take a stronger stand was violence against women, which was given a platform plank of its own, largely to report the president's record on the issue. The platform also promised support for women-owned businesses.

The Republicans
Through the 1990s, the Republican party's stance vis-à-vis feminism remained oppositional. The Christian Coalition has solidified its place as a core constituency within the party, and remains a firm opponent of both feminist and gay/lesbian activism. The party's loss in the 1992 and 1996 presidential elections may serve to temper its harsh stance on social issues, but this remains unclear. Certainly, the party's majority position in Congress since 1994 pushes in the opposite direction.

The 1992 "year of the [Democratic] woman" phenomenon prompted representational responsiveness within the Republican party. In 1991, Republican activist Glenda Grunwald formed WISH List, which contributes to Republican pro-choice women. As was discussed in Chapter 2, WISH List claims to have contributed approximately $370,000 to pro-choice Republican women in 1994, and the establishment of this new organization provoked competition. Republican leaders were concerned that WISH List's pro-choice stance could be damaging to the party, and they apparently sponsored the formation of the Women's Leadership Network in response. The Network was a PAC that funded women Republicans regardless of their position on abortion. Its charter members have been described as "a who's who of [Bush administration] White House wives," including Vice President Dan Quayle's wife, Marilyn, and former RNC chair Lee Atwater's wife, Sally (Mundy 1992, 17). By 1994, the organization was listed as terminated by the Federal Election Commission. In 1993, then House Minority Leader Newt Gingrich organized the twelve Republican women in the House into a "buddy" system for potential women candidates, and the RNC used its satellite communication system to beam advice to female candidates (Rosin 1995, 20).

After the Republican landslide in the congressional and senatorial midterm elections in 1994, women were elected to leadership posts in both the House and Senate conferences. In the Senate, Connie Mack was elected conference secretary, and in the House Susan Molinari was elected conference vice-chair and Barbara Vucanovich was elected conference secretary (Congressional Quarterly 1995). The women brought into Congress

by these efforts were a qualitatively different group from their predecessors. Six of the seven newly elected Republican women in 1994 were anti-
choice, and most had roots of some sort in pro-life or Christian right
groups (Melich 1996, 284; Rosin 1995). House Speaker Newt Gingrich recognized the potential symbolic appeal of these women and fostered their
careers, meeting with them on a weekly basis (Rosin 1995). In essence, the
Republicans successfully co-opted the feminist electoral project, subvert-
ing it into a campaign for the election of anti-feminist women.

Certainly, the Republican party's policy stance has remained anti-feminist. At the 1992 convention, pro-choice Republicans, bolstered by coalitions of moderate Republicans, made an all-out effort to remove abortion
from the party's platform. The leaders of the two pro-choice organizations
within the party – Mary Dent Crisp and Ann Stone – testified before the
party's platform committee, arguing that the party risked electoral losses
because of its inflexible position on the abortion issue. Arguing that pro-
choice voters were becoming single-issue voters, Stone told the platform
committee that the anti-abortion language in the platform was "a millstone
around our pro-choice candidates' necks" (Stone 1992). Unconvinced, the
platform committee retained the same anti-abortion language that had been
in the platform since 1980. The platform document also retained the same
language celebrating the party's historic commitment to the rights of
women, but rejecting quotas or preferential treatment. There was no mention of child care or other issues of particular importance to women.

The same was true of the party's 1996 platform document. In the name
of equality before the law, the party pledged to "vigorously enforce anti-dis-
crimination statutes" and rejected "distortion of those laws to cover sexual
preference." This commitment to equality before the law also translated
into the party's "scorn [for] Bill Clinton's notion that any person should be
denied a job, promotion, contract or a chance at higher education because
of their race or gender" and support for federal legislation ending affirmative action in California Proposition 209. Despite renewed efforts by pro-
choice activists within the Republican party, the platform once again
endorsed a constitutional amendment to protect "unborn children" and
strongly criticized Clinton's decision to veto a ban on partial-birth abortions. In short, there was little difference between the content of the 1980
and 1996 Republican platforms, at least in terms of feminist issues.

Conclusion
The most remarkable characteristic of the US party system's response to
feminism is the polarization that began in 1980 and has persisted to the
present day. Although moderated somewhat in recent years, this polarization has become a perennial characteristic of the American partisan

landscape and, from all appearances, will not change without a major realignment or other external event. The polarization of the US party system has meant that every election is an important event for American feminists, who are under constant pressure to remain vigilant in their efforts to limit the power wielded by anti-feminist Republicans. In contrast to this, the moderate, centrifugal response of the Canadian party system to feminism has meant that Canadian feminists (at least until recently) have been able to regard elections as events of only moderate political importance. It is to the Canadian political parties and their less dramatic responses to the women's movement that we now turn.

5

Moderate Endorsement: Canadian Parties Respond

Unlike its American counterpart, the Canadian party system has not polarized in response to feminism. None of the major Canadian political parties was transformed by feminism, but all altered their internal practices and policy stances to some degree in the decades after feminists first mobilized in the early 1970s. Of the three political parties in the pre-1993 party system, the social democratic NDP was the most responsive, and the right-leaning Progressive Conservatives the least. The relatively stable pattern of moderate partisan responsiveness was disrupted in 1993, when a federal election resulted in a complete reordering of the Canadian party system, including the emergence of the overtly anti-feminist Reform party, which became the official Opposition in 1997. Even the entry of an anti-feminist party did not polarize the Canadian party system, however. Rather, feminism all but disappeared from the national political landscape in the mid-1990s.

The Canadian Party System

During most of the period covered by this study, there were three major political parties in Canada: the centrist Liberal party, the right-of-centre Progressive Conservative party, and the social democratic NDP. The two former political parties have traditionally been considered "brokerage" parties that rotate in and out of office, while the New Democratic party has been characterized as a somewhat more ideologically driven mass party that has never moved beyond third party status.

Although the Liberals and Conservatives have rotated in and out of office, the rotation has been uneven, with the Liberals governing for much of the twentieth century. This was the case during the period of this study. Under the leadership of Pierre Trudeau, the Liberals formed the government from 1968 until 1979, and again from 1980 until 1984. After almost a decade as the official Opposition, the party under the leadership of Jean Chrétien once again formed the government in 1993 and was re-elected in

1997. The party occupies the centre of the political spectrum, but tends to shift its ideological disposition according to electoral calculation. Through the 1970s, the Liberals faced serious competition from the social democratic NDP, and as a consequence tended to occupy the centre-left of the political spectrum. In the 1990s, facing competition from the Reform party in English Canada and struggling to manage the country's fiscal woes, the Liberal party has moved towards the centre-right of the Canadian political spectrum.

The Progressive Conservative party formed a minority government for nine months in 1979 under the leadership of Joe Clark. After four years in opposition, with a new leader, Brian Mulroney, and a more clearly defined fiscal conservatism as its ideology, the party was elected with a massive majority in 1984, and was re-elected with a smaller majority in 1988. The PC party governed for nine years and was then soundly defeated in the 1993 federal election, plummeting to a mere two seats in the House of Commons and losing official party status. A substantial number of PC supporters in the West and rural Ontario shifted their allegiance to the new right-wing populist Reform party, which became the third-largest party in the House after 1993. Many former PC supporters in Quebec defected to the new separatist Bloc Québécois in 1993, making the Bloc the official Opposition. Under the leadership of Jean Charest from 1993 to 1997, the PCs were able to rebuild at least some of their party organization and mount a credible national campaign in the 1997 election, winning twenty seats. The party's present ideological stance is somewhat ambiguous: it entered the 1997 election campaign positioning itself almost as far to the right as the Reform party (although not on social issues) but drifted towards the centre throughout the course of the campaign.

The New Democratic party is a fairly conventional social democratic party with close ties to trade unions. Over the past thirty years, its ideological stance has moderated somewhat in an effort to increase its electoral appeal. Although it has never formed either the government or the official Opposition at the national level, the NDP consistently won a sizeable number of seats in elections between 1968 and 1988. In the 1993 election, however, it was reduced to a mere nine seats and lost its official party status. In 1997, it increased its share of the seats to twenty-one.

The two new entrants to the Canadian political arena are the Bloc Québécois and the Reform party. In 1984, Conservative leader Brian Mulroney won support from Quebec voters sympathetic to the idea of some form of sovereignty for Quebec by promising to broker a new constitutional arrangement acceptable to the government of Quebec. The new constitutional arrangement – the Meech Lake Accord – recognized Quebec as a distinct society, and met the other conditions set out by the Quebec government. When it became clear that the accord would not be ratified by all the provinces, Mulroney's support in Quebec collapsed and several Quebec MPs left the PC caucus. They eventually formed the Bloc Québécois, a party committed to the separation of Quebec from the rest of Canada. With considerable support from the provincial Parti Québécois, the Bloc ran candidates in Quebec in the 1993 federal election, winning fifty-four of the province's seventy-six seats in the House of Commons and becoming the official Opposition in Ottawa. In 1997, the BQ won forty-four seats, dropping to third place in the House. The party is united behind the cause of Quebec nationalism but lacks ideological cohesion on other matters. While BQ supporters and leaders span a considerable ideological range, the party has tended to espouse a centre-left stance on issues unrelated to Quebec nationalism.[1]

The Reform party was also catapulted to national prominence in 1993. Formed five years earlier as a Western Canadian protest party, Reform was a vehicle for discontented Westerners and disaffected Tories. Positioning itself as a right-wing alternative to the unpopular Mulroney government, and as a populist voice for Canadians who believed they had been excluded from the constitutional negotiations of the late 1980s and early 1990s, the Reform party was well situated to benefit from the downfall of the Conservatives in 1993.[2] The party won fifty-two seats in 1993 and sixty in 1997, fulfilling party leader Preston Manning's desire to supplant the Bloc as the official Opposition.

Pre-Mobilization

Prior to the mobilization of the contemporary women's movement, women's participation in Canadian party politics tended to take the form of political "housekeeping." Women's involvement in the Liberal and Conservative parties was channelled into ladies' auxiliaries that provided important support to party organizations, but had little policy or other influence. Although the CCF (which later became the NDP) had no separate women's organization, women were involved in maintaining party organizations and running party social committees, including holding bake sales and the like. Among the activities considered appropriate for women, however, was public education, which gave CCF women the opportunity to engage in the substance of politics. Despite this, the party was resistant to women playing too visible a role, so very few women were nominated as candidates for the party (Sangster 1989, 118-28).

The secondary position of women in the political parties gave rise to periodic challenges. In the 1930s, for instance, women in the CCF organized to pressure the party into addressing the concerns of women, particularly farm women, wage-earning women, and women on relief

(Sangster 1989, 131-2). By the late 1960s, women in all three political parties were growing discontented with their auxiliary role. At a meeting of NDP women in 1968, for example, one participant reported that "many more women inside the party ... would like to run for public office ... but are prevented from doing so because of home responsibilities" (Eady 1970b). Similarly, in 1964, Liberal organizers experienced a crisis of confidence over the future of the Liberal women's auxiliary, and the Women's Liberal Federation initiated an informal consultation that elicited expressions of concern over the federation's aging membership and overemphasis on social activities. Although the Liberals chose not to amalgamate the federation at the time, it was unable to address the fundamental problems, so pressure for change continued to mount.

The Conservative party experienced the least pressure for change. To the extent that Tory women were discontented, it was because of the limited role they were allowed to play in campaigning. In response to Ontario women's assertion that "men should be reminded that we can do more than be runners for the Party and lickers of stamps at election time," the PC national women's association president responded that "we must be vigilant about discrimination against women, [but] we must also guard against the attitude of the carping fishwife." She went on to exhort members to be ready to open an election office: "Every woman knows how to create a home and many know how to run an office. Here is your opportunity to create a 'home' for your local campaign which is clean, bright, efficient and friendly. We have had enough of dirty, smoke-filled campaign headquarters" (Harrison Smith 1964). Conservative women also responded with some caution towards the emerging women's movement. In 1968, the president of the PC women's association confided to another party official that she thought the proposed Royal Commission on the Status of Women was "a waste of money" (MacAulay 1968). Nonetheless, when the time came, the PC women's association joined with the other two parties to advocate the formation of the commission that would launch second-wave feminism in Canada.

Initial Responses to Feminism

After the Royal Commission on the Status of Women reported in 1970, activists in traditional women's organizations joined together, albeit somewhat acrimoniously, with more militant young women to form the Ad Hoc Committee on the Status of Women to lobby the federal government for implementation of the commission's recommendations. In major urban centres, women were forming consciousness-raising and political action groups. Under the leadership of Doris Anderson, a journalist with feminist leanings, even English Canada's mainstream women's magazine *Chatelaine* was making the integration of women into electoral politics a *cause célèbre*.

This emerging activism and gradually changing climate of ideas affected all three major Canadian political parties, albeit to varying degrees. The women's organizations affiliated with the parties all became founding members of the Ad Hoc Committee on the Status of Women. The political party most immediately and directly affected by second-wave feminism was the NDP, which played host to a feminist mobilization closely related to other struggles inside the party at the time. The Liberal party experienced an influx of liberal feminist activists intent on working through the party to achieve social change, and was also motivated to respond to the emerging movement for electoral reasons. The Progressive Conservatives were the least affected, but even this staid party of the right felt reverberations from the changing times.

The New Democrats

Feminist mobilization in the late 1960s and early 1970s profoundly affected the NDP. By 1970, the party had become a hotbed of feminist organizing as young partisan activists also involved in women's liberation groups became vocal in their criticisms of the party and insisted that the NDP become the partisan political advocate of the women's liberation movement. One document activist women circulated in 1970 called on the NDP to "support the movement for the liberation of women ... advocate special measures to end inequality ... [and] make special efforts within the party and in extra-parliamentary activity to assist the development of the women's movement" (no author 1970b). In contrast to the entry of feminist women into the US Democratic party at roughly the same time, this mobilization was not a case of extra-partisan groups moving into the party. Rather, it was committed NDP women whose emerging feminist consciousness called into question their involvement in the party. In the words of one of these women, Krista Maeots Laxer: "If the party continues to structurally exclude women's liberationists by rebuffing their every effort, while at the same time doing nothing significant to change the position of women itself, then it will lose many of its progressive young women. They will get tired of fighting in the NDP and will concentrate all their efforts on the community" (Laxer 1970, 4). Unlike their American counterparts, the NDP women's threat was not that they would try to take over the party, but rather that they would abandon the party in favour of direct action.

The NDP feminist mobilization was integrally linked to the Waffle movement within the party. The Waffle was composed of radical activists, many of whom were students or academics, who wanted the party to "waffle to the left" (Morton 1986, 92). The 1969 Waffle Manifesto espoused a strong economic nationalism, driven by concerns about American domination of the Canadian economy and by a critique of American society as militaristic and racist. Although the economic nationalism of the Waffle was uniquely Canadian, its critique of the United States had much in common with that of the student and new left movements south of the border. Just as US feminism emerged partially out of civil rights, peace, and student movements, a significant segment of socialist feminism in Canada emerged out of the Waffle. Many of the young women involved in the Waffle were committed to its socialist ideals, but became disillusioned by the treatment of women within the faction. In the words of one such activist, "in 1971, we started to organize a women's movement, a feminist movement in the party, because the fact is that the Waffle was just as chauvinist as every other structure in the party, and a lot of women came very rapidly to see this" (Hilda Thomas, quoted in Lewis 1993, 335). Waffle women went through a process of reaction against the sexism of their male colleagues and thus honed their consciousness as feminists. This sexism notwithstanding, the Waffle responded positively to its internal feminist mobilization, "providing an arena for the development of an analysis and policy proposals that integrated socialism and feminism in a new way" (Vickers et al. 1993, 50-1).

The impact of the emerging women's movement was not limited to the young women involved in women's liberation organizations. Rather, the character of women's participation changed dramatically during the late 1960s. New Democratic party treasurer Mary Eady in 1970 reported that the activity of women's groups inside the party was evolving as women were beginning to discuss feminist topics and becoming active in the community on a range of issues (Eady 1970b, 7). Similarly, reports from provincial representatives in the 1970 Participation of Women Bulletin spoke of profound changes. In British Columbia, it was reported that there were few party women's groups left in the province because women had grown more interested in direct action through the NDP itself. The Manitoba representative reported that there were many groups whose membership now included younger, more active women. These groups, "while still performing many valuable services such as fundraising, banquets, election work etc. ... are now busy discussing pollution, marijuana ... and so on" (NDP POW, *POW Bulletin* 1970).

This feminist mobilization and consequent growing discontent among NDP women led to calls for changes in party rules and party policy. These demands included more women as candidates (Eady 1970b), support for the policy agenda of the women's movement (Laxer 1970; no author 1970a; 1970b), and representational guarantees for women within the NDP. The most powerful of these invoked the party's socialist ideology. In the words of Krista Maeots Laxer, "I find it particularly frustrating to hear NDP men and women both repeating the old adage that women should run for party positions on an individual basis, according to their own individual merits, competing equally with their fellow male socialists. Has it not sunk in yet, after 50 years of recorded precedent, that this system does not work? ... Fellow socialists, when did we become liberals? When did we accept the liberal myth that equal opportunity exists, and therefore all we have to worry about is running elections without corruption?" (Laxer 1970, 4).

The newly mobilized feminists in the party came into conflict with the male NDP establishment at the party's 1971 leadership convention. This meeting was already fraught with conflict, as the leadership race pitted the Waffle's James Laxer against establishment candidate David Lewis. Even in this atmosphere of conflict, the debates on the "woman question" were described by one observer as "perhaps the most bitter debates of the week" (Cross 1971, 4). Delegates to the convention defeated a resolution calling for equal representation of men and women on the federal council. The NDP's resolutions committee had drafted a plank on women that one feminist activist described as "a watered down, misleading and mutilated version of the cogent and accurate resolutions submitted by women from across the country" (Kidd 1971, 8).

Seeing this weak plank as an insult to women, feminists tried to have the resolution deferred and called for a national convention of NDP women within a year. These efforts were unsuccessful, and, reflecting the hostility of significant segments of the party to feminism at that time, union delegates serenaded the defeated feminists with a chorus of "Solidarity Forever" (Cross 1971). It is not surprising that many feminists were disenchanted with the NDP in the aftermath of the 1971 convention. Varda Kidd, among others, called the party on its apparent double standard, asking, "Since when in the history of this party have special measures, designed to eliminate discrimination and exploitation, been considered undemocratic? The demand of the unions for special representation was not shouted down, especially by women, as favouritism" (Kidd 1971, 8).

After this inauspicious beginning, relations between feminist women and the NDP establishment became less openly conflictual. In 1974, the party sponsored a national conference for NDP women. The conference was unquestionably feminist in tone and content. Delegates to the conference endorsed the *BC Women's Manifesto*, a blistering condemnation of the treatment of women in Canadian society and a thinly veiled attack on the NDP provincial government in British Columbia's record on issues of importance to women. It is significant that this meeting of NDP women endorsed a document that saw feminism and socialism as inextricably linked, claiming that "there can be no liberation for women within the confines of a capitalist society, nor can there be a socialist society which is dependent upon the oppression of women" (BC POW Committee 1974, 5). Moreover, feminist women in the NDP began to define themselves as a cohesive political force. Addressing the conference, BC MLA Rosemary Brown (1974) provided a rallying cry: "We have to withhold our support from candidates or leaders or any members running for this party who have not demonstrated a clear commitment to this principle. We must not, indeed dare not, hesitate to make all levels of the party aware that the feminists accept the liberation of women as a priority issue and expect its leaders, officers and representatives to do so, unequivocally." The federal NDP's response to the endorsement of the *BC Women's Manifesto* offers a clear illustration of efforts to moderate the claims of its feminist constituency. Objecting to the "unnecessarily strident language" in the manifesto, as well as the unsuitability of the severe criticisms of an NDP provincial government, federal party leader David Lewis approved a statement on women's rights that watered down the original document. Accordingly, this statement omitted the critique of the BC government and dropped the manifesto's references to the "oppression" of women, speaking instead of "discrimination" against women (NDP 1974). Although it tempered the rhetoric of the BC manifesto, the party's statement on women's rights committed the federal council to full support of the movement for the liberation of women, and to a range of policies of particular interest to women, including free twenty-four-hour child care, maternity leave, changes in labour and pension laws, bans on sexual stereotyping in textbooks and on exploitative advertising, decriminalization of abortion, and improved access to birth control, among others (NDP 1974). In short, the party endorsed the key elements of the feminist policy agenda.

A sign of the NDP's increased responsiveness to feminism in the aftermath of the Federal Women's Conference was the redefinition of the role of the party's women's organizer. The position was established in 1961, when the new party was formed, and was eliminated in 1968 (Bashevkin 1993, 125). The 1971 convention passed a resolution calling for the appointment of a federal women's organizer. An organizer was appointed, but the role was ambiguously defined until 1974, when there was a debate within the federal executive regarding the definition of the position, pitting those who thought that the position should be a "general political organizer who happened to be female" against others who thought that the organizer's primary function should be as a feminist advocate within the NDP. This debate resulted in a decision to make the women's organizer responsible for coordination of women's activities in the party, promoting NDP policy for women, and developing liaison with other women's groups. The new organizer, Anne DeWitt, soon became an advocate for feminist women within the party establishment. In 1975, the Participation of Women (POW) Committee voted to recommend that the federal women's organizer act as a caucus watchdog to ensure that the NDP caucus take positive action on all questions relating to women that were raised in the House of Commons.

A second, and more visible, outcome of the Federal Women's Conference was the candidacy of a feminist woman in the NDP 1975 leadership contest. Rosemary Brown's leadership bid resulted directly from the mobilization of feminist women within the party in the early 1970s. The BC delegation came to the party's women's conference in 1974 determined to secure the support of delegates for the candidacy of a woman in the upcoming leadership race (Brown 1989, 154). Delegates passed a resolution to run a woman candidate, and established a search committee to find a feminist candidate (no author 1974). The committee identified Brown, a BC MLA who had spoken at the 1974 conference, as a highly desirable candidate. In January of 1975, the NDP's POW passed a resolution calling on provincial POW representatives to write to Brown urging her to run and offering her their unanimous support (POW 1975). In her memoir, Brown recalls that it was the cause of women that "catapulted" her into the race, and that appeared to engender the most hostility to her candidacy. The campaign itself was explicitly feminist, with "feminism and socialism" as its theme (Brown 1989, 148-9).

With backing from NDP feminists and leftist, Brown was prepared to mount a highly competitive campaign. Because of her support base, the party establishment considered her a serious threat. The outgoing leader, David Lewis, along with former CCF leader Tommy Douglas, the three NDP premiers at the time, and "most of the other influential figures in the party" persuaded Ed Broadbent to reconsider his decision not to run for the NDP leadership. Broadbent gave in to this pressure, and went on to win the leadership. Brown placed a respectable second, with 648 votes on the final ballot to Broadbent's 948 (Morton 1986, 173).

The Liberals
Unlike the NDP, the Liberal party did not experience a spontaneous feminist mobilization among its membership in the early 1970s. Rather, younger women already active in the party continued the challenge they had launched in the late 1960s to the circumscribed roles the Liberals assigned to women. In the words of one such woman, "You started to get professional women into the party ... we had been trained, we had degrees ... it seemed such a waste not to use it" (interview 24/03/94). These women were joined by feminist activists with a pragmatic bent who decided to take their struggles for women's equality inside the governing party. At

another level, the party's leadership perceived the political mobilization of women as significant, and tried, in an admittedly clumsy and reluctant manner, to woo this new electoral constituency.

Hoping to come to terms with the emerging women's movement, and possibly to buy the government some time before responding to the Report of the Royal Commission on the Status of Women, the Liberal party formed a Task Force on the Status of Women in 1971. The three members of this task force crossed the country mainly meeting with Liberals, but also receiving submissions from interest groups. With a mandate to publicize the RCSW's report, solicit public opinion on its recommendations, and formulate a set of recommendations for consideration by the government, the task force presented seventeen policy proposals to the party, including calls for pay equity, establishment of a federal human rights commission, development of a national day care program, improved pensions for homemakers, availability of birth control information, removal of abortion from the Criminal Code, and public or party funding for political campaigns in order to increase the number of women elected (LPC 1972).

These proposals were then presented to the Liberal party's consultative council (consisting of over 2,000 partisan activists who "voted" on proposals by mail).[3] To the extent that this consultative council accurately represented their views, partisan activists were supportive of the feminist policy agenda as defined by the RCSW. Three-quarters of council members supported public funding for day care centres, and over half agreed that abortion should be removed from the Criminal Code. This call for decriminalization echoed a resolution passed at a national party convention in 1970, which advocated removal of abortion from the Criminal Code and reform of procedures so that abortion would be fairly, quickly, and uniformly available (NWLC 1982a, 38). On the other task force recommendations, support from partisans ranged from 60 percent to 80 percent (LPC 1972).

Despite this support, the government took little action on most of the recommendations. Abortion was not removed from the Criminal Code until the Supreme Court struck it down in its 1988 Morgentaler decision, and Canada has never had a national child care program.[4] The Trudeau government took no action on the task force's recommendations regarding equal rights for Native women, an issue that festered until the Charter of Rights and Freedoms forced the Mulroney government to take action in the mid-1980s. The Liberals did move towards public funding for elections in 1974, responding to concerns about the increasing cost of running for office (see Stanbury 1991). The question of pension-splitting was not resolved until the late 1970s. In short, the task force and the party membership (as represented by the consultative council) were more progressive on feminist issues than was the party-in-government.

Under pressure from women inside and outside the Liberal party to act on the RCSW's recommendation that the parties nominate more feminist candidates, Trudeau ordered senior organizers to recruit women as candidates for the 1972 federal election. This effort was reasonably successful in Quebec, where the party recruited eight women from the ranks of moderate feminists (Sharpe 1994, 93-4). The most prominent of these was Monique Bégin, a founding member of the Fédération des femmes du Québec and executive secretary of the RCSW. In the rest of Canada, party organizers were more resistant to this directive, and only two women were nominated, neither of whom was elected.

One of these women, Aideen Nicholson, ran a feminist campaign drawing on support from members of the Ontario Committee on the Status of Women. These women had decided to try to capture a Liberal nomination in Toronto and, after examining the possibilities and consulting "friendly" women with greater experience in partisan organizing, they selected the downtown riding of Trinity, which had a large population of Portuguese Canadians. Convinced that a woman could not win an "ethnic" riding, the party postponed the nomination for as long as possible in the hope of recruiting a man to run against Nicholson (interview 24/03/94). Nicholson won the nomination, but lost the election by a narrow margin. It was not until the 1974 election that the Liberal party outside Quebec, embarrassed by the 1972 results, made an effort to find women candidates to run in winnable ridings in English Canada. As a result, Nicholson and four other women from outside Quebec were elected under the Liberal banner in 1974.

The Liberal party's effort to come to terms with the emerging feminist movement in 1972 was not limited to candidate recruitment. Prior to the 1972 campaign, the party's national director and senior campaign strategists met with the women's organizer, Marie Gibeault, and two other Liberal women to devise a plan to attract the "women's vote." The opinion polling industry was still in its infancy, but the party had some evidence that women might be an important constituency in an election that promised to be tightly contested. When party strategists briefed the Liberal caucus prior to the election, they identified their target voters as all voters aged eighteen to twenty-five, women aged twenty-six to thirty-four, and women and men aged thirty-five to forty-nine. Despite an apparent need to focus on female voters – particularly those younger women most likely to be affected by the emerging women's movement – there is no evidence that party strategists prepared any targeted appeals for women voters, although they did target ethnic voters, environmentalists, and others (Wylie 1972).

The plan to capture the women's vote involved appointing female co-chairs for every provincial campaign committee, recruiting women candidates, putting a statement dealing with women in the party's platform, and making a series of announcements illustrating the government's commitment to status-of-women issues. In hope of appealing to women working outside the home, emphasis was placed on the Liberal government's record of promoting equality of opportunity in the workplace. Despite these plans to address women's concerns during the election, the first draft of the party's campaign statement did not make specific reference to the government's commitment to improve the status of women until Gibeault insisted that one be added (Myers 1989, 50). In short, the Liberals were less responsive than the NDP to the emerging feminist movement, both in terms of numerical representation of women and policy responsiveness.

The National Women's Liberal Commission
As feminism percolated through society and the Liberal party in the early 1970s, the fate of the Women's Liberal Federation of Canada (WLFC) came into question. Already plagued by an aging and declining membership, the WLFC was dealt a serious blow when the Royal Commission on the Status of Women recommended that the political parties integrate their women's organizations into the regular party. Nonetheless, WLFC activists resisted change, not only because they were reluctant to lose an organization to which they had devoted time and energy, but also because their experience in the Liberal party in the 1950s and 1960s made it difficult for these women to conceive of being integrated into the mainstream of the party on anything approaching an equal footing with men.

On the initiative of younger Liberal women, many with feminist sympathies, the National Women's Liberal Commission (NWLC) was formed in 1973. Unlike its predecessor, the NWLC was constituted as an internal constituency group rather than an auxiliary. All female party members were automatically members of the commission and were eligible to attend its meetings and vote in its internal elections. While the Women's Liberal Federation of Canada had one seat on the national party's executive, the new NWLC had seven. Its purpose was to assist the party in selling Liberalism to women voters, push for legislation on issues directly affecting women, and encourage women to run as candidates. This transition was not without acrimony; there was an ongoing dispute regarding transfer of funds from the WLFC to the NWLC, prompted by resentment among the WLFC stalwarts of the loss of their organization. According to Bashevkin (1993, 128), the NWLC "evolved as an uneasy alliance between older auxiliary and newer feminist elements."

The NWLC executive struggled to define the organization in relation both to the party and to the flourishing women's movement. Activists worked to create a place for themselves in party affairs, planning strategy in advance so their presence was felt at party meetings and conventions, particularly policy forums. Espousing an explicitly feminist policy agenda, the commission worked as an advocate for feminist stances on issues such as abortion, child care, and pensions.

While the NWLC activists' primary objective was to find a meaningful place for women in party affairs, their secondary focus was making connections to the emerging women's movement. These women identified with the women's movement, sympathized with its policy agenda, and were in several cases actively involved in movement organizations. Executive members sought out representatives of women's organizations in their provinces and reported the contents of these discussions to the national executive. These Liberal feminists were eager to have the NWLC seen to be part of the broader women's movement. In 1974, the NWLC's national executive adopted a motion affirming that women's groups within political parties are as concerned as any other group with improving the status of women, and calling for inclusion of a female representative of each of the three Canadian major political parties in all meetings and functions relating to International Women's Year in 1975 (NWLC 1974).

The Progressive Conservatives

The Conservatives were slower to respond to the emerging women's movement in the early 1970s. Pressure for change – both from within the party and from outside – was met with considerable resistance. The correspondence files of the PC women's association during this period reveal a degree of pressure for change from within. For instance, one riding association women's group in Saskatchewan wrote to the party's national director in 1973 to ask him about their role "as women" in the party, telling him that "we want women to get involved in a meaningful way. We're looking for a new identity" (Einarson 1973). Liam O'Brian, PC national director at the time, passed this on to Alene Holt, the head of the women's association of the PC party, for a response. This was not the only communication of the kind directed to Holt. In a letter written later in 1973, she reported having been criticized by the provincial president of the Saskatchewan PC women's association for failing to attend the Women for Political Action Conference (to which she had not in fact received an invitation). The letter went on to complain that "as if that wasn't enough I received a memo from Mrs. Kay Beck ... in connection with [John Munro's] statement on the Status of Women, plus a letter from Don Matthews ... all requesting or suggesting that we should have a Status of Women committee on our National Executive" (Holt 1973b). Holt was not enthusiastic about the suggestion. Like many other women who had been involved in party politics in a more traditional manner, she was uneasy about the new meanings being assigned to women's participation in the partisan political arena.

Nonetheless, some Conservative women were struggling to come to terms with the emerging women's movement. The president of the Ontario PC women's association, Joyce Bowerman, made a speech in 1973 advocating that the party come to terms with the new movement, telling her audience that "the women's movement isn't just limited to the few noisy rebels we hear about, or to particular social and economic classes. It is affecting young girls who are thinking that maybe Daddy's field such as law, medicine, pumping gas ... or selling might be the model for their job destiny. Women are staying at work or going back to it, and are not willing to live with inequities in pay or treatment. This cannot but affect politics, so let's keep up with the changes and get their commitment to our party" (Bowerman 1973). Bowerman also chaired a panel entitled "Run, Lady, Run" at the 1974 annual meeting of the national PC women's association. The three Members of Parliament on the panel – Gordon Fairweather, James McGrath, and Flora MacDonald – presented very different messages about the role of women in politics. Fairweather and MacDonald both spoke about women's participation in political life and recognition of women's contribution to Canadian society, while McGrath encouraged PC women, as consumers, to contribute to bringing consumer complaints to the annual meeting (PCWAC 1974).

PC policy statements on women revealed a fair degree of responsiveness to feminism in the early 1970s. During the 1972 election, the party promised legislation to protect women from dismissal during pregnancy and to provide maternity leave, to make day care facilities available to all female federal employees on a contributory basis and encourage industry to follow suit, and to provide federal assistance for training child care workers (PC 1972a). The party's stance on the question of abortion was somewhat more ambiguous. The PC's campaign document included a table showing an increasing rate of abortion, and then went on to promise to place the issue before the House of Commons, allow time for a meaningful debate, and study the medical, sociological, and psychological effects of abortion leading to a revision of the abortion laws (ibid.). Despite this apparent intention to enact more restrictive legislation on abortion, the PCs did promise to make birth control information available to women free of charge (a controversial stance in some circles at the time).

By 1975 (International Women's Year) the Conservatives had adopted a more explicitly feminist rhetoric on the woman question. The party's *Program for Women in Canada* boldly asserted: "It is time for action, not words. Widespread discrimination against women still exists ... It is Progressive Conservative Policy that changes must be made which will guarantee in law the right of Canadian women to equal rights with men and, as a corollary, equal responsibilities ... Progressive Conservatives must do everything possible to end the all too evident lack of interest and the unconscionable delay in rectifying injustices against women" (in Chong 1975). Despite this rhetoric, the PCs remained slow to develop policy on issues of importance to women, the role of the women's association remained that of an auxiliary, and there was little evidence of changing roles for women in the party.

Flora MacDonald was the first woman to run for the party's national leadership. Her leadership bid in 1976 was ultimately unsuccessful, but it did break down a barrier for women within the party. MacDonald ran a populist campaign, appealing for small contributions and support from the public as well as party members. For the most part, she tried to downplay her sex, claiming that she did not attempt to seek support because she was a woman, but that she had to show that a woman could mount a national campaign and establish an effective organization (Winsor 1976). She did appeal for contributions from women of all political parties, but her organizers reportedly thought this was a mistake, as it played up her "liabilities" (Newman 1976). In short, feminism was at best a nascent force in the Conservative party in the early 1970s.

Party Responsiveness in the Trudeau Years
After the initial flurry of response to feminism, the three major Canadian political parties at the time settled into a fairly stable pattern of moderate endorsement of feminist policy issues and gradual inclusion of women in partisan elites. Throughout the period, the NDP remained the party most responsive to feminism, while the two mainstream parties lagged behind.

Representational Responsiveness
All three political parties were slow to integrate women into partisan elites during the Trudeau era. After the initial burst of enthusiasm for women candidates, progress was slow. As Figure 5.1 shows, less than 10 percent of PC and Liberal candidates were women. The NDP nominated considerably more female candidates than the other political parties, but this did not translate into a greater proportion of MPs. Throughout the Trudeau era, women represented less than 10 percent of any political party's parliamentary caucus.

Women won some modest representational gains inside the extra-parliamentary wings of the political parties during this period. An important measure intended to enhance women's participation in the NDP came in 1977, when the party reconstituted its Participation of Women Committee. First created in 1969 "to assist and encourage women's participation in all forms of political activity," POW was originally appointed by the federal council. The 1977 amendment changed this, allowing provincial conventions to elect POW representatives as specially designated delegates to the federal council (Bashevkin 1993, 125). This increased the power and legitimacy of the organization within the party.

In 1980, the Liberals established an ad hoc committee on affirmative action, made up of officers of the NWLC and the Liberal Party of Canada (LPC). Backed by a statement of support from the party leader and president reaffirming the party's commitment to equal opportunity for and greater participation by women through affirmative action, the NWLC drew up an action plan, and began to collect data on the representation of women (NWLC 1982b). The baseline data collected in 1980 found substantial underrepresentation of women throughout the party. With 50 percent of LPC member organizations reporting, the participation rate on national party executives and committees was found to be 75 percent male and 25 percent female. The action plan established that women should be recruited not only as party members but for elected executive positions at all levels and as political candidates and emphasized that "the system for identifying qualified women should not be more stringent for women than it is for men" (NWLC 1980). It also advocated that the party develop training

Figure 5.1

Percentage of women candidates, 1974-97

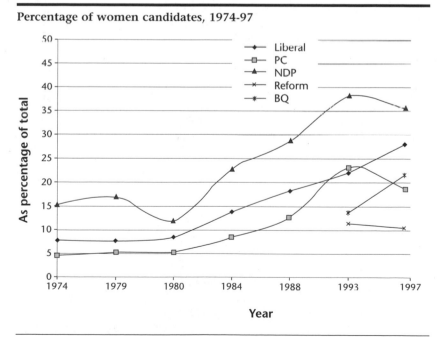

Source: Calculated from Elections Canada data.

programs directed at women and eliminate gender bias in party materials.

The first female presidents of political parties in Canada were Joyce Nash, elected to head the NDP in 1975, and Iona Campagnolo, elected Liberal party president in 1982. Campagnolo, a former Cabinet minister and self-identified feminist, was recruited to run as a channel for activist anger and to draw media attention away from internal party squabbles. Even though Campagnolo had Pierre Trudeau's backing, she experienced strong resistance to her candidacy. As she reported to Sydney Sharpe (1994, 166-7), "The night of the vote, I had to get off the convention floor, the hatred was so palpable ... In the morning, I found little bits of paper, full of hate, misogynist hate, at my door." Campagnolo won the presidency, but faced a daunting task running a party with profound divisions between its parliamentary and extra-parliamentary wings.

Policy Responsiveness

In keeping with their initial responses to the mobilization of feminism, the three political parties varied from left to right in their policy responsiveness to feminism during this period. The NDP endorsed most of the key items on the feminist agenda, while the Conservatives were slow to respond. The policy responsiveness of the governing Liberal party is more difficult to cat-

Figure 5.2

Percentage of women elected, 1974-97

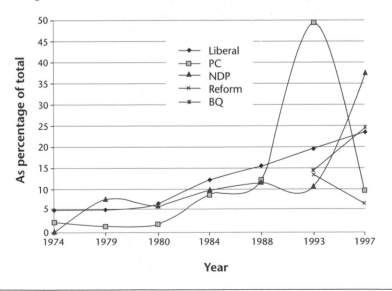

Year

Source: Calculated from Elections Canada data.

egorize. The party's relatively weak extra-parliamentary wing appeared quite open to a feminist policy agenda, but the response of the more powerful parliamentary party was bounded by its role as government and by Trudeau's ambivalence towards feminism. Further complicating the matter, the practice of government funding for women's groups and the access to policy makers afforded to these groups fostered the emergence of a symbiotic relationship between organized feminism and the Liberal government. This caused the government to take for granted the allegiance of feminists. This assumption fuelled the government's political miscalculations when introducing an entrenched Charter of Rights and Freedoms into the Canadian Constitution, a strategic error that would prove a crucial turning-point in the politicization of Canadian feminism.

The NDP

By 1975, the New Democratic party had endorsed virtually every policy stance espoused by major feminist organizations. It had adopted a resolution advocating a pro-choice stance on abortion in 1967, and its statement on women's rights in 1975 pronounced its support for public child care programs, maternity leave, and changes to labour law. As feminists raised new issues, they were generally incorporated into party policy.

Although formally committed to feminist policy stances, the parliamentary party did not always give them high priority. Judy Wasylycia-Leis, the NDP's women's organizer from 1977 until 1980, reports that she would "lobby and pester and nag and get through to Ed [Broadbent] on the issues. I would show up at daily executive meetings of caucus; I'd have my issues, day care, pensions, reproductive choice, affirmative action; I'd lose more often than I'd win but gradually women's issues began to be raised in Question Period" (in Steed 1988, 256). The party's commitment to feminist issues won it praise from feminists during election campaigns. During the 1979 election, the president of NAC noted: "The NDP entered the election campaign with well worked-out positions on a wide range of women's concerns. Mr. Broadbent was the first party leader to raise women's issues in the course of the campaign ... He was also the only leader to mention women's concerns and equality rights in the television debate ... [NAC] generally rates the NDP highly on its treatment of women's issues" (NAC 1980). In short, the NDP was open to the feminist policy agenda, even if these issues did not figure prominently in the party's electoral or parliamentary strategy. The NDP's openness to feminism is not particularly surprising, given the strength of the feminist constituency within the party. Moreover, Canadian feminism has tended to be statist in character, so the movement and party were in tune with one another ideologically during this period.

The Liberals

The Liberal response to feminism through the 1970s was not nearly as positive as might be expected from a government pursuing an agenda intended to create a "just society." Trudeau was the dominant figure in both the Liberal party and the government throughout this period, and he was not particularly sympathetic to feminism. As Judy LaMarsh (1968, 307-8), a Cabinet minister under Lester Pearson, observed, Trudeau had "little understanding of women as people. He talks about civil rights, but it would not even occur to him that inequality because of sex alone haunts half his people." This assessment captures the Liberal government's mixed policy responsiveness throughout the 1970s. The government funded women's organizations and wanted to appear responsive to the newly mobilized women's movement, yet the burden of pushing for policy change fell on the small band of women in the Cabinet who frequently found themselves at odds with the prime minister.

The extra-parliamentary wing of the party appeared to respond quite favourably to feminism. Between 1970 and 1980, delegates to Liberal party conventions adopted several policy resolutions addressing issues that feminist women in the party advocated. These included decriminalization of abortion (in 1970), equal pay for similar work (1970), modifying the Canada Pension Plan (1973), amending federal legislation identified by the RCSW as discriminatory (1973), amending the Divorce Act (1978), amending the Indian Act to give women equal status (1978), and including equality rights in a new or revised constitution (1978). Delegates also passed several resolutions advocating greater representation of women in the party and in government (NWLC 1978b, 38-9).

The significance of these resolutions should not be overestimated, as the extra-parliamentary party was very weak relative to the parliamentary party at the time. According to McCall and Clarkson (1994, 310), in the 1970s "the lay party fell into a virtual coma ... with its disheartened members merely going through the motions of conducting policy discussions at their biennial conventions ... Given the general belief that the Trudeau cabinet scorned advice emanating from any but their own bureaucrats, policy debates were perfunctory and resolutions were passed by the hundreds simply because no one bothered to oppose them." Clearly, the extra-parliamentary party's willingness to adopt policy resolutions on feminist issues should not be overstated. A better indicator of party responsiveness is the action taken by the government.

The parliamentary party (essentially synonymous with the government) was less responsive to the feminist policy agenda. The government's relationship with the women's movement was complex, largely because of its practice of funding feminist organizations. In the late 1960s and early

1970s, the federal government funded citizens' organizations, primarily youth, cultural, and official language minority groups. This practice was so extensive that the period from 1970 to 1972 has been referred to as the "great Ottawa grant boom" (Pal 1993, 47). In light of this, it is not remarkable that the federal government acted quickly on the RCSW's recommendation that women's organizations be funded. This began in 1972 when a grant was made available for the conference where NAC was founded. In the next fiscal year (1973-4), a total of $223,000 was made available to women's organizations through the Secretary of State's Women's Program. This increased to $2.5 million in fiscal 1974-5, the International Women's Year. Subsequently, funding to women's organizations ranged from $400,000 to $955,000 (ibid., 220). The only criteria for these grants were to advance the equality of women, increase public understanding, and promote the organizational development of women's groups (ibid., 219).

The motives for this funding remain a matter of some controversy. It was rooted at least in part in the Trudeau government's ongoing preoccupation with national unity, and represented an effort to foster national community by facilitating the development of pan-Canadian organizations that shared the centralist, statist orientation of the Trudeau government (see ibid., 251). Some feminists have argued that government funding was intended to exert control over these organizations. In an editorial in *Canadian Forum*, NAC activist Marjorie Cohen argued that "the line between cooperation and cooptation is a thin one, and it can become a hair's breadth when an organization's whole existence depends on not making the government too mad. This becomes a subtle muzzle on activity" (in Pierson et al. 1993, 87). Whether intentionally or inadvertently, Liberal government funding of women's groups did contribute significantly to the creation of a symbiotic relationship between the women's movement and the Liberal party, as the fledgling groups quickly became dependent on government funding and did not seek to establish a significant funding base other than government.[5]

Tracking the government's action on party policy resolutions of importance to women, the NWLC found that government action had fully or partially implemented the party resolutions on many of these issues. In 1977, the government enacted the Canadian Human Rights Act, prohibiting discrimination on the basis of age, sex, and marital status, and established the principle of equal pay for work of equal value within the federal government.[6] It also passed legislation allowing Canada and Quebec Pension Plan contributions to be split upon divorce and protecting CPP and QPP contributors temporarily leaving the labour force to raise children. In 1978, the government amended the Canadian Labour Code to eliminate pregnancy as a basis for lay-off and dismissal, and introduced the Child Tax Credit. The NWLC optimistically labelled as "under consideration" the resolution calling for future appointments to federal boards and commissions to represent male-female population distribution realistically (NWLC 1982b).

There were several resolutions on which the Liberal government took no action. Most notable was the resolution calling for the decriminalization of abortion, an issue the government was unwilling to reopen. Equal rights for status Indian women was also listed as "under consideration," but no action was taken on the issue until 1984. In addition, the government failed to implement resolutions advocating that the Human Rights Commission collect data on the impact of pay equity legislation and calling for family law reform.

Despite the NWLC's efforts, Trudeau was apparently uninterested in appearing responsive to feminist issues. NAC president Lynn McDonald reported that in the 1979 election, Trudeau (like the other two major party leaders) refused to participate in a debate on women's issues. While his NDP and PC counterparts addressed women's issues during the campaign, Trudeau neither met with NAC representatives nor addressed women's issues explicitly (NAC 1980). The Liberals chose not to release any policy statements in the campaign, relying on the government's "Towards Equality" program. NAC was critical of this program, largely because it promised further studies in areas in which NAC believed action could be taken without further study (NAC c. 1980).

In the 1980 campaign, perhaps humbled by his party's loss in 1979, Trudeau agreed to meet privately with NAC leaders. The other two party leaders had agreed to public meetings with the women's group. The private meeting ended when Trudeau stormed out saying, "You can't prove good faith with people who accuse you of being cynical" (in Ritchie and Cohen 1981, 13). A partial record of this meeting subsequently published in *Canadian Forum* shows Trudeau to have been dismissive of women's concerns. When NAC questioned changes to Unemployment Insurance that eliminated a large portion of part-time workers (disproportionately women), Trudeau replied that it was the Liberals who had introduced UI in the first place, but then revealed that restricting women's access to the UI system was in fact the intent of the changes. According to Trudeau, "our job as a government was to try and tighten up the system so that there would be less abuse. Our intention certainly was not to discriminate against any particular category, whether it be based on sex or on region or on age. But statistically, I think it's fair to say, I stand corrected if necessary, that we found that it was mostly the young people and mostly the female sex which was ripping off the system" (in ibid., 9). When pressed on the issue of equal rights for Indian women, Trudeau played the role of professor in a Socratic dialogue, and refused to commit to take action on the issue, blaming the problem on Indian men.

Even more revealing, however, were Trudeau's more general comments about his government's record on status-of-women issues and the hints about the political dynamic surrounding these issues within his government. In a remarkably frank admission, Trudeau told NAC representatives that "I can only give you my word that I won't systematically oppose anything which is progress towards greater respect for the status of women ... We've made some substantial progress in implementing ... [the RCSW's] recommendations ... to bring equality when we could do it, shall we say, without difficulty. And you may say, well, there's no great merit in doing it if there was no difficulty. No, but at least it proved that we have a will to act when there are no obstacles in society to that acting" (in Ritchie and Cohen 1981, 12). The message from Trudeau to feminists was "trust us" – an attitude that created considerable difficulty for the Liberal government months later when the Charter debate was under way. At the 1980 meeting, Trudeau told NAC representatives, "You'll have to take our word for it that we are sincere in attempting to improve the status of women within our society." He went on to say that "maybe we don't move fast enough, maybe the women members of Parliament or ministers we have aren't on the ball enough, pushing us in that direction. I say that, I think, rhetorically because I have been pushed very actively by them" (in Ritchie and Cohen 1981, 10). Apparently, the government was only as responsive to organized feminism as its small group of women ministers and caucus members were persistent and vocal.

The conflict between Trudeau and these women surfaced at other times during the meeting. When Trudeau asserted that it was mainly women who were abusing the UI system, MP Aideen Nicholson raised doubts about the quality of research, which Trudeau quickly brushed off. When pressed on the issue of equal rights for Indian women, Trudeau replied that "I think in fact our position has been demonstrated as a couple, three of our women Ministers who have been acting almost illegally ... I mean they've refused to sign orders disenfranchising women. So, in a sense, all through the last part of our government ... all those orders are stacked up, and I suppose some Indian men could take an injunction against our Government and our Ministers for not having done their duty. What can you do when women Ministers want to break the law in order to help other women?" (in Pierson et al. 1993, 81). In other words, the government's inaction was to be excused because women in the Cabinet were acting on behalf of Aboriginal women. Just as Judy LaMarsh had to represent Canadian women's interests within Pearson's Cabinet because no one else was there to do it, the women in Trudeau's Cabinet were assigned responsibility for this "separate sphere." Certainly, the transcript of Trudeau's meeting with NAC lends credence to Sharpe's (1994, 93) assertion that within the government Trudeau "publicly invited women to join the game, but privately dealt them a weak hand."

When we examine this mixed record of policy responsiveness for the period from 1970 until 1979, the Liberal government cannot be described as unresponsive to the policy agenda of the organized women's movement, yet it was not fully responsive. During this first decade of contemporary feminist mobilization in Canada, national feminist organizations placed high priority on issues relating to employment and income security. It was on these issues that the Liberal government was most responsive (Bashevkin 1996). Thornier cultural issues such as abortion or equal rights for Aboriginal women posed a greater problem for the government. Recalling Trudeau's admission that the government acted only when there was an absence of resistance, it is not difficult to explain this mixed pattern of responsiveness.

During the final Trudeau government (1980-4), the women's organization inside the party remained a vigorous, if not always influential, force within the party under the leadership of two women who were decidedly feminist in outlook: Irma Melville (1980-2) and Lauris Talmey (1982-4). Throughout her term, Melville was a vocal proponent of women's issues within the party, and she did not hesitate to take fellow Liberals to task for slights to women or women's interests. Under Melville's leadership, the NWLC increased its mailing list from 643 names in 1980 to 3,688 in 1982.[7] In 1982, the commission produced a set of Guidelines for Political Action as a resource for women interested in forming women's clubs at the constituency level. In addition to practical advice regarding party rules and procedures and ways to attract members, the document encouraged women to speak out on issues of importance to women: "It is imperative that women speak up about women's issues to other women, society as a whole, decision-makers and government. Feminist public speaking can help people understand the issues involved in the women's movement and ease the 'women's libber' stereotype" (NWLC 1982b, 8). The commission document offered a moderate definition of feminism – "any person who believes in social, legal, political and economic equality for women" – but was willing to identify itself with a still-controversial social movement.[8]

Despite these efforts, the Liberal party did not become any more responsive to feminism in its last mandate under Trudeau's leadership. In preparation for its July 1980 national convention (before the Clark government fell), the party's policy committee produced a discussion paper setting out party philosophy. This paper placed heavy emphasis on both economic and foreign policy, reflecting a move away from the "just society" agenda.

Although it was designed as a discussion paper, not a platform statement, the peripheral attention to issues raised by the women's movement reflects the limited responsiveness of the party to these concerns. Only two of the seventy-four pages of the document addressed women and, as usual, the controversial issue of abortion was ignored despite mounting pressure for change (LPC 1980). The discussion paper advocated an affirmative action program for women and minority groups and provision of affordable, high-quality child care, but made no mention of a national child care program, or even of any government involvement in child care. Similarly, it advocated assuring homemakers' financial security by "pressing for improved survivor benefits [and] allowing [homemakers] to contribute to pension plans" (LPC 1980, 29). The document also noted the issue of "wife battering" and argued that adequate crisis centres should be made available, but did not specify whether the state was to provide this service. In short, the era of the interventionist state and the "just society" were over, at least within the Liberal party.

The Charter of Rights and Freedoms
Returned to office after a nine-month exile in opposition, Pierre Trudeau was determined to use his final mandate to repatriate the Canadian constitution and introduce an entrenched guarantee of rights. The story of Liberal mismanagement of equality rights provisions in the proposed Charter reveals a great deal about the limits to the party's responsiveness to feminism. The Liberals' handling of the issue sparked a remarkable mobilization of Canadian feminists that, in turn, set the stage for all three political parties' sudden interest in women's issues during the 1984 election.

The first part of the fight over the Charter of Rights and Freedoms centred around the wording of equality rights provisions, pitting feminists, the NDP, and some federal Conservatives against the Liberal government. Shortly after the federal government announced its intention to initiate constitutional discussions in the spring of 1980, NAC proposed a series of regional consultations for women to develop a constitutional position. In June 1980, Justice Minister Jean Chrétien turned down NAC's request for funding for constitutional research (Vickers et al. 1993, 111). The government-appointed Canadian Advisory Council on the Status of Women (CACSW), which had become more active and professionalized under the leadership of former journalist Doris Anderson, planned a conference on the constitution for September of 1980. Vickers et al. (1993, 112) report that "women's hopes for the CACSW conference were that partisan conflict would be avoided by virtue of the careful, academic approach that was being planned." These hopes were in vain, however, as a strike by translators forced cancellation of the CACSW conference.

This cancellation meant that NAC's mid-year conference in Winnipeg would be the only opportunity for a major conference dealing with the constitution. The Winnipeg meeting was to have been supplemented by a series of regional meetings. This did not come to pass, however, as the federal government told NAC that there was no federal money available for the conference (Vickers et al. 1993, 112). The federal government's consistent refusals to fund NAC activities relating to the constitution, particularly when coupled with events that came later, support NAC president Lynn McDonald's contention that the withholding of government funds was a deliberate effort by the Liberal government to manipulate and co-opt feminist organizations.

With no government funding, and no independent source of financing, NAC was forced to replace its plans for a series of regional meetings and the Winnipeg conference with a one-day meeting in Toronto on 18 October 1980. As Vickers et al. (1993, 112) note, "Given the fact that many of the opponents of an entrenched Charter were from Quebec and the West, this contraction to a Toronto meeting would have a contingent that was better disposed to the government position and, hence, more vulnerable to potential attempts by representatives of government to influence its views." The record is not clear on precisely what transpired at the conference. Nancy Connolly, a special assistant to Status of Women Minister Lloyd Axworthy, attended the meeting and pressed for a resolution supporting entrenchment of the Charter. The extent of her involvement and influence at the meeting is, however, contested. NAC president Lynn McDonald, an NDP activist who opposed entrenchment, told Ottawa journalist Elizabeth Gray that Connolly had let it be known that the meeting's final resolution "should show unequivocal support for the Government's position" and that Connolly leaned on the chair of the meeting, Beth Atcheson, who succumbed to pressure and wrote another draft of the resolution (Gray 1981). Atcheson's account of the conference was somewhat different. She claimed that she had redrafted the resolution in part because of discussions with a group of seven or eight people, including the aide, and that the majority of women attending the conference clearly supported entrenchment (Vickers et al. 1993, 112). The next month, the NAC executive forced McDonald to write a letter to the *Globe and Mail* "setting matters straight," as well as letters of apology to Connolly and Atcheson. McDonald acquiesced, as she believed that Gray had misrepresented her statement about how government influence had been wielded.

Compounding these tensions, Axworthy's address to the NAC conference outraged the women in attendance. Chaviva Hošek (1983, 286) reports that Axworthy "completely misread his audience, its understanding of the issues and the intensity of its concern. He simply told the assembled group to 'trust' his government to come through with a better wording of the Charter. Most of the audience was outraged at being treated with such condescension." With tensions within women's organizations over the constitution already high, and in the face of mounting animosity towards the Liberal government in some feminist circles, Axworthy apparently decided that CACSW's rescheduled conference on the constitution (which was to be held in mid-February of 1981) should be cancelled. In early January, when CACSW president Doris Anderson was out of Ottawa for a day, Axworthy met with the other five members of the CACSW executive. All of the CACSW executive members, including Anderson, were Liberal appointees and one, Wyn Gardner, had campaigned for Axworthy in the past.[9] Anderson alleged that at the meeting, Axworthy exerted pressure on the council's executive to cancel the 13-14 February conference because it might prove embarrassing to the government (Lavigne, 1981a). Axworthy denied having manipulated the executive, but acknowledged having discussed the February conference with them (Lavigne 1981b). After trying unsuccessfully to have the full council reverse the executive's decision to cancel the conference, Anderson resigned her post as CACSW president on 21 January 1981. With the opposition parties calling for Axworthy's resignation from the status of women portfolio, five CACSW council members followed Anderson's lead and resigned their seats on the council.

Axworthy's blatant effort to manipulate the CACSW sparked considerable anger from women's organizations. Several groups and individuals banded together as an ad hoc committee and organized a conference in Ottawa for the same day as the cancelled CACSW conference. There was a distinctly partisan air to the acrimony, as simmering partisan tensions within the women's movement finally boiled over. Former NAC president Laura Sabia (who had once run as a PC candidate) was quoted asking, "What the hell good are women's opinions when already the Charter of Rights has gone to Westminster? That's baloney. It's so easy to fool some of these women, especially when they're nice Liberal women" (in Lavigne 1981c). In light of these partisan tensions, the ad hoc committee was careful to ensure that its conference would not be used for purely partisan purposes, and excluded partisan women of all stripes from speaking at the conference (Hošek 1983, 290).

Feminist Liberal women were put in a difficult situation during the Charter debate, but their actions make it clear that their first loyalty lay with the party. It appears that they were not as taken aback by Axworthy's "trust me" posture as were other feminists. As Hošek (1983, 289) notes, women active in the party felt that informal influence was the most effective way to have women's interests reflected in the constitution. Lorna Marsden publicly rebuked feminist protesters, saying she thought the whole exercise was a waste of political energy since she could have won the changes the feminists wanted in two hours behind closed doors with the legal team drafting the Charter in the Department of Justice (McCall and Clarkson 1994, 313).

The second stage of the Charter battle involved a large-scale mobilization of feminists of all partisan stripes to pressure the provincial premiers to include section. 28. Unlike the earlier stage of the battle, partisan conflicts were muted in this stage as women cooperated across party lines to win guarantees of equality. As one woman involved in the fight observed, political parties – and the Liberals in particular – were in awe of the political muscle of the women's movement after the Charter episode (interview 15/03/94).

Evidence suggests that in the final two years of its mandate, the Trudeau government tried to repair its image on issues of concern to women. In 1982, NWLC president Irma Melville, former NAC president and Liberal party platform committee chair Lorna Marsden, and feminist legal activist Mary Eberts briefed the political planning committee of Cabinet regarding women's issues (NWLC 1982c). The same year, the government appointed the first woman justice to the Supreme Court and introduced reforms to the Criminal Code to establish a "rape shield" provision that protected female complainants in rape trials.

By 1984, the government had taken action on some of the issues identified in the 1980 discussion paper and a few others. In 1983, it implemented a system of affirmative action within the federal public service that applied to women as well as Aboriginal people and the disabled. In addition, the government set up a voluntary program offering consultative services to employers interested in establishing affirmative action programs and to federal Crown corporations and corporations receiving federal contracts. The Liberals did not establish any sort of national child care program, although they did make funds available through the Canada Assistance Plan for child care subsidies for low income families. As well, they doubled the child tax deduction in 1983, allowing parents to deduct a greater proportion of child care costs from taxable income.

On the perennial issue of equal rights for status Indian women, the Trudeau government was finally prodded into action in 1984, mere months before the equality rights provision of the Charter was to come into effect. The government introduced legislation in June of 1984 removing the section of the Indian Act that denied status to Indian women who married non-Indians, and introduced a measure allowing the names of such women and their children to be entered on an interim band list, from which the band council might authorize entry on the regular band list within two years. The legislation was passed by the House, but had not been passed by the Senate by the last day of the session, so it died on the Order Paper.

The government also took several actions that at least gave the appearance of policy responsiveness in advance of the 1984 election. To deal with the thorny question of employment equity and child care, a Royal Commission and a task force were established. Neither the Abella Commission (dealing with employment equity) nor the Cooke Task Force (dealing with child care) reported prior to the 1984 election, however. In addition, plans to revise the Canada Pension Plan were announced in the 1984 federal budget, but were not implemented before the election was called. These reforms included continuing survivor benefits after remarriage, automatic splitting of CPP benefits when the younger spouse reaches sixty-five, and a split of credits upon divorce.

Funding to women's organizations through the Secretary of State increased at a rapid rate through the final Trudeau mandate. In 1979-80, the total Women's Program grants and contributions totalled almost $900,000. The next year, this figure increased to $1.29 million, and in 1981-2, the figure jumped 116 percent to $2.78 million. Funding to women's groups increased only slightly the next year, but in 1983-4, with a federal election in the offing, it increased by an additional 43 percent to $4.2 million. In the election year (1984-5), the funding of women's groups increased by another 119 percent to $9.3 million (Pal 1993, 221). Thus, in the course of the last Trudeau government, total funding to women's organizations increased by 235 percent.

The Progressive Conservatives
In the mid-1970s, feminism began to have a somewhat stronger impact on the Conservative party. In 1976, the party selected the youthful and relatively progressive Joe Clark as its leader. Clark was considered a "red" or moderate Tory, and was married to Maureen McTeer, a woman who kept her own surname and had a career outside the home. One of the first signs of feminism's early effect on the party came with the controversy among activists (especially women) over McTeer, or Clark, as some of them insisted on calling her.

The same year that Joe Clark was elected party leader, the national president of the PC women's association reported to the party president that the women's association faced a crisis over changing understandings of gender roles: "I have found in each Province a group not receptive nor responsive to the existing Women's Association, but at the same time not altogether adverse to the idea of such an association provided that it move into the contemporary society ... I do believe there is a role, particularly in light of the ramifications of International Women's Year. There is indeed a new awareness amongst women, the NDP is making the most of it and the Liberals paying lip service." Out of this sense of discontent regarding women's roles in the party came a movement to reform the role of the women's association and to appoint a women's organizer for the party. The national association continued to lobby for this until 1981.

At this time, the party began to adopt more fully developed positions on issues of importance to women. Recounting the 1979 federal election, the leader of a major feminist organization noted that "the Conservatives came into the campaign with the least developed policy on women, but by the end had addressed a wider range of issues than any other party ... We are especially pleased with their proposals on contract compliance and equal pay for work of equal value, which are new developments in Conservative policy ... In some cases, the principle is good, but specifics are missing" (NAC 1979). During the 1980 election campaign, the party promised action to encourage women to enter "non-traditional" occupations, to implement pay equity in the federal public service and among federal contractors, to remove the section of the Indian Act that removed treaty status from women who married non-Indian men, and to remove the spousal exemption from the sexual assault law and reclassify sexual assault as a form of violent assault rather than a separate category of criminal activity. The PC's position on the issues of parental leave and child care were less likely to please women's groups, however. The party made no firm commitments on reforming maternity leave and even though the party considered the problem of child care urgent, its only commitment was to hold a federal-provincial consultation on the issue. On the question of abortion, Joe Clark promised only that his party would continue to treat the matter as a free vote in the Commons, and endorsed the general direction of the law at the time (PC 1980).

It was not until 1981, humbled by losing office after only nine months, that the PCs began to take organized feminism seriously. This was part of a broader effort to update the party's image, hoping to appeal to younger urban voters by jettisoning its image as a party dominated by elderly rural activists. An internal memo from Barbara Ford, the newly appointed director of the women's bureau, captures this: "Currently the PC party does not attract the Professional, under 35 and ethnic women's vote in Canada. In fact, women view the PC party as being 'staid and old,' while the Liberals are viewed as 'demonstrating a fine blend of grass roots kind of ideology and a forward moving image.' The first step in attempting to attract these voters to the party is to attack the image problem. The image that must be created is of 'young, competent progressive' and this image must be maintained on a *consistent* basis." Like their Republican counterparts in the United States, the Conservatives had a woman problem. Unlike the GOP's electoral deficit among women, however, the PCs did not face this difficulty because of blatantly anti-feminist stances. Rather, they were simply perceived as behind the times.

The Conservatives' response to their woman problem was similar to the Republicans' insofar as it emphasized promoting women within the party. Unlike the Republicans, however, the PCs also tried to attract women voters through appeals based in moderate liberal feminism. In 1982, for instance, the director of the women's bureau circulated a clipping from NAC's newsletter to all Tory MPs. The clipping featured a listing of "what MPs said in the House" on issues relating to women. Although the director refrained from commenting on the contents of the clipping, the message was clear: Tory MPs were receiving far more "brickbats" than "bouquets" from the feminist group (Ford 1981).

Comparison

By the early 1980s, all three Canadian political parties had endorsed feminist stances on several issues of particular importance to women. When the three party leaders debated women's issues during the 1984 election, there were few matters on which they took widely divergent stances. Feminists in the studio audience clearly favoured the NDP because of the party's longer history and greater credibility on their issues. Nonetheless, the two brokerage parties espoused moderate feminist stances on a range of topics, whether credibly or otherwise.

Within all three parties, activists were moderately supportive of feminist policy stances. Not surprisingly, the support for a pro-choice stance on abortion and government-provided child care was greatest among NDP activists. Moreover, support for these positions was considerably stronger among women in each party. Nonetheless, differences among parties (especially between the NDP and the other two parties) were greater than the differences between men and women within each party on these issues.

The Mulroney Years

The landslide election of the Progressive Conservatives under the leadership of Brian Mulroney in 1984 brought the Trudeau era to an end. To the extent that any decade has an ideology, the 1980s were a decade of "the new conservatism" in Anglo-American countries. Although less ideologically driven and more open to compromise, Mulroney was Canada's answer to Margaret Thatcher and Ronald Reagan. His government ushered in a new era of retrenchment and restructuring in the name of competitiveness. Coming to power after decades of Liberal dominance, the PCs seized the initiative throughout their first mandate leaving the opposition parties to react.

Relations between the government and organized feminism were acrimonious throughout this period, in large part because of the growing opposition of feminist organizations to Mulroney's neo-liberal agenda. Compounding this, the Mulroney government (with the support of the other two major parties) embarked on a program of constitutional amendment that many major English Canadian feminist organizations opposed, both on procedural grounds (objecting to decisions reached by "eleven White men behind closed doors") and substantive grounds (mainly concerns regarding the primacy of the Charter). As a result, relations between feminist organizations and all three Canadian political parties soured considerably by 1993.

Despite this, all three parties remained moderately positive in their responses to feminism during this period. Unlike the US Republicans, the Canadian Conservatives did not come to define themselves in opposition to feminism. Rather they lagged somewhat behind the two other Canadian parties in endorsing moderate feminist stances on a range of issues. For all three parties, representational responsiveness outstripped (and arguably supplanted) policy responsiveness.

Representational Responsiveness

Women made representational gains within the political parties during this period. In 1983, the NDP adopted a resolution guaranteeing gender parity on both the federal executive and the federal council (a larger body that is the primary party decision-making organ between conventions). With the exception of union delegates to the federal council, there is gender parity on this body. This has translated into a substantial increase in the number of women, from just over 20 percent in 1977 to 42 percent 1989 (Whitehorn and Archer 1995, 7). Similarly, the party's executive was "balanced" by sex so that women held roughly half of the vice-presidential positions. The party's constitution also stipulates that either the president or associate president must be a woman (ibid.). Since 1985, the post of party president has always been held by a woman. Whitehorn and Archer (ibid.) attribute this long succession of female presidents to "the shift in the party's base of support and a desire to project a progressive image."

In 1986, the Liberals adopted a rule requiring that half their vice-presidential positions be held by women. This measure was dropped, however, in 1990. Since then, the only representational guarantee for women has been seven seats allocated to the National Women's Liberal Commission on the party's sixty-nine-member national executive (NWLC 1994a, 55). Not surprisingly, the proportion of women on the party's national executive dropped after 1990, from 38 percent of the total committee in 1990 to 33 percent in 1994 (Bashevkin 1993, 79; NWLC 1994a, 55). The representation of women on other national party committees ranged from as low as 13 percent on the financial management committee to 50 percent on the constitutional and legal affairs committee. On other committees, women were usually approximately 25 percent of the members (NWLC 1994a, 55).

Although the only guarantee for women's representation on the PC national executive is the inclusion of representatives of the party's women's association, women have made up half or over half of the party's governing body in recent years. Bashevkin (1993, 79) reports that in 1983 women made up 50 percent of the national executive, and in 1993 women held 58 percent of seats on the body. In 1983, newly elected party leader Brian Mulroney appointed the first woman to serve as national director of the party, a move that "shocked the caucus and backroom boys" (in Sharpe 1994, 113). The mid-1980s were a period of burgeoning activism for women in the Conservative party. As part of its effort to change the party's image and attract women voters, the party's women's bureau organized PC women's caucuses in major Canadian cities. Designed to help women acquire leadership, organizational, and political skills to participate in the mainstream of party politics, the caucuses emphasized networking and "access to power" for women.

In 1990, the Liberal party adopted a constitutional amendment requiring that 50 percent of all convention delegates be women (Bashevkin 1993, 97). This did not translate into gender parity, however, as ex officio delegates were predominantly male. Nonetheless, women made up 47 percent of delegates to the 1990 Liberal leadership convention.[10] At PC conventions the proportion of women increased substantially over time, but varied depending on the convention's political importance. At a minimum, the party's constitution required that at least two of the six delegates selected from each constituency be women, thereby establishing a floor of one-third representation of women among constituency delegates. Fewer women were delegates to leadership conventions, as illustrated most vividly by the two PC conventions in 1983. At the first – a policy convention – women were over 41 percent of the total delegates. At the leadership convention where Brian Mulroney was elected several months later, women were only 28 percent of the delegates. Similarly, at the 1989 PC convention, women were 46 percent of delegates, but at the 1993 leadership convention, they were only 34 percent of delegates (see Table 5.1).

Curiously, the NDP is the only party that did not employ any representational guarantees for conventions. In a recent study of party conventions in Canada, John Courtney speculates that the absence of quotas may lie in the NDP's history of devolving principal responsibility for determining the character of convention representation onto its various parts, notably the affiliated trade unions and local constituency associations. He also suggests that the underrepresentation of women at conventions was not perceived as a problem by the party, since between 26 and 37 percent of constituency delegates have been women (Courtney 1995, 147). Certainly, the proportion of women attending NDP conventions has increased steadily since the early 1970s. As Table 5.1 shows, women have gone from being a quarter of delegates in the 1970s to almost 40 percent in 1989. It is noteworthy that this steady upwards trend was not interrupted in 1989, the party's first leadership convention since the mid-1970s.

Parliamentary Parties

Even as organized feminism shifted its attention away from partisan politics, and particularly from the project of electing women, women in the political parties became ever stronger advocates for women's involvement in internal party affairs and electoral politics, focusing particularly on the election of women to the House of Commons. This shift in emphasis is not surprising. The extra-parliamentary wings of Canadian political parties play a limited role in policy making; activists are better placed to affect the party's choice of candidates than its choice of policies. Moreover, liberal feminists were advocating the election of women both as a means to an end and an end in itself, women were playing a more prominent role in party affairs, and, with women more firmly entrenched in professions and business, the number of women whose qualifications matched those of male recruits was growing. There was also pressure from outside the political parties: the Canadian Advisory Council on the Status of Women issued two reports advocating greater participation of women in political life in 1986 and 1990, and in 1990-1, the Royal Commission on Electoral Reform and Party Finance (RCERPF) held a series of consultations with the political parties on a variety of issues, including ways to increase the number of women elected.

As Figure 5.1 shows, the percentage of women candidates nominated by the NDP has steadily increased over time, from less than 16 percent in 1974 to 38 percent in 1993. This has not, however, automatically translated into significant numbers of women elected. In an effort to retain the

Table 5.1

Women at Canadian party conventions

Liberals		PC		NDP	
Year	%	Year	%	Year	%
1968 (L)	18	1967 (L)	19	1971 (L)	26
		1981	33	1979	26
1982	38	1983a	41	1981	35
		1983b(L)	28	1983	31
		1989	46	1987	33
1990	47	1993 (L)	34	1989 (L)	37

(L) denotes a leadership convention.
Sources: Bashevkin (1993, 75); Whitehorn and Archer (1995).

profile of a national political party (and to benefit from a public funding formula based on the number of candidates a party nominates), many NDP candidates ran in ridings where they had virtually no chance of winning. Thus, many of the women running as NDP candidates were essentially sacrificial lambs. In fact, the proportion of women in the NDP caucus has lagged behind that of the other two major Canadian political parties in some years (see Studlar and Matland 1994).

The NDP is the only Canadian political party that tried to implement an affirmative action program for women and other underrepresented groups as candidates. The first iteration of this plan, set in motion after the 1988 election, tried to evade the tricky question of how to apply a quota when each decision-making group (the members of the constituency association) selected only one candidate. It clustered several federal ridings together and applied a quota to the group of ridings. This ultimately did not prove workable, so a policy approved by the 1991 NDP national convention gave the federal council the power to oversee greater female involvement in each region. The most significant power given to the federal council under this plan was to freeze nominations for an entire cluster of ridings until a more inclusive nomination process had been achieved (Whitehorn and Archer 1995, 8-9). Even before the affirmative action program was put into place, the national NDP was placing considerable pressure on constituency associations to nominate women. In a 1991 survey of constituency associations, Carty (1991, 68-9) found that 90 percent of the NDP associations felt real pressure from their party to adopt special provisions to ensure equal treatment for women, while 80 percent of the associations reported adopting special measures for women. In contrast to this, the majority of PC and Liberal associations characterized the pressure from their party as "just talk," and only one-third of associations adopted special measures.

Within the Liberal party, there was a marked change in emphasis towards the election of women in the late 1980s and early 1990s. The National Women's Liberal Commission adopted a new statement of purpose in 1987 that put far less emphasis on pursuing policy stances favourable to women and far greater emphasis on nominating and electing Liberal women (NWLC 1987). In its presentation to a party reform commission in 1991, the NWLC advocated a quota of 50 percent women candidates on the grounds that "voluntary measures to increase the participation of women have not been successful. Only mandatory affirmative action programs have produced the desired effect" (NWLC 1991, 9). The women's commission also advocated expenditure limits for nomination contests and an extension of tax credits to nomination campaigns. Although the NWLC's appearance before the party reform commission predated the release of the Report of the Royal Commission on Electoral Reform and Party Financing by several months, the recommendations of the party commission echoed those made by the Royal Commission. The RCERPF had engaged in an extensive process of consultation with the parties and had held a symposium focusing entirely on the election of women, thereby creating considerable opportunity for exchange of ideas.

Although the Liberal Party of Canada did not adopt these recommendations, it took several steps to ensure that more women were elected. In addition to appointing nine women candidates, the LPC launched the "Judy Campaign," which brought together the efforts of the NWLC, the Judy LaMarsh Fund, and the parliamentary Liberal women's caucus under the leadership of Liberal Deputy Party Leader Sheila Copps. The Judy Campaign entailed informal efforts to recruit women candidates, a mentorship program linking new candidates with experienced ones, a contribution of $2,000 to the campaigns of all women running for the Liberal party, campaign colleges for women candidates and their staffs, and a manual entitled *Walk, Talk and Knock*. This manual, distributed to Liberal candidates of either sex, caused a brief media controversy because it devoted several pages to wardrobe advice for women candidates.[11] The manual also included an extensive briefing on "gender issues" including employment equity, education and training, women and poverty, and health and legal issues of particular importance to women (NWLC 1993). The briefings on these issues were thorough, and occasionally explicitly critical of the Mulroney government's record, but enunciated no Liberal party positions on the issues.

Given the emphasis that the NWLC placed on the election of women, one might have expected a sharp increase in the number of Liberal women elected. In fact, the number of women running for the party and the number of women elected did increase in 1993. As Figure 5.2 (p. 148) demonstrated, however, the rate of increase between 1988 and 1993 was no greater than the rate of increase between 1980 and 1984, or between 1984 and 1988. Moreover, Liberal women, once nominated, were no more likely to be elected in 1993 than in 1988. More Liberal women were elected in 1993 than in 1988 because more were nominated, not because success rates for female candidates increased.

Although lagging slightly behind the two other Canadian political parties in this regard, the Progressive Conservatives have steadily increased the number of women running for election under the party's banner as well as the proportion of women in the party's parliamentary caucus, especially since 1984. The 1993 figures are anomalous – it was clear that the party was going to lose the election, so numerous seats were opened up, probably contributing to the almost 100 percent increase in the number of women candidates. Moreover, impressive as the gender parity in the PC caucus looked in proportional terms, the fact remains that the caucus had only two members. After the 1997 election, however, the proportion of women in the PC caucus declined to only 10 percent.

The crowning achievement of the campaign to make a place for feminist women within the New Democratic party was the election in 1989 of Audrey McLaughlin as party leader. When Ed Broadbent announced his intention to step down as leader in 1988, women in the NDP conducted what McLaughlin called "an on-going, cross-Canada strategy meeting" to decide which women inside or outside the caucus should "carry the banner" for feminist NDP women (McLaughlin 1992, 52). When other, more prominent and experienced women such as Marion Dewar, Johanna den Hertog, and Alexa McDonough made it clear that they would not run, McLaughlin stepped into the race with their full backing. Compared with these women, McLaughlin was a political neophyte – she had only been elected to the House of Commons in a 1987 by-election and had a limited history of involvement in the party. Support from women, and particularly from feminist women, was important to McLaughlin's campaign and eventual election as leader. In a study of delegates to the convention that elected her, Thomlinson (1992) found that women, and particularly those who had attended the women's caucus meeting at the convention (a proxy for attitudinal feminism), were significantly more likely to vote for McLaughlin in the leadership contest. McLaughlin was the first woman elected leader of a major Canadian political party.

In the 1990 Liberal leadership contest, held to choose a successor to John Turner, who had succeeded Trudeau, Sheila Copps mounted the first candidacy of a woman for that party's leadership. This came some fifteen years after women had first contested the leadership of the two other major political parties. Copps's campaign was not explicitly feminist in message, and she was only slightly more successful among female delegates than male (see Table 5.2). The experience of mounting her leadership campaign made Copps a vocal proponent of spending limits on leadership and nomination contests as a means of levelling the playing field for women candidates. She placed third in the leadership contest, and was subsequently appointed deputy leader of the party and then deputy prime minister by the victor, Jean Chrétien.

The prospect of almost certain defeat in the 1993 election may account for the election of a woman to lead the Conservative party that year. At its 1993 leadership convention, the party chose Kim Campbell to head it into the upcoming election. Campbell had been a Social Credit member of the British Columbia legislature, and ran for the federal Conservatives in 1988. Mulroney appointed her to the Cabinet, giving her a series of challenging portfolios. She was made minister of justice just in time to be given responsibility for ushering controversial abortion legislation through the House of Commons, and later was appointed minister of national defence. Having spent only four years in Ottawa at the time she was elected party leader, Campbell had less federal experience and shallower roots in the Conservative party than most contenders for a national party leadership usually have. Within the space of a year, Campbell went from being the first woman to serve as minister of national defence, to the first woman to serve as prime minister, to the leader of the party that experienced the worst electoral defeat in Canadian history. She did not win her seat, and resigned as party leader shortly after the election.

At the 1993 leadership convention, women delegates were significantly more likely to support Campbell's candidacy than were men. On the first ballot, 46 percent of men and 57 percent of women reported voting for Campbell. Among delegates who supported the ideas of the women's movement, 47 percent of men and 62 percent of women supported Campbell on the first ballot (calculated from Appendix, data set: Progressive Conservative Delegate Survey 1993). Clearly, the prospect of a female leader who identified herself as feminist was more appealing to women than men in the party, and more appealing to Conservatives sympathetic to feminism.

The fact that the first two women to lead major Canadian political parties both led their parties into electoral disasters of unprecedented proportions has not gone unremarked. Various observers have attributed the losses experienced by the NDP and the PCs to the leadership of McLaughlin and Campbell, respectively. Certainly, neither was a particularly experienced or skilful political leader. That said, it appears more credible to argue that both women were elected leaders more because of their sex than their other characteristics. McLaughlin stepped into the

Table 5.2

First ballot support 1990 Liberal leadership contest, by gender

Candidate	Men		Women	
	%	(n)	%	(n)
Chrétien	56	(465)	54	(342)
Martin	27	(217)	27	(169)
Copps	11	(86)	13	(82)
Others	7	(53)	7	(44)

Note: Total percentages in Chapter 5 tables do not always equal 100, due to rounding.
Source: Appendix, data set: Liberal Party Delegate Survey 1990.

leadership race only after other women with more experience and deeper roots in the party decided not to run; Campbell was promoted by the Tory elite largely as a gimmick – a woman from Western Canada – being grasped by a party facing an almost certain electoral defeat. These failures should not be understood as an indictment of women's capacity to lead political parties; rather, they should be understood as a symptom of the difficulties faced by women building political careers inside the political parties at the time.

Policy Responsiveness

If representational and policy responsiveness went hand in hand, we would expect that the period from 1984 to 1993 would have been positive in terms of progress on women's issues. The reality, however, is not that straightforward. All three Canadian political parties' emphasis on representational gains outstripped their efforts to respond to feminist issues. Nonetheless, all three Canadian parties remained moderately responsive to feminism throughout this period, and none came to define itself in opposition to feminism in the manner of the US Republicans.

The New Democratic Party

For most of the Mulroney era, the NDP remained a strong proponent of feminist issues. Notably, the party remained faithful to its pro-choice stance when the Mulroney government tried to recriminalize abortion in 1989. The NDP was also in tune with the women's movement's shifting policy emphasis, sharing NAC's opposition to privatization, cutbacks to government services and programs, and entry into continental free trade arrangements. Given this harmony between movement and party agendas, particularly when coupled with the election of a woman with feminist backing as party leader, one might expect that the late 1980s and early 1990s would have been a period of heightened NDP responsiveness to feminism. In reality, however, this was not the case.

The NDP under McLaughlin's leadership did not prove fertile ground for a resurgence of feminism inside the party. In the words of Marion Dewar, "We [feminists] popped her in there, and she had no constituency in the party" (in McLeod 1994, 35). The women who had championed McLaughlin's cause during the leadership race were not available to support the new and inexperienced leader. Consequently, McLaughlin relied heavily on staff members, who were resented by the caucus, and she was ultimately unable to fulfil the promise of her candidacy.

Moreover, tensions between social movement organizations and the NDP mounted during this period, fuelled by the experience of the Ontario NDP in power, the perceived betrayal of the party by the Action Canada

Network (an anti-free trade group that had endorsed Liberals in some constituencies in 1988), and NAC's increasingly oppositional stance. By 1993, a senior provincial party official wrote a memo condemning the "single issue" focus of social movement organizations and noting that "their agenda is not our agenda" (McLeod 1994, 123).

A significant rift between NAC and the NDP emerged during the debate over the Charlottetown Accord in 1992. The federal NDP caucus joined with the PCs and Liberals in supporting the accord as a last chance to buy constitutional peace in the county, but NAC decided to oppose the accord in solidarity with Aboriginal women, who were angry about being excluded from negotiations and concerned that the recognition of an inherent right to Aboriginal self-government would remove Aboriginal women from the guarantees of equality entrenched in the Charter of Rights and Freedoms. NAC's president, Judy Rebick, became a high profile opponent of the accord, which was defeated in a national referendum. As NAC leaders expected, their decision to oppose the accord alienated the organization's allies in the NDP caucus.

This tension was exacerbated by NAC's actions in the 1993 election, when Rebick's successor, Sunera Thobani, told reporters that the NDP had ignored the concerns of women just like the Liberals and Conservatives. This statement was met with considerable anger on the part of feminists in the NDP. In the words of former MP Joy Langan: "The women's movement – I'm talking about NAC – very much used us when I was a Member of Parliament to get access to people, to set things up for them. And we are feminists, in a party with good strong feminist policies that are very much like NAC's policies. Where was NAC in the federal election? No political party met their criteria. No political party did anything or said anything that was of any value ... They were busy being non-partisan and saying 'no-bo-dee reflects our views'" (in McLeod 1994, 124-5). Feminist activists allied with the NDP took issue with these complaints. In a submission to the Party Renewal Conference in 1994, Judy Rebick (1994) argued, "The process of coalition-building among the social movements ... should be a source of strength to the NDP ... Many activists have turned to the social movements for their political activity ... because these movements provide more meaningful political activity for their average members. This should be seen as a challenge to the party rather than a threat." Despite Rebick's protests, the events of the early 1990s introduced an element of tension into the alliance between feminists and the NDP that may not be readily mended.

That said, the NDP remained the party most closely in harmony with the women's movement's policy agenda. In response to a policy questionnaire that NAC sent to the three major political parties prior to the 1993 election, the NDP indicated its support for a national child care program, strong action on violence against women, increased spending on social programs, and improved access to abortion services. Like NAC, the party was strongly opposed to the government's changes to immigration rules making it more difficult for women from developing countries to qualify for visas as domestic workers. The NDP was also the only party to share NAC's continuing opposition to NAFTA (Léger and Rebick 1993).

The Liberals

Feminist activity within the Liberal party during the Mulroney era has a great deal in common with feminist organizing around PACs in the United States. Motivated at least in part by a belief that electing women would foster political change, these activists sought equality for women in the formal political arena. As the success of this campaign mounts, its connections to the policy questions that once motivated it fade away. As journalist Charlotte Gray (1994) noted after attending an NWLC convention, the pervasive view among NWLC activists is "an unspoken assumption that most women inhabit a loftier plane than men, and would make the House of Commons a 'nicer' place."

While NWLC activists considered themselves feminists and believed they have common cause with the women's movement, their first loyalty was to the party. They considered themselves an integral part of the party. In its brief to the LPC's reform commission in 1991, the NWLC executive criticized the influence of "special interest groups" within the party, arguing that "such groups have used the party as a forum for their beliefs, but have not contributed to the strength of the party. This must not continue to happen" (NWLC 1991, 10). This thinly veiled jab at Liberals for Life inadvertently demonstrates the NWLC's identification of itself with the party. It is not a "special interest group," presumably because its members and activists are loyal partisans willing to place the party ahead of their cause.

In short, activists in the NWLC were feminists, but their feminism had little in common with that of NAC. The growing social distance between partisan feminists and women's movement activists meant the NWLC became a less effective conduit for feminist concerns to be communicated to the party. It also meant that Liberal women were more likely to identify with the party than with the women's movement.

Liberal policy in the 1993 election revealed a moderate degree of responsiveness to the movement's stance on more traditional status-of-women issues, but a fairly limited degree of responsiveness on the broader economic issues to which NAC had begun to give priority. On the question of child care, the party indicated a commitment to the development of a program, but gave no timetable for implementation (Léger and Rebick 1993,

19). The LPC strongly supported the principle of employment equity, and indicated a commitment to mandatory quotas and timetables with sanctions for non-compliance (ibid., 36). The party also promised to reinstate the court challenges program, which provided grants to defray the costs of mounting Charter challenges, and said it was committed to including gay and lesbian rights in the Canadian Human Rights Act. The party supported the recommendations of the report of the parliamentary sub-committee on the status of women regarding violence against women, which included gun control and gender sensitivity training (ibid., 6).[12] The Liberals also indicated their intention to repeal a provision requiring foreign domestic workers to have completed a six-month training course because it discriminated against applicants from countries where such courses were not available. On the question of the North American Free Trade Agreement, which had become a high-priority issue for NAC, the Liberal position was that, if elected, they would renegotiate, but not abrogate, the agreement (ibid., 30). The Liberal party did indicate a general commitment to maintaining social programs, especially health care, but it did not promise to repeal the cap on the transfers to provinces under the Canada Assistance Plan, the federal-provincial device that transfers federal funds to social assistance programs delivered by provincial governments.

The Progressive Conservatives

During its nine years in office, the Progressive Conservative party's responsiveness to feminism was mixed. The Mulroney government directly antagonized feminist organizations by cutting their funding and reducing their access to the policy process. Feminist leaders were alarmed by the apparent sympathy that an anti-feminist organization, REAL Women, won from elements within the Conservative party. In 1985, REAL Women lobbied to receive public funding through the Secretary of State's Women's Program (which had previously funded only feminist organizations) and approximately thirty members of the PC caucus met representatives of the organization (Pal 1993, 147). Even more alarming to feminists was the government's decision to fund a conference sponsored by REAL Women. This was, however, the only occasion of federal government funding to an anti-feminist organization. In 1989, Cabinet ministers refused to attend the major national feminist organization's annual parliamentary lobby, breaking a tradition of annual consultation with NAC instituted in 1976. That same year, the government froze the budget of the federal Women's Program and subsequently reduced it, thereby substantially reducing the funds available for operating grants to feminist organizations (ibid., 147).

The antagonism between feminist groups and the Mulroney government was not based solely on these questions of access, however. Rather, many Canadian feminists took issue with the Mulroney government's neo-liberal economic agenda, which involved privatization of government-owned corporations, entry into continental free trade arrangements, elimination of restrictions on foreign investment, and reduction of government spending on a variety of programs, including social programs. NAC and several other organizations opposed this agenda, arguing that women would be disproportionately harmed by these changes. As the reforms were introduced, feminist groups became progressively more involved in "popular sector" coalitions mobilizing in opposition to the PC policy agenda. One issue that caused particular controversy was child care. During the 1984 election campaign, the PCs had promised to introduce a national child care program. The government introduced legislation establishing such a program during its first mandate, although it was considered inadequate by most women's and child advocacy organizations. The government allowed the legislation to die in the Senate when it called the 1988 election, and it did not make any effort to develop a national child care program during its second mandate.

On questions unrelated to the role of the state in regulating the market and not requiring significant government transfers, the Mulroney government's record was considerably more positive, although not uniformly so. This mixed record can be attributed in large part to the difficulty the government experienced in managing "women's issues." The government caucus was divided on these, with socially conservative MPs advocating a "family values" agenda pitted against more progressive members of the caucus, including several women who considered themselves feminists (Young 1996, 91). As party leader, Mulroney found himself trying to mediate between competing factions in the party on these issues while trying not to alienate a perceived community of "women voters." When faced with one such controversy within his caucus, the prime minister was reported to have chastised MPs advocating socially conservative stances on the grounds that he "didn't spend all this time improving the status of women in government to have this kind of difficult press" (in Vienneau 1991, A2).

Abortion proved a particularly difficult issue for the Mulroney government. In the wake of a 1988 Supreme Court decision striking down the abortion law (which essentially delegated the question to committees of doctors who could grant or deny access to abortion), the government struggled to find a way to regulate access to abortion without alienating voters or caucus members aligned on either side of the debate. In 1989, with its caucus severely divided on the question, the government introduced legislation banning abortion, except when the physical, mental, or psychological health of the pregnant woman was at risk in the opinion of the doctor performing the procedure. This legislation was intended to satisfy both sides by recriminalizing abortion on the one hand but creating a gaping loophole to allow doctors to perform abortion at their discretion on the other (Brodie 1992, 98). As in other parliamentary systems, parties in the Canadian House of Commons usually exercise considerable party discipline on their members. On "moral" issues such as abortion and capital punishment, however, the practice has emerged of allowing members to vote their conscience. In the case of the abortion legislation, only the members of the federal Cabinet were expected to vote in favour. This legislation passed in a free vote in the House of Commons but was defeated by a coalition of pro-life and pro-choice senators in a tie vote. This defeat was, ironically enough, partly the result of the efforts of several of the Conservative women Mulroney had appointed to the Senate. After this defeat, the government made no further efforts to regulate abortion. It is noteworthy that the Tories' proposed legislation was not nearly as limiting as anti-abortion legislation advocated by the US Republicans. At no time did the Conservatives try to make abortion absolutely illegal or unconstitutional, nor did they try to prevent public funds from being used for abortions. In comparative perspective, then, the Conservative compromise appears moderate.

The same can be said of other PC initiatives on "moral issues" related to feminism. When the Supreme Court struck down portions of the law governing sexual assault, the minister of justice consulted extensively with women's organizations to introduce new "no means no" sexual assault legislation (see Bashevkin 1996, 230). In response to the murder of fourteen women at a Montreal university in 1988, the government initiated a task force to study violence against women and passed significant gun control legislation that was backed by many of the women in the PC caucus, but opposed by the party's rural and Western members, a strong constituency within the caucus (see Young 1996). The government also established a task force to report on the question of violence against women, and a Royal Commission dealing with new reproductive technologies. Both became mired in conflict and were perceived by many feminists to be mainly symbolic (Bashevkin 1996, 231). Even so, on these moral issues, the Conservative record is not consistent with that of an anti-feminist party.

The ideological divisions within the PC caucus mirrored those found within the extra-parliamentary party. Surveys of delegates at the party's 1983 and 1993 leadership conventions found evidence of some support for feminist policy stances, particularly among women. Moreover, there is evidence to suggest that feminist women constituted a distinctive ideological grouping within the party. Delegates to these conventions reported a considerable degree of support for feminism and women's equality in their responses to survey questions. At the 1993 convention, delegates were asked their opinion of the ideas of the women's movement, and over half indicated support or strong support. This is consistent, moreover, with their support for feminist stances on abortion and child care. While only 44 percent of delegates to the 1983 convention believed that there should be no restrictions on access to abortion, 71 percent of delegates at the 1993 convention considered abortion a private matter between a woman and her doctor. Similarly, while 34 percent of delegates to the 1983 convention advocated increasing government spending on day care, 41 percent of respondents in 1993 agreed that the federal government should establish a national child care program either immediately or when finances improve (calculated from Appendix, data sets: Progressive Conservative Delegate Survey 1983 and 1993). Clearly, some of the difference between the two conventions can be understood as an artefact of question wording, but it is remarkable that after almost a decade of a PC government failing to fulfil its promise to implement a national child care program, 41 percent of delegates were still advocating federal government involvement in the issue.

Comparing the attitudes of delegates to the 1983 PC convention with public attitudes on the same questions, it is clear that partisans are more conservative than the public. Table 5.3 shows that despite increased support for a pro-choice position on abortion among delegates in 1993, party activists were still less supportive than the public. While only 71 percent of respondents to the 1993 PC survey adopted a pro-choice stance, 84 percent of respondents to a 1987 Gallup survey advocated a pro-choice position. PC supporters were even more likely than other members of the public surveyed to espouse a pro-choice position, with 87 percent of PC-leaning respondents adopting the pro-choice position. On the question of day care, partisans were even more distant from the public and the PC-leaning public, although partisans did move in the direction of the public on the issue between the 1983 and 1993 conventions. While 41 percent of PC delegates in 1993 advocated creation of a national child care program now or when finances improve, 56 percent of the general public and 49 percent of PC-leaning respondents to a 1987 Gallup poll agreed that child care is a government responsibility.

There were notable differences between male and female delegates on these issues in both the 1983 and 1993 surveys. In both years, women expressed greater support for women's equality. Table 5.4 shows that there were gender gaps of eighteen points in 1983 and seventeen points in 1993 on the question of whether "more should be done to achieve women's equality." A more subtle pattern of gender differences emerged when delegates to the 1993 convention were asked whether they supported or

Table 5.3

Public and PC delegate opinion compared (%)

	Public				PC-leaning public				PC activists			
	All	Women	Men	Difference (W – M)	All	Women	Men	Difference (W – M)	All	Women	Men	Difference (W – M)
Abortion												
July 1975 (agree with)	84	83	85	-2	90	89	90	-1				
July 1983 (agree with)	83	81	85	-4	87	84	90	-6				
May 1988 (legal)	84	84	84	0	87	89	84	5				
1983 survey									44	56	40	16***
1993 survey									71	79	67	12**
Child care a government responsibility												
April 1982	46	48	43	5	42	46	37	9				
January 1985	52	54	50	4	47	50	44	6				
October 1987	56	59	52	7*	49	58	43	15*				
1983 survey									34	39	32	7
1993 survey									41	47	38	9*

*** χ^2 statistic significant at $p < .001$
** χ^2 statistic significant at $p < .01$
* χ^2 statistic significant at $p < .05$

Sources: Gallup poll data from the Canadian Institute of Public Opinion, Carleton University; PC data from Appendix, data sets: Progressive Conservative Delegate Survey 1983 and 1993.

opposed the ideas of the women's movement. Table 5.5 demonstrates that men were almost as likely as women to support the ideas of the women's movement, but that women were more likely than men to indicate strong support or opposition to the ideas of the movement. There were also gender differences in ideological self-placement in both years, with men more likely to place themselves to the right of centre in the party and women to place themselves at the centre or left of centre in the party. In 1993, the gender differences were larger (see Table 5.6).

The New Canadian Party System (1993-2000)

The Canadian political party system was shattered in the 1993 election. Two of the major political parties (the NDP and the Conservatives) lost official party status in the House of Commons and were replaced by the Bloc

Table 5.4

More/same amount/less should be done to achieve women's equality, 1983 and 1993 PC convention delegates compared by gender

	1983***			1993***		
	Male % (n = 709)	Female % (n = 221)	All % (n = 930)	Male % (n = 533)	Female % (n = 246)	All % (n = 779)
Less	17 (122)	11 (25)	16 (147)	32 (171)	21 (52)	29 (223)
Same	55 (389)	43 (94)	52 (483)	43 (228)	37 (90)	41 (318)
More	28 (198)	46 (102)	32 (300)	25 (134)	42 (104)	31 (238)

*** χ^2 statistic significant at $p < .001$
Sources: Appendix, data sets: Progressive Conservative Delegate Survey 1983 and 1993.

Table 5.5

PC delegates' attitudes towards the ideas of the women's movement, by gender, 1993***

	Men (n = 825) %	Women (n = 453) %
Strongly support	3	12
Support	50	46
Oppose	38	33
Strongly oppose	8	10

*** χ^2 statistic significant at $p < .001$
Sources: Appendix, data sets: Progressive Conservative Delegate Survey 1983 and 1993.

Québécois and the Reform party. The outcome of the 1997 election made it clear that the breakdown of the old party system was not merely an anomaly; rather, it signalled a period of transition to a new party system.

In this new party system, responsiveness to feminism declined. At first, there were positive signs: the prime minister's senior policy advisor, Chaviva Hošek, was a former president of NAC, and in 1993 Liberal women MPs banded together to form a women's caucus within the party. Despite this, the Liberal government did little in the way of responding to feminist policy issues. It proved incapable of fulfilling its promise to implement a national child care program, and it made many women's and children's lives more difficult when it restructured federal transfers to the provinces (resulting in cutbacks in social programs and education). The overarching dynamic of the Liberals' first mandate was deficit reduction to stave off a fiscal crisis perceived to be looming on the horizon, and to respond to the Reform party's successful calls for fiscal austerity. In this context, there was little potential for feminist activism except in defensive mobilizations.

A significant characteristic of the new party system is the entry of two new political parties and the demise of the NDP and the Conservatives. This change in the cast of characters has had profound consequences for the representation of women. Although the Bloc has proven to be an ally for feminists, its narrow basis in Quebec and its separatist ideology have prevented it from taking strong stands on national issues. In both its representational practices and its substantive policy stances, the Reform party has proven hostile to the representation of women. This hostility is of particular significance because Reform has replaced the NDP as the dynamic element of the emerging party system.

Table 5.6

Left-right self-placement in the PC party, by year and gender

| | 1983* | | 1993*** | |
	Men % (n = 715)	Women % (n = 217)	Men % (n = 531)	Women % (n = 238)
Left	11 (78)	8 (17)	14 (75)	26 (61)
Centre	29 (209)	38 (82)	36 (192)	39 (93)
Right	60 (428)	54 (118)	50 (264)	35 (84)

*** χ^2 statistic significant at $p < .001$
* χ^2 statistic significant at $p < .05$
Sources: Appendix, data sets: Progressive Conservative Delegate Survey 1983 and 1993.

In numerical terms, inclusion of women in the Reform party follows roughly the same pattern as that of the other political parties: the higher the fewer. Although no comprehensive statistics are available regarding the participation of women in the Reform party, a study based on the constituency association executive lists available on the Internet for fifty-eight constituency associations revealed that 24 percent of riding presidents listed were women, as were 12 percent of vice-presidents, 30 percent of treasurers, and 58 percent of secretaries.[13] More striking, and arguably more significant, is the pattern of women's representation among Reform candidates and MPs. As Figure 5.1 shows, the party had fewer candidates than any of its competitors in the 1993 election; in 1997, the number of women running under the Reform banner *declined,* as did the proportion of women in its caucus. With women making up just over 5 percent of the party's parliamentary caucus after the 1997 election, Reform has achieved the lowest rate of representation of women of any major Canadian political party at the federal level in fifteen years.

The Reform party has resolutely avoided taking a position of any kind on women's issues, arguing that there are no problems specific to women, but simply social or family issues. It is telling that this stance was recommended by a party task force led by Preston Manning's wife (Flanagan 1995). Because the party does not recognize women as a political group, questions of gender and, more specifically, gender equity disappear from political discussion. As Tracey Raney has demonstrated in her work on Reform, the party's conceptualization of citizenship and equality rely on equal treatment for undifferentiated citizens; public policy should not take into account difference of any sort. Reform's rejection of difference extends to the argument that social groups that claim to be different undermine the stability of the community (Raney 1998, 90). The party's ideological commitment to a highly formalized notion of equality means that it will not endorse policies (like child care, for example) intended to address systemic, rather than direct, discrimination.

As a result, the party's policy platform is on most issues antithetical to organized feminism. Reform opposes state-funded child care, affirmative action, abortion on demand, and public financing for feminist organizations; on at least one occasion, Preston Manning has mused out loud about eliminating maternity benefits provided under the national unemployment insurance system (Sigurdson 1994, 268). In 1999, the party's parliamentary caucus championed the cause of Beverly Smith, a homemaker who was taking her claim that Canadian tax law discriminated against single-income two-parent families to the United Nations. Although this policy is not necessarily antithetical to feminism, Reform's other statements advocating traditional family form suggest that Reform's motivation was to encourage traditional single-income families, rather than to increase the alternatives available to women with small children.

Although Manning and several senior party office-holders are evangelical Christians, their anti-feminist stances do not appear to stem simply from their Christian beliefs. The party's rhetoric of populism would render such efforts politically risky. In Manning's own words, "As a populist political party, the Reform party accepts a political agenda that comes from its consultations with Canadians. Since most Canadians do not have strong or explicit Christian commitment, that agenda will not be a specifically Christian agenda" (in Flanagan 1995, 8). Rather, the driving force behind Reform's antipathy to feminism appears to lie in its firm belief that feminists, like other "special interest groups" have come to wield a disproportionate influence in Canadian politics which in turn has contributed to the construction of an intrusive, inefficient, and expensive welfare state (Archer and Ellis 1994).

Although the Reform party has not adopted policies relating explicitly to women, its platform does include policies directed towards strengthening the family. The core of these policy proposals are changes to the Income Tax Act designed to facilitate, and perhaps even encourage, one parent to stay at home with children (Reform Party of Canada 1999). Although gender neutral on the surface, these policy stances do suggest an assumption of traditional family forms. The suspicion that Reform's intent is to reduce the role of the state in providing caring services and returning such services to the family (mainly women) is supported by Manning's public statements to the effect that "family is the most important primary caregiver in our judgement" (Manning, cited in Raney 1998, 127).

The Reform party appears to have ties of some sort to anti-feminist and pro-family groups. For instance, the web-page of the Canada Family Action (CFA) coalition, a Christian group opposed to abortion, extension of rights to homosexuals, and opposed to tax discrimination against single-income families) features a guest column by Reform MP Rob Anders entitled "How to Get Involved in Canadian Politics," which provides a step-by-step guide to capturing a constituency association (http://family-action.org/archive/getinvolved.html). Although there are no formal ties between the Reform party and the leading anti-feminist group REAL Women, the latter organization apparently has some proprietary sense towards the party. In the group's November/December 1998 newsletter, REAL women endorsed Reform's United Alternative initiative, arguing that "a realignment of our political parties is desperately needed to end our one-sided political system. There *must* be a strong, national alternative to the Liberal party, for the sake of democracy, if nothing else" (REAL Women 1998). Giving members registration information for the UA conference, REAL Women told its members "we *must* attend this convention so that there will be a large critical mass of social conservatives who will not be overruled by those who merely fiscal conservatives [sic] ... Please consider attending this Convention with as many friends, neighbours and relatives as you can muster together, in order to change the course of Canadian politics" (ibid.). Although political parties have little control over who endorses them, REAL Women's interest in Reform seems to speak to a relationship of some sort between the two organizations.

The character of the emerging Canadian political party system is still in transition. Of the most immediate significance in this regard is the Reform party's effort to transform itself into a new party with broader geographic appeal. If Reform fails in its attempt to create the United Alternative, then it seems reasonable to accept that the conclusions drawn above will continue to apply. If Manning's effort to create a new party is successful, future prospects are less clear. The policy resolutions adopted at the founding conference for the United Alternative do not appear to deviate significantly from Reform party policy on social issues. As in Reform party policy documents, women and gender equality are not mentioned, but recognition for "the family as the essential building block of a healthy society" is prominent in the resolution on social themes (Policy Declarations, http://www.unitedalt.org/committees/policydraft.html). There is no evidence that the new party will move away from the individualist conception of representation embedded in Reform party practice. Although Reform has released no information regarding the gender breakdown of the UA conference delegates, it is noteworthy that only two of the twenty steering committee members were women.[14] In short, as long as either the Reform party or the UA remain the dynamic element in the emerging party system, prospects for women's representation remain limited. Even if the constellation of parties changes, the individualist conception of representation and the underlying politics of the constrained state appear to bode ill for women's representation.

The emergence of Reform has the potential to reverse some of the gains made by women's organizations inside the parties over the past thirty years. It is particularly noteworthy that just as the Reform party emerged as a significant party of English Canada, the New Democratic party was decimated. The decline of the NDP put a stop to the dynamic towards greater representation of women that the party had created. In its place emerged the Reform party, with its refusal to recognize women as a political group or to encourage women's candidacies. It is not surprising, then, that the election of women has dropped from the political agenda since the 1993 election, and that the upwards rate of change has declined somewhat. This dynamic can be seen more clearly in women's candidacies than in women elected. Figure 5.1 (p. 147) shows that the proportion of female candidates declined between 1993 and 1997 for the New Democratic, Conservative, and Reform parties. The Liberal party continued to increase the number of women nominated, as did the Bloc Québécois.[15] When the Conservative party undertook a major internal reorganization in the aftermath of its devastating electoral defeat in 1993, it disbanded the national PC women's association and removed all requirements for gender balance at national meetings, on the national council or in the management committee (Keone 1999). This brought the PCs in line with the undifferentiated membership model espoused by Reform.

In substantive terms, issues of importance to women have all but disappeared from the policy agenda of government. As Janine Brodie (1998, 21) notes, in the 1993 election "the federal parties were virtually silent about so-called women's issues. Indeed the two major parties obviously felt gender was so irrelevant that they could refuse to debate women's issues as they had in the two previous federal campaigns without paying any electoral penalties." As already discussed, this can be attributed in part to the fiscal climate in which the party system is emerging. But it also has to do with the dynamics of party competition in the emerging system. With the Liberals and Conservatives both competing primarily against Reform in English Canada, women's issues have become peripheral to the contest for votes.

Conclusion

The Canadian political party system was slower to respond to the mobilization of feminism than its American counterpart, and its response has been far more moderate. In contrast to the American party system's dramatic polarized response, there have been differences only in degree and timing in Canadian parties' espousal of moderate liberal feminism. The question of how we can account for this difference and the broader question of what potential this suggests for feminists to transform the partisan political sphere forms the focus of Chapter 6.

6

Can Feminists Transform Party Politics?

Since 1970, feminist movements on either side of the 49th parallel have worked to fulfil liberal democracy's promise of political equality for all citizens by working within the organizations that hold the keys to the gates of government: political parties. As we have seen in previous chapters, US feminists have pursued this project with greater vigour than their counterparts to the north. In both countries, the success of feminists in opening up political parties and electoral politics to women's participation has been mixed.

In this chapter, we examine three questions. First, how can we account for the differences in the US and Canadian women's movements' involvement in the formal political arena? Second, what consequences have these differences had in terms of the responsiveness of political parties to feminism? Finally, we return to the question posed at the beginning of the book: can feminists transform party politics?

Movement Strategies
Throughout the period from 1970 to 1997, both the Canadian and the American women's movements engaged with the partisan political process, albeit to varying degrees. Neither entered into a permanent, exclusive relationship with a political party, but both fostered ties with them. Over time, voices contesting this partisan engagement grew stronger inside both movements, prompting some movement organizations to try to establish alternative routes for political engagement. This does not support the new social movement theorists' contention that women's movements, as "new" movements, are predisposed away from the formal political process. Rather, both women's movements share a contradictory relationship with political parties and electoral politics. In identifying the movements' aversion to the pragmatic deal-making and vote-chasing that characterize brokerage parties, the new social movement theorists are accurate. What they fail to capture,

however, is the equally powerful lure of partisan and electoral politics drawing movements into this sphere. These contradictory impulses are manifested by the coexistence within movements of multipartisan and apartisan
strategies.

Within the context of this contradictory relationship, the engagement
of the American and Canadian women's movements with electoral politics followed widely divergent trajectories. In the United States, the
women's movement became increasingly involved in electoral politics and
developed closer ties with the Democratic party, while the Canadian
women's movement became less involved in electoral politics over time.
The Canadian movement's multipartisan stance gradually evolved into a
largely apartisan orientation in the early 1990s; in recent years, ties to the
NDP have been partially restored.

In part, these divergent trajectories can be attributed to differences in
the ideological character of the two national movements. The US women's
movement is remarkable in comparative terms for its hegemonic liberal
feminism. Had radical or socialist feminist strains been stronger within the
American women's movement, its focus on electoral politics might well
have been muted, or at least contested more vociferously within movement circles. By the same token, the relative strength of socialist and radical feminism within the Canadian women's movement constrained the
extent of the movement's engagement with the formal political arena.
Had liberal feminism remained the dominant ideological tendency within
NAC, the Canadian women's movement might well have retained its
moderate focus on electoral and partisan politics.

These ideological differences do not entirely explain the diverging trajectories of the two movements, however. The liberal orientation of the
women's movement in the United States did not change over time – if
anything, radical feminism has become a more important ideological
strain in the 1990s – yet the movement's focus on electoral politics has
intensified since the 1970s. In Canada, the causal linkages between
changes in the ideological orientation of NAC and its electoral and partisan engagement are clearer. As socialist and radical feminism became the
dominant tendencies within NAC in the mid-1980s, the organization's
electoral orientation shifted. That said, the shifts within NAC were in part
related to changes outside the women's movement – the neo-liberal
Mulroney government galvanized leftist feminists within NAC.

In essence, the ideological characters of the two movements interacted
with elements of the opportunity structure to determine electoral and partisan strategies. Fixed elements of the political opportunity structure have
affected the direction of women's movement organizations' strategies, and
this has been reinforced by more variable political arrangements such as

party systems and characteristics of political parties.

Differences between the political institutions of Canada and the United States, as outlined in Chapter 1, had profound effects on the strategies employed by women's movement organizations in the two countries. Most notably, the US congressional system has invited, even required, the involvement of the women's movement in the formal political arena, while the Canadian parliamentary system has had the reverse effect. The US congressional system is characterized by the autonomy of individual legislators to pursue their policy interests or agendas with little constraint from party leaders or organizations. In the absence of strong party discipline, individual legislators' patterns of support or opposition to a movement's legislative agenda is open to scrutiny. The very weakness of US political parties in this regard, particularly when coupled with the transparency of the US political system, creates strong incentives for American feminist organizations to engage in the electoral arena in an effort to elect their members and allies to Congress, where they can exercise a clear and visible impact on policy. In contrast to this, the Canadian Parliament is characterized by a high degree of party discipline imposed on legislators, the limited influence and autonomy of legislators, and the shroud of secrecy surrounding the internal workings of parliamentary party caucuses. This set of institutional arrangements creates few incentives for movement organizations to focus on the electoral arena, as the election of their individual allies seldom appears to affect policy outcomes.

In essence, the two countries' legislative institutions create different incentives for their two women's movements. The autonomy and policy effectiveness of American legislators encourages feminist organizations to involve themselves in the project of electing individual women to Congress. To the extent that the Canadian system creates any incentives for movement organizations to engage in the formal political arena, it is not so much in the realm of electing individual women as in trying to influence the national parties. Given these institutional differences, one might expect to find Canadian feminists focusing their efforts on infiltrating political party organizations at the national level. In fact, this has not been the case in any sort of systematic way. It is the US women's movement that has engaged in a far more comprehensive way with party organizations or, more precisely, with the Democratic party at the national level.

This can be explained with reference to the organizational characteristics of political parties in the two countries. While US political parties are open, permeable organizations, Canadian political parties are relatively closed, cohesive entities. The kinds of incursions that American feminists (and, for that matter, anti-feminists) have made into American party politics would not be possible in the Canadian context. Canadian political parties react with considerable hostility when interest groups try to "capture" party organizations. This reaction is integrally related to the strength of political parties within the Canadian parliamentary system. Because of the strict norms of party discipline within the parliamentary arena, control of or influence within a Canadian political party is a source of considerable power. This stands in contrast to weak American political parties, which are easy to infiltrate, but which exercise little control over policy outcomes. Disciplined, programmatic political parties like those found in Canada would be ideal vehicles for a movement if they could be captured. The very cohesion that would make these political parties useful vehicles, however, makes the parties more defensive and thus effectively precludes this strategy. Ironically, it is the weakness, not the strength, of US political parties that invites intervention by the women's movement.

An additional institutional factor that affected the two movements' involvement in the electoral arena during the period of this study was the availability of litigation as a political strategy. For the American women's movement, the legal route appeared promising in the 1970s (as the Supreme Court at the time appeared open to feminist claims, most notably in its landmark ruling in *Roe* v. *Wade*). With Reagan's election to the presidency in 1980 launching a sustained effort to change the ideological composition of the Supreme Court, the legal route became an unlikely avenue for pursuing a feminist policy agenda. Just as the legal route was closing, or at least narrowing, for US feminists, it opened for Canadian feminists. The entrenchment of the Charter of Rights and Freedoms in the Canadian Constitution in 1982, complete with equality rights provisions Canadian feminists had fought to include, appeared to open a new route for feminist activism in the country. Considerable effort among liberal feminists was devoted to forming an organization to spearhead litigation under the Charter. Thus, resources that might otherwise have focused on the electoral arena were focused on the judicial route in the late 1980s and, to an extent, the 1990s. (Ultimately, the Charter has not proven nearly as beneficial to feminist causes as many had originally hoped, and most feminist efforts in recent years have been focused on a largely unsuccessful defensive effort to try to prevent the Court's broad interpretations of the rights of the accused from harming women's interests in cases of rape and violence).

The political party systems in the two countries have shaped the partisan orientations of the movements. In broad terms, both national women's movements have been drawn towards partisan engagement because of the possibility of influencing public policy and allowing women's entry into political elites. Despite this appeal, neither movement has found political parties to be ideal coalition partners. The periodic emergence of apartisan stances in both national movements illustrates the unwillingness of movement leaders to subordinate the interests of the movement to a political party's electoral agenda.

The US women's movement has tended towards a partisan relationship with the Democratic party, while the Canadian women's movement has remained multipartisan, with strong apartisan tendencies growing since the mid-1980s. The US two-party system, combined with the polarization of the two political parties around social issues, has contributed to the closer ties that the American women's movement has with the Democratic party. In contrast to this, the three-party system in place until 1993 offered Canadian feminists a broader partisan choice. Because significant numbers of feminist activists were allied with at least two of the three major Canadian political parties, women's movement organizations could not enter into a closer relationship with any one party without alienating a significant internal constituency (Rebick 1992). (This was compounded by the practice of providing public funding for women's movement organizations in Canada). Once the Canadian party system changed, introducing the anti-feminist Reform party and drawing the Liberals to the right, there was greater potential for alliance between the women's movement and the NDP. Moreover, by 1993, interpersonal ties between NAC and the Liberal party were much weaker, so internal considerations did not provide the same sort of constraint. As a consequence, the ties of the Canadian women's movement to the NDP have grown stronger in the late 1990s.

What, then, have been the effects of the divergent strategies employed by these two national women's movements? Ironically enough, the Canadian women's movement appears to have been more successful than its American counterpart in affecting the representation of women, at least in numerical terms. The proportion of women in the Canadian House of Commons has increased at a consistently faster rate than the proportion of women in the US Congress. Of course, this cannot be attributed simply to movement strategies, as different structural features of the two electoral and candidate selection systems have had an important effect on the rate of change in the numerical representation of women. A more important indicator of the women's movements' "success" lies in the reactions of political parties to feminism. To what extent have parties adopted feminist policy issues into their policy platforms? What role do women play in party affairs? To what extent do gender and feminism coincide within the party? It is to these questions that we now turn.

Partisan Responses

The established political parties in Canada and the United States varied considerably in their responses to organized feminism. At one end of the spectrum, the Canadian NDP was host to a significant feminist mobilization in the early 1970s that has affected party policy and practice to the present day. At the other end of the spectrum, the US Republican party has come to define itself in opposition to feminism. To make sense of the patterns of partisan responsiveness, it is necessary to consider two dimensions: variations among the political parties and variations between the two national party systems. Reviewing the patterns of responsiveness to the women's movement, we can conclude that political parties are not inherently inhospitable to feminism. Their responsiveness is determined by the fit between movement and party ideology and by the promise of electoral benefit. Moreover, the character of a party's response will be determined at least in part by the strategies adopted by feminist activists within the party, which are in turn shaped by the characteristics of parties and the sets of incentives embedded in party structures.

Variation among Political Parties

The established political parties in the United States and Canada varied in the extent, the timing, and the character of their reactions to mobilized feminism. These patterns suggest a great deal about the factors that affect partisan responsiveness to social movement mobilization.

The least responsive political parties in terms of both representation and policy were the US Republican party and, more recently, the Canadian Reform party. Since 1980, the GOP has defined itself in opposition to the policy stances of organized feminism, as has the Canadian Reform party since its formation in 1987. Both parties have ties to anti-feminist groups, although this is more clearly the case for the Republicans. In addition, the Republican party's anti-feminist policy stances are far more clearly espoused and overtly expressed than those of the Reform party.

Relative to the Republicans or Reform, the Canadian Progressive Conservatives responded more positively to feminism. Although initially slow to respond to the mobilization of organized feminism, the Conservatives did eventually try to appeal to women voters through moderate liberal feminist policy stances and by promoting the candidacies of women. Moreover, the party never adopted overtly anti-feminist stances on social issues. In this sense, the Conservatives can be understood to have been considerably more responsive to feminism than either the Reform party or the Republicans.

The Democratic party was highly responsive to the women's movement when it first emerged, resulting in a close alliance between movement organizations and the presidential wing of the party through the 1970s and early 1980s. The alliance culminated in the 1984 nomination of Geraldine Ferraro as the party's vice-presidential candidate. After a devastating loss in the 1984 election, the relationship between Democrats and feminist organizations became more distant. Although party elites continued to display attitudinal support for key women's movement positions, platform commitments on these issues were increasingly vague and couched in moderating language.

As with the Democrats, the Canadian Liberal party was initially fairly responsive to the mobilization of feminism, but grew less so over time. From 1970 until they were defeated in 1984, the relationship between movement organizations and the governing Liberal party was symbiotic in character, a term that implies mutual reliance, if not affection. The Liberals never endorsed the policy agenda of the women's movement in the wholehearted way that the Democrats did in the early 1970s. From 1985 until 1993, relations between women's movement organizations and the Liberal party became considerably more distant. As ties with movement organizations weakened, the feminist agenda within the party came to centre on the project of electing women, a preoccupation that complemented the party's single-minded effort to form the government in 1993. Once elected, the party pursued a fiscally conservative agenda that put it at odds with organized feminism. The formation of a women's caucus within the party's parliamentary caucus did little to raise the profile of women's issues during this period.

Of the five major North American parties, the New Democratic party was the most responsive to the organized women's movement. It endorsed the key elements of the movement's agenda early in the 1970s, and feminist women became a powerful and numerically substantial force within the NDP. Although the NDP remained a staunch proponent of feminist stances on policy issues, the numerical representation of women in the party's parliamentary caucus and in party leadership became an increasingly prominent focus of feminist activism within the party over time. Nonetheless, in terms of policy, the NDP remains the most responsive of the political parties included in this study.

Ideology

This pattern of responsiveness (represented graphically in Figure 6.1) suggests that ideological congruity between movement and party plays a significant role in determining party responsiveness. When political parties are ranked from least to most responsive, the resulting ordering coincides precisely with the parties' placement on an ideological spectrum from right to left. Moreover, looking at the patterns of congruence between changes in party ideology and responsiveness to the women's movement, the connection becomes even more clear. In the late 1960s and early 1970s, "new left" and liberal forces were gaining a foothold within the Democratic party, making it more hospitable to the emerging women's movement. Through the period from 1972 to 1993, the movement's fortunes within the party waned as the fortunes of moderates and conservatively inclined southern Democrats rose. That said, the presence of a radical liberal stream within the NDP made it a logical host for feminist activism.

Although the ideological fit between Canadian women's movement organizations and the LPC was not as close as that between the US movement and the Democrats, there were some points of connection between movement and party in the 1970s. The dominant ideology of NAC during this period was liberal feminism, which accepted "politics as usual" as an operational code, and which emphasized issues centring on economic equity for women.[1] The agenda of the Liberal party during this period centred on the pursuit of the "just society," an agenda that emphasized a moderate redistribution of wealth and state intervention to achieve a measure of social justice. The congruence of these two ideological agendas facilitated the movement-party relationship and sparked a measure of party responsiveness on feminist issues. Subsequently, the ideological fit between women's movement organizations and the Liberal party declined, the feminism of Liberal partisans and the feminism of movement activists became distinct entities with little commonality, and informal communication between the two diminished. The Chrétien government's pursuit of a fiscally conservative agenda during its first mandate from 1993 to 1997 put it at odds with the ideological stance of NAC.

There has always been a considerable degree of ideological congruence between Canadian feminism and the NDP. Canadian feminism has always encompassed a socialist strain absent in the US women's movement. The NDP was host to a feminist mobilization when women active in the party (and especially in the Waffle movement) applied the logic of socialist theory to the situation of women, and concluded that socialism and feminism were integrally linked. The congruence between the socialist strain present in the Canadian women's movement and the moderate democratic socialism of the NDP has facilitated relations between the women's movement and the party throughout the period covered by this study.

Type of Response
Recalling the two dimensions of partisan responsiveness – policy and representation – we again find variations among the political parties. The stark pattern that Gotell and Brodie (1991) posit whereby political parties are highly responsive in representational terms and unresponsive in policy terms does not hold, although there is some tendency in that direction. The most pronounced case of this is the US Republican party, which promoted women in political elites while simultaneously opposing the movement's policy agenda. In a less pronounced manner, both the US

Democrats and the Canadian Liberals also drifted away from policy responsiveness towards representational responsiveness in the 1980s and 1990s. In both cases, however, this can be attributed at least in part to the efforts of feminist activists inside the party to foster representational responsiveness, usually based on the assumption that policy responsiveness would ensue. The least degree of disjuncture between representational and policy responsiveness is found in the Canadian NDP. Even in this case, feminist activists within the party in the late 1980s focused on electing a woman to the leadership of the party because they thought this would reshape party policy and practice, a strategy that met with little success. What this pattern suggests is not so much a vindication of Gotell and Brodie's assertion as the conclusion that activists' strategies affect partisan responsiveness and that the relationship between representational and policy change is more complex than Gotell and Brodie's analysis asserts.

Figure 6.1

Party responses to feminism

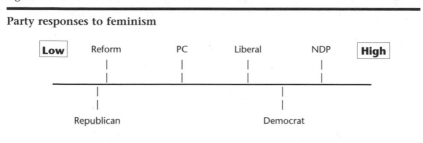

Timing
The responsiveness of political parties to feminism has also varied over time. Both US parties and the Canadian NDP and Liberals responded positively to the women's movement when it first mobilized. All of these political parties (with the possible exception of the NDP) were motivated at least in part by desire for electoral benefit. After the initial flurry of interest, the parties' responsiveness waned somewhat. The Canadian Conservatives were relative latecomers, coming to terms with the feminist policy agenda only in the early 1980s. Once again, electoral concerns were the motivating factor – the party was trying to appeal to women voters and shed its "backward" image.

Over time, all the political parties have become less responsive to the organized women's movement. This may not appear to be the case at first glance, as the number of women in political elites is increasing, and none of the political parties except the GOP has abandoned its commitments to the feminist position on key issues. What has waned, however, is momentum. Political parties are generally not responding to newer issues raised by women's movement organizations, and even the growing number of women in party elites is largely a continuation of trends established in the 1980s.

Within the pattern of declining momentum, it is also possible to identify certain "moments" when political parties were more responsive. The closest alliance between the Democratic party and American women's movement organizations came in 1972 and 1984, when it appeared that the women's movement might be able to contribute to electoral success for the party's presidential nominee. In both years, the Democratic party lost the presidency by a wide margin, and consequently turned away from women's movement organizations. Similarly, the closest relationship between the Canadian women's movement and the Liberal party came in the early 1970s when the movement appeared to hold electoral potential for the party, and in the early 1980s after movement organizations had mounted a powerful lobbying campaign to ensure that gender equality would be fully protected in the new Charter of Rights and Freedoms. These observations lend support to the party competition model of partisan behaviour, as political parties were most open to engaging with women's movement organizations when they saw the potential for electoral benefit.

National Variations
There is also considerable cross-national variation in the pattern of party responses. The most notable variation in this regard is not in the degree of responsiveness, but in the pattern of activism within the parties. In the American case, feminist activism is not organic to the political parties. To the extent that it is present, it is brought into the party by autonomous organizations that enter into affiliations with the party. Canadian political parties do not tolerate the same direct involvement of non-partisan organizations in internal party affairs. This was illustrated by the NDP's resistance to the Waffle and, more recently, by the Liberal party's efforts to shield itself from incursions by pro-life groups. Thus, this pattern of response suggests that party characteristics partially determine the character of internal feminist activism.

Applying the logic of "nested games" to the activism of women within the Democratic, Liberal, and New Democratic parties (where they have been most active), we can make sense of these patterns of variation. Tsebelis's idea of nested games – games involving conflict between different actors occurring within other games – is useful in this regard, in particular because it challenges the conception of political parties as coherent and homogeneous strategic players. Applying the concept to the study of political parties, Tsebelis argues that British Labour activists who appear to be following a wholly irrational (in Downsian terms) strategy of replacing their MPs, thereby contributing to the party's defeat, are in fact behaving rationally because in the long run these actions enable the activists to create a reputation for toughness which mean their views are taken more seriously. When feminist activism within the political parties is examined in this light, substantial cross-national differences emerge: women have been far more willing to challenge the Democratic party from within, becoming involved in factional disputes and sometimes putting the interests of feminism ahead of the party's electoral fortunes. In contrast to this, women in the Canadian Liberal and New Democratic parties have tended to submerge their differences within the party in order to present a uniform public face. What this cross-national variation suggests is that activists are responding to very different imperatives: feminists in the Democratic party win respect for being conflictual, while feminists in the Canadian parties are best able to achieve their objectives by behaving loyally. Again, this suggests that activists' actions within a political party are shaped by organizational context.

The Movement-Party Relationship

Having concluded that the strategies of the organized women's movement are shaped by political opportunity structures, and that the responses of political parties to overtures from the movement are shaped by ideology, competitive calculations, and the strategies adopted by feminist activists, what can be concluded about the final product: the movement-party relationship?

First, the movement-party relationship is at least in part an exchange relationship. In this view, leaders of movement organizations engage with political parties in order to advance the movement's policy agenda and include its adherents in political elites. Party leaders engage with movement organizations in the hope of enhancing the party's electoral success. For a movement-party alliance to develop, both the movement organizations and the party organizations must have resources to exchange. A political party that is electorally unsuccessful has little to offer movement leaders. By the same token, movement leaders who have little to bring to the table are unlikely to find allies among the leadership of political parties. For movement and party leaders alike, entry into an alliance entails costs; such an alliance may close off other avenues of political cooperation, and the leaders will spend some of their political capital defending the alliance to movement adherents or partisan activists who oppose it. Thus, the potential benefits of such an alliance must outweigh the costs.

The resources available to movement organizations in exchange relationships with political parties are electoral benefit, legitimacy, and tangible campaign resources (volunteers and financial contributions). When compared with unions, new social movement organizations are seldom able to muster these resources in sufficient quantities over an extended period. Melucci (1980) has gone so far as to argue that new social movements cannot bargain with political parties because they lack the highly structured cohesive organization that can reliably deliver electoral resources. Lending credence to this argument, a study of the influence of the AFL-CIO, the National Education Association, and NOW endorsements on candidate support and prenomination activity in caucuses in Michigan, Virginia, and Iowa in the 1984 Democratic presidential primary found that NOW's endorsement had no significant effect on members of women's groups (Rapoport et al. 1991). The authors of this study speculate that NOW's endorsement was less influential than the AFL-CIO's or the NEA's because NOW has less history of involvement in partisan politics, no base in the workplace, and a less hierarchical top-down structure than the other groups. There is certainly an element of truth in these assessments: neither Canada nor the United States has a women's movement organization with the same clout within a political party over an extended period as have trade unions.[2] That said, women's movement organizations in both countries have periodically mustered sufficient resources to make the parties take notice. Moreover, by tapping into the expanding financial resources available to professional women in the United States, American women's movement organizations (most notably the PAC EMILY's List) have won a place within the congressional wing of the Democratic party.

In exchange relationships with movement organizations, political parties can offer the following resources: inclusion of movement adherents in political elites and inclusion of elements of the movement's policy agenda in the party platform and in government policy, if the party is elected. It is the inclusion of the movement's issues in public policy that offers the greatest incentive for movement leaders to engage with political parties. The process of lobbying government for changes in laws, regulations, and policies is slow and arduous, and in many cases fruitless. A government that has made commitments on issues of importance to the movement before it is elected, and that is accessible to movement representatives is a far less formidable target for lobbying efforts. Thus, political parties can hold out the promise of considerable benefit to movement organizations if they engage with them.

Clearly, a political party's attractiveness is determined to a considerable extent by its electoral success. All the political parties included in this study are "major" political parties, in that they have experienced fairly consistent electoral success over the period being covered. That said, their electoral fortunes have varied. The US Democrats held a majority of seats in the Senate and the House of Representatives for most of the period 1963 to 1993, but elected only two presidents (Carter in 1976 and Clinton in 1992). Conversely, the Republicans held the presidency but not Congress. The Liberal Party of Canada formed the federal government from 1970 to 1984, with one nine-month interruption, and won power again in 1993, while the NDP was the perpetual third party throughout this period. The inability of the NDP to form a government certainly limited its appeal to more pragmatic or instrumental activists who sought access to power through their electoral engagement.

Second, the ideological predisposition of both movement organizations and political parties provides boundaries or constraints to the movement-party relationship. Even if such a relationship had appeared mutually beneficial to party and movement leaders, the US women's movement and the Republican party could not have entered into a close relationship because of ideologically grounded objections from movement adherents and partisans. Expressed in other terms, the costs of alliance are higher when there is no congruity of ideological approach. Thus, the ideology of both movement and political party organizations constitutes a boundary to the possibility of movement-party engagement.

Third, institutions matter. The institutional context provides both movement and party leaders with resources and structures the sets of incentives and disincentives to which movement and party leaders respond. The US congressional system creates great incentives for American women's movement leaders to engage in electoral politics. The strength of political parties in the Canadian system makes them an appealing ally for Canadian women's movement organizations, but their cohesion makes the cost of engagement high.

Finally, affinity between movement and party leaders can play a role in establishing or cementing a movement-party alliance. In part, this affinity reflects the ideological "goodness of fit" between movement and party organizations, but there is more to it than simple ideological affinity. Rather, activists and leaders in either movements or political parties can have dual loyalties, and can understand their movement and partisan activism to be complementary. Thus, they are loyal to both and are willing to overlook lost elections and occasional failed promises. While intangible, this affinity can cement alliances that do not yield the anticipated benefits.

Party Systems
In addition to variations among political parties, the two national party systems differed substantially in their responses to feminism. In short, the US party system polarized in response to the women's movement, while the Canadian party system did not. This pattern is, from several perspectives, counterintuitive. From the point of view of political culture, one would expect that Canada, with its "Tory touch," would provide an hospitable environment for social conservatism, while the United States, with its homogeneous liberal culture, would not support social conservatism. In fact, the reverse is true. Moreover, employing Sartori's (1976) theoretical

approach to the study of political party systems, one would expect the American two-party system to be highly centripetal (tending towards the centre) while the Canadian three-party system would be somewhat more divergent. This rests on Sartori's argument that two-party systems tend to be characterized by centripetal patterns of ideological placement of political parties and multiparty systems by centrifugal patterns. Once again, this does not prove to be the case. How, then, can we explain this difference?

Women's Movement Strategy

One plausible explanation for this divergence would look to the alliance strategies of feminist organizations in the two countries. Did the two women's movements adopt different strategic orientations towards political parties, and, if they did, can these differences account for the divergent responses of the two countries' political parties to feminism? As discussed in detail above, American and Canadian women's movements differed both in the intensity of their focus on partisan politics and in their partisan orientations.

At first glance, differences in the two movements' partisan orientation appear to offer an explanation for the cross-national difference. As organized feminism in the United States was clearly allied with the Democrats; the Republicans could dismiss feminism and seek electoral benefit from alliance with anti-feminism. While there may be some truth in this, it must be noted that US feminist organizations became most closely allied with the Democrats *after* the Republicans renounced their support for the Equal Rights Amendment and became staunchly pro-life in 1980. Thus, the partisan orientation of the women's movement may have subsequently entrenched the anti-feminism of the Republicans, but it does not account for the initial adoption of the stance. Moreover, the Canadian women's movement became just as outspoken an opponent of the PCs in the mid-1980s as American feminists were of the Reagan Republicans, yet the Conservatives were not provoked into adopting an explicitly anti-feminist stance. That said, it should be noted that Canadian feminists never developed as close an alliance with one of the political parties as the American movement did with the Democrats, so Canadian women's movement organizations were not providing the same kind of partisan cues to their attentive public. As a consequence, Canadian feminists could not be as easily written off as an electoral constituency by the Conservatives as activist women were by the Republicans. Thus, the strategies of the women's movements provide only a partial explanation for the divergence.

Party Competition

Another approach would be to look at opinion structures in the two countries. Employing a rational choice or party competition model, we would expect that a polarized public would produce a polarized party system. Rational choice and neo-institutionalist approaches to the study of political parties emphasize their competitive aspect, characterizing political parties as vote maximizers that privilege the goal of winning elections above all else. The founder of this approach to the study of political parties, Anthony Downs (1957, 28), argues that "parties formulate policies in order to win elections rather than win elections in order to formulate policies." Parties' policy stances, in this view, are best understood as a means to electoral success rather than statements of deep-rooted belief. Elaborations of this theory have suggested that when the electorate's opinion tends towards the centre, political parties will converge in their policy stances, trying to appeal to the median voter. When opinion is divided, however, political parties will polarize in their policy stances, each one catering to a distinct opinion grouping (Ware 1996, 321-6). If a Downsian approach were to hold in this case, then, we would expect to find that the American public has polarized around feminist issues, while the Canadian public tends towards the centre. (In other words, we expect to find a bimodal distribution in the United States, and a unimodal distribution in Canada).

An examination of the relevant distribution of opinion in the Canadian and American electorates does not, however, lend credence to this approach. Although attitudes towards feminism and abortion are different in the two countries, the bulk of voters espouse moderate positions. Canadians and Americans do not differ substantially in their support for feminism. Surveys taken in both countries in 1992 asking respondents if they considered themselves feminists found that 29 percent of US and 32 percent of Canadian respondents (of both sexes) answered in the affirmative (Perlin 1997, 137). Similarly, 78 percent of US respondents in 1980 and 77 percent of Canadian respondents in 1982 agreed that there are not enough women in responsible positions in government and business (ibid., 136). Surveys trying to measure the extent of traditional attitudes towards women have produced inconsistent results in comparative terms. A 1988 American study found that 41 percent agreed that "it is much better for everyone involved if man achieves outside the home and a woman takes care of home and family." In Canada, surveys taken in 1983 and 1989 found that 48 percent and 47 percent of respondents, respectively, agreed that "women are going to have to go back to the traditional role of wife and mother," while a study in 1990 found that only 25 percent agreed that everyone would be better off if women were satisfied to stay at home and raise children (ibid., 135). In short, while there appear to be some differences in general attitudes towards women's equality in the two countries, they are not stark.

There are subtle cross-national differences on the divisive abortion issue, but they do not lend credence to the party competition model. As Table 6.1 shows, Canadians have since the early 1970s been somewhat more likely to support a pro-choice stance and Americans somewhat more likely to support a pro-life stance on abortion. The majority of respondents in both countries, however, have taken a middle of the road position advocating some restrictions on access to abortion.[3] This is not the polarized distribution of opinion that would lend support to the party competition model.

Political parties make targeted appeals on issues that will influence distinct groups of voters. The existence of a highly mobilized, articulate anti-feminist pro-life movement in the United States creates a constituency for the Republican party that does not exist to the same extent in Canada. The extended battle over ERA ratification contributed to the mobilization and organization of this powerful anti-feminist movement, rooted in part in socially conservative religious groups. In contrast to this, anti-feminism is not nearly as influential or organized a force in Canada (Erwin 1993). Moreover, the religiosity that drives at least some portion of American social conservatism is less prevalent in Canada than in the United States. According to Nevitte et al. (1993, 26) Canadians are less religious, on the whole, than Americans. The 1981 World Value Survey found that 62 percent of Americans scored "high" (nine or ten on a ten-point scale), compared with 45 percent of Canadians. Similarly, in 1990, 58 percent of Americans and 38 percent of Canadians qualified as "very religious." Finally, US pro-life and Christian right groups have been far more engaged in partisan politics than their Canadian counterparts. The pro-life forces seeking to influence partisan politics in Canada have focused their attentions either on the Liberal party or on the project of forming their own (electorally unsuccessful) political party, Christian Heritage, in the 1980s. The reluctance of conservative Christian groups to engage with established political parties in Canada can probably be attributed to impermeable character of Canadian political parties. In this sense, it mirrors the Canadian women's movement's more distant ties with established parties (see Young 1996).[4] The significance of this for understanding Republican party behaviour is twofold. First, Christian conservatives constitute a sizeable and mobilizable electoral constituency. Second, as noted above, Christian conservatives and anti-feminists represent an extremely powerful group within the Republican party, so party leaders must weigh their policy agenda against electoral concerns.

Electoral Calculation
Finally, it is possible that the divergence in the responses in the two party systems to feminism can be attributed to the various parties' electoral calculations. In particular, the existence of an electoral "gender gap" in the United States and the relative absence of one in Canada might account for

the differences in the responses to feminism of the right-of-centre parties.

In the United States, women's partisan preferences have gradually shifted, so that since 1970 more women identified with the Democrats than the Republicans (McGlen and O'Connor 1995). This trend became more pronounced over time, peaking in 1984 (see Figure 6.2). In Canada, women were more supportive than men of the governing Liberals through the 1970s and early 1980s. As Figure 6.3 shows, this gap narrowed considerably in 1984, when women joined with men in voting for the PCs and ousting the Liberals. The gap grew again in 1988, an election that revolved around the question of continental free trade – an issue on which there were substantial gender differences (see Bashevkin 1989). The gap all but disappeared in 1993 as male PC supporters shifted their support to the Reform party in greater numbers than women.

It must be noted that these gender gaps in partisan identification and voting behaviour are not simple phenomena. Even though gaps are perceived as resulting from women's difference from men (or deviation from a male norm), women do not necessarily produce these gaps. In fact, the most celebrated gender gaps – in US presidential elections in 1980, 1984, and 1988 – were produced not by women moving towards the Democratic party but by men shifting towards the Republicans at higher rates than women (Bendyna and Lake 1994, 239). Moreover, gender gaps are rooted not so much in the issues usually identified as "women's issues" like abortion or child care as they are in other policy areas. In both countries,

Table 6.1

Attitudes towards abortion: Canadians and Americans compared

	Legal/ all circumstances (%)	Legal/ certain circumstances (%)	Never legal (%)
United States			
1975	21	54	22
1980	25	53	18
1988	24	57	17
1992	33	51	14
Canada			
1975	23	60	16
1983	23	59	17
1988	24	60	14
1992	31	57	10

Note: The 1992 US figure is based on two surveys averaged, and the 1988 Canadian figure is based on three surveys averaged.
Source: Nevitte et al. (1993, 21).

attitudinal gender gaps have tended to appear on issues relating to social welfare and use of force rather than explicitly gendered issues such as abortion or equal rights for women (Everitt 1996; Bendyna and Lake 1994). Thus, gendered differences in voting behaviour have been aptly characterized as the difference between "economic man" and "social woman" (Gidengil 1995). Finally, women do not constitute a monolithic group, so gender gaps are not produced so much by all women versus all men as they are by certain groups of women. In both countries, gender gaps are produced by the distinctive ideological location and partisan preferences of a relatively small group of women who tend to be well-educated professionals and who are more likely to remain unmarried or delay marriage (Miller 1988; Wearing and Wearing 1991).[5]

As Figures 6.2 and 6.3 show, both right-of-centre parties were confronted with substantial electoral gender gaps throughout the 1980s and, in the case of the PCs, through most of the 1970s as well. Yet their responses to greater unpopularity among women were not the same. In the 1984 and 1988 presidential elections, Republican presidential candidates were able to narrow the gender gap without eschewing their party's opposition to abortion and the ERA. This strategy assumed that "activist-type" women who

Figure 6.2

Gender gaps in US presidential elections, 1968-92

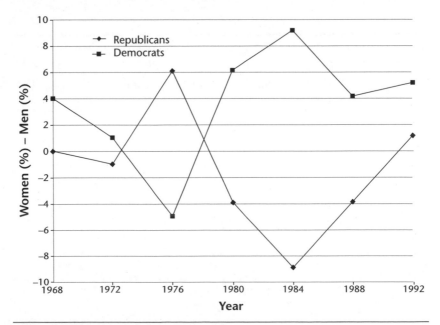

Source: Calculated from Stanley and Niemi (1994).

held strong opinions on these issues were likely to be staunch Democrats, and that the gender gap could be diminished sufficiently by recognizing women's increased participation in the workforce. As noted above, Reagan campaign strategists profiled professional women, using them to deliver the message that Reagan's policies allowed women to get ahead in the marketplace (Kirschten 1984). Similarly, Bush's chief policy advisor on gender gap issues urged Bush and other GOP candidates to stress that their policies, by creating a booming private sector, generated opportunities for women to advance their families' well-being (Blustein 1988). This strategy was apparently successful, as Bush was able to reduce a gender gap as large as twenty-five points prior to the election to a mere four points on election day. Crucial to note here is that, until 1992, the Republicans held a monopoly on the presidency that the gender gap was insufficient to end. It is also noteworthy that throughout the 1980s, some 32 percent of women were registered as Independents, in contrast with an average of 40 percent of men (Bendyna and Lake 1994, 242). Thus, women were less likely to count themselves among the swing voters who decide elections.

In the Canadian case, gender differences do not play out as simply, in part because of the three-party system, and in part because of the flexible partisanship and shifting electoral coalitions that characterize Canadian politics. Some commentators (notably Gotell and Brodie 1991) suggest that this means Canadian political parties will never be fully responsive to

Figure 6.3

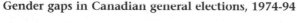

Gender gaps in Canadian general elections, 1974-94

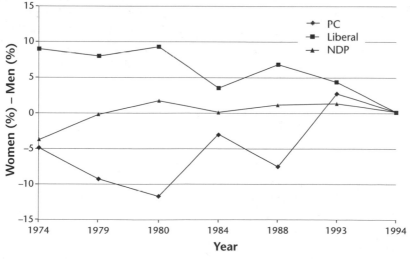

Sources: Calculated from Wearing and Wearing (1991) and the 1993 Canadian Election Survey, Institute for Social Research, York University.

feminism. Arguably, however, ambiguities surrounding the electoral choices of Canadian women have created enough uncertainty about the "women's vote" that parties have tried not to offend women or to allow feminist issues to become so polarized that they would influence women's voting behaviour (Black 1985). This may be changing, however, as there is every reason to believe that the Reform party is writing off groups of women voters in precisely the same way that the Republican party has.

More significant, perhaps, is the fact that the Canadian women's movement has not made a concerted effort to use the gender gap as a political resource. The reasons for this are complex, but stem at least in part from the direction of gender differences in voting. It is the moderate Liberal party that has benefited from the gender gap, not the left-of-centre NDP that has been the Canadian party most responsive to the women's movement. Because of their ambivalent relationship with the Liberal party (and with party politics more generally) Canadian feminist leaders have not constructed a political meaning for gender differences in the Canadian electorate in the same way that US feminist leaders did in the mid-1980s. This, along with the different pattern of gender differences in voting in the Canadian electorate and the different logic of competition in the two party systems, has made the Conservatives and Republicans respond differently to gender gaps. As a consequence, the US party system polarized, while its Canadian counterpart did not.

Summary
To explain the two party systems' divergence in response to feminism, it is necessary to draw on several of the partial explanations outlined above. The Republican party's oppositional reaction to feminism is rooted in the organizational and numerical strength of anti-feminist and Christian right groups in the United States and their ability to win a place as an extremely influential constituency within the party. The substantial gender gap in voting behaviour and the close alliance between organized feminism and the Democratic party prompted the GOP to make cosmetic attempts to appeal to women (by promoting women in the party) and to appeal to women on a narrow range of economic issues. It did not, however, cause the party to reconsider its explicitly anti-feminist platform planks until the party lost the presidency in 1992. By then, the Christian right was so firmly entrenched within the Republican party that efforts to modify the anti-feminist stance inevitably failed. In contrast to this, the absence of a thriving organized anti-feminist movement in Canada combined with the more ambiguous partisan cues of the Canadian women's movement to make the Progressive Conservatives far less hostile to feminism than their American counterparts. The presence of a perceived group of "women vot-

ers" who could not be written off by a party operating in a system where electoral coalitions are unstable and cleavages constantly shifting meant that the Conservatives continued to try to appeal to the female – and even feminist – electorate by adopting moderate feminist stances on a variety of issues. As a consequence, the Canadian system converged on the centre, while the American system polarized.

Can Feminists Transform Party Politics?

Clearly, the reactions of political parties to feminism are shaped by a number of factors – ideology, anticipated electoral benefit, internal party politics, and the strategies pursued by movement organizations. This analysis returns us to the central concern of this study: can feminists transform party politics? The debate among feminists surrounding this question centres on the question of whether political parties are merely male-dominated, and thus transformable by women (the liberal feminist view) or inherently patriarchal (the radical feminist view). The research presented in this book lends some support to both sides in the debate among feminists. Bolstering the liberal feminist argument is evidence that movement organizations' engagement with political parties in both countries yielded gains in terms of numerical representation of women and expansion of the political agenda to include "private" issues such as reproduction and child care. Even though the progress on these issues was not as rapid or as far-reaching as feminists might wish, over the past three decades we have witnessed considerable change in the composition of partisan elites, understandings of the "appropriate" political role for women, and the range of issues considered to be political. Women's participation in party affairs has in large measure been normalized. Given the centrality of political parties in structuring political life in advanced industrialized democracies, this is an essential element of democratic citizenship. As such, the significance of the battles women have fought to secure their place in party politics should not be understated.

Notwithstanding this progress, some evidence presented in this book supports the claim that an inverse relation exists between the numerical representation of women in partisan elites and substantive responsiveness to the movement's policy agenda. The number of women in partisan and legislative elites has increased steadily over the period studied, but policy responsiveness has not kept pace. Feminist activists within the political parties have come to focus their attention on the numerical representation of women as an end in itself. Thus, a political action committee – EMILY's List – that exists to give money to women candidates has become the most dynamic player among US feminist organizations, the women's organization inside the Liberal party has chosen the election of Liberal women as its foremost goal, and feminist women in the NDP became complacent once they had elected a woman as party leader. In short, none of the major North American political parties has been entirely transformed through engagement with the contemporary women's movement.

Before discussing the reasons for this, we must first consider the question of what characterizes a "transformed" political party. First, there would be gender parity in the elite cadres of a fully feminized political party, either through representational guarantees or because all of the informal barriers to women's equal participation in partisan elites had been eliminated. In time, half of the parliamentary or legislative caucus would be women. The qualifier "in time" is added here in recognition that incumbency acts as a barrier to a rapid change in the composition of a legislative caucus.[6] In the interim, a truly feminized party would be marked by meeting or exceeding gender parity among non-incumbent legislators after each election. The leader of this political party might be of either sex, but the position of leader would not be out of reach to a woman, and a female leader's failures in the position would not be immediately attributed to her sex.

A political party transformed by feminism would include feminist stances on policy issues in its electoral platform, where they would figure prominently, not merely as an afterthought or addendum. As the party developed new policies on a range of issues, their gendered dimensions would be considered and incorporated into the policy. If elected, the party would move to enact these policies with the same speed and diligence that it acted to implement its other platform commitments.

None of the political parties discussed in this book meets all these criteria. Each has approached gender parity on some party body, but none has achieved it in all party organizations. More significantly, no political party has achieved gender parity in its legislative caucus (with the exception of the two-member PC caucus after the 1993 election). Although some policy gains have been won, feminist issues have seldom figured prominently in any of the parties' policy platforms. The possible exception to this is the Canadian NDP, which has consistently included feminist issues in its platforms, although its willingness to implement those policies once elected has never been put to the test at the federal level.

If political parties are not inherently opposed to feminism, why has the influx of feminist women into the partisan political arena in the past thirty years not had a more thoroughly transformative effect on party politics? To answer this question, we must recall the argument presented above: the movement-party relationship is, above all else, an exchange relationship. When women's movement organizations have appeared to be able to offer political parties what they most desire – electoral success – parties have welcomed these organizations into the partisan fold and have adopted the movement's issues as their own. In the words of one Canadian party activist, "It's the strength of the voice of the women's movement that has helped to wake the parties ... If something's marketable they'll grab it, and if it happens to have breasts, fine" (interview 10/02/94). The moments when engaging with the women's movement appeared to promise electoral success have, however, been few and far between because the political resources available to movement organizations are limited. As a consequence, there are profound constraints in the extent to which feminists can hope to transform party politics, and the limited resources available to them provide the boundaries of this constraint.

Votes are, of course, the currency of party politics. Given this, one might expect that the politicization of a group that forms just over half of the electorate would capture the attention of vote-seeking parties. To understand why this has not been the case, we must recall the limitations in the magnitude of the gender gap and the extent to which it is rooted in adherence to feminism. In short, gender gaps in voting intentions have only rarely been of sufficient magnitude to affect party behaviour.

The other resource that feminist organizations have employed in their dealings with political parties is money. In the United States, the success of EMILY's List has bought a place for women at certain Democratic party tables (usually found in back rooms). At first glance, this does not appear to be a rousing victory for the feminist cause – one might well argue that women have excelled at playing the morally ambiguous Washington money game. Yet we should not dismiss this achievement too quickly. American women are citizens of a country whose highest court has declared that in the realm of electoral politics, "money is speech."[7] It follows, then, that those who lack money have little political voice. There is no question that the regulation of campaign finance in the United States is perverse and favours monied interests, but if women's groups are able to solicit enough contributions from the emerging class of well-heeled professional and managerial women to buy their way into the corridors of power, why should they be held to a higher standard of conduct than their male counterparts? Moreover, if we consider it a laudable goal that women's rates of political participation match those of men, there is no reason why the contribution of cash to candidates should be placed in a separate category from voting, working on a campaign, or running for office.

Unlike their American counterparts, Canadian feminists have not entered into the political money game in an effort to influence political parties. All three of the major federal parties have established funds for women candidates, but these operate on a much smaller scale than their American counterparts and have considerably less impact on the number of women running because they contribute to women candidates only after they have won their party's nomination. Moreover, because these organizations exist inside the political parties, and tend to raise funds through dinners held at party conventions, they do not draw a broader range of women into the political process.

There are several barriers to the emergence of an organization analogous to EMILY's List in Canada. First, because Canadian electoral law provides for spending limits for both political parties and individual candidates during elections and for the reimbursement of a substantial proportion of parties' and candidates' expenses, money is not as essential to Canadian politics as it is to US politics. Thus, it does not constitute the same kind of barrier to women candidates and solutions centred on funding are less likely to be chosen by Canadian activists. Second, the provision of an extremely generous political tax credit makes it far more attractive to contribute directly to a candidate or a registered political party able to provide a receipt for income tax purposes rather than a contribution to an organization unable to provide such a receipt.[8]

Feminist Futures and Party Politics

There is little reason to believe that the future of party politics in either Canada or the United States will be wholly feminist. That said, the breakdown of barriers to women's participation in electoral politics means that women have become an integral part of the partisan political sphere, both in national legislatures and party back rooms. Not all of these women are feminists; in fact, some have launched political careers by becoming high-profile opponents of feminism. Nonetheless, many of these women who have entered the partisan political arena have feminist sympathies. These women constitute a resource for feminist activists in lobbying for policy change or fighting to prevent erosion of the gains that have been made.

The progress that feminists have made in opening the formal political arena to women's participation may appear disappointing from some perspectives. Certainly, the transformation envisioned by activists at the beginning of the current cycle of mobilization has not been realized. Moreover, few would have foreseen the subversion of the feminist electoral project by anti-feminists. Even taking this into account, feminist efforts to transform party politics in the United States and Canada must be judged a success: to a considerable degree, feminists have caused the realization of liberal democracy's promise. Even if the presence of anti-feminist women in public office is anathema to the feminist political agenda, it is a victory for women's efforts to transform liberal democracy to recognize women's full citizenship.

Appendix: Data Sets and Scales

Data Sets

Convention Delegate Study 1972
Warren E. Miller, Elizabeth Douvan, William Crotty, and Jeane Kirkpatrick, *Convention Delegate Study of 1972: Women in Politics* (ICPSR 07287).
Universe: All delegates to the 1972 Republican and Democratic national nominating conventions.
Method: Mail.
Cases: 2,587.

Convention Delegate Study 1980
Warren E. Miller, M. Kent Jennings, and Barbara G. Fara, *Convention Delegate Study, 1980* (ICPSR 08367).
Universe: Respondents to the 1972 delegate study and all delegates to the 1976 and 1980 Republican and Democratic national conventions.
Method: Mail.
Cases: 5,406.

Convention Delegate Study 1984
Warren E. Miller and M. Kent Jennings, *Convention Delegate Study, 1984* (ICPSR 08967).
Universe: Delegates to the 1984 Republican and Democratic national conventions.
Method: Mail.
Cases: 5,076.

Party Elite 1974

John S. Jackson III and Robert Hitlin, *Party Elites in the United States, 1974: Democratic Mid-Term Conference Delegates and Sanford Commission Members* (ICPSR 8206).

Universe: The universe for the conference delegates was the 2,043 delegates certified as eligible to attend the conference. For the Sanford Commission, the universe was the 161 official members of the commission.

Sampling: A systematic random scheme was used to select one-third of conference delegates. Survey questionnaires were mailed to all members of the Sanford Commission.

Method: Mail.

Cases: 430.

Party Elite 1976

John S. Jackson III and Robert A. Hitlin, *Party Elites in the United States, 1976: Democratic Mid-term Conference Delegates* (ICPSR 8207).

Universe: All 985 official delegates to the 1976 Democratic National Convention.

Sampling: A systematic random design selected every third name on randomly ordered lists of delegates.

Method: Mail.

Cases: 520.

Party Elite 1978

John S. Jackson III, *Party Elites in the United States, 1978: Democratic Mid-term Conference Delegates* (ICPSR 8208).

Universe: All 1,380 official delegates to the 1978 Democratic Mid-Term Party Conference.

Sampling: Questionnaires were mailed to all delegates. Those who returned the questionnaire constituted the sample.

Method: Mail.

Cases: 622.

Party Elite 1980

John S. Jackson III and Barbara Leavitt Brown, *Party Elites in the United States, 1980: Republican and Democratic Party Leaders* (ICPSR 8209).

Universe: All Democratic and Republican county chairs, all Democratic and Republican state chairs, all National Convention delegates for both parties and all members of the Democratic and Republican national committees in 1980.

Sampling: A systematic random scheme was employed to sample Democratic and Republican county chairs and national convention delegates for both

parties. Lists for these groups provided by the national parties or assembled from state election authorities were entered randomly and then a 1-in-3 skip interval was used. Questionnaires were mailed to all state chairs and all members of the Democratic and Republican national committees. Returned questionnaires constituted the sample.
Method: Mail.
Cases: 2,319.

Party Elite 1984
John S. Jackson III, David Bositis, and Denise Baer, *Party Elites in the United States 1984: Republican and Democratic Party Leaders* (ICPSR 8617).
Universe: All Democratic and Republican county chairs, all Democratic and Republican state chairs, all national convention delegates for both parties, and all members of the Democratic and Republican national committees in 1984.
Sampling: A systematic random scheme was employed to sample county chairs and national convention delegates for both parties. Questionnaires were mailed to all members of the DNC and RNC and returned questionnaires constituted the sample.
Method: Mail.
Cases: 2,308

Washington Post, Democrats, 1988
Washington Post, Washington Post Democratic Convention Delegate Poll (ICPSR 9068).
Universe: Delegates to the 1988 Democratic National Convention.
Sampling: Random.
Method: Telephone.
Cases: 504.

New York Times, Democrats, 1988
New York Times, New York Times Democratic Convention Delegate Survey, 1988 (ICPSR 9217).
Universe: Delegates to the 1988 Democratic National Convention.
Sampling: Random sample of delegates within two strata: super delegates and regular delegates.
Method: Telephone.
Cases: 1,059.

ABC News/*Washington Post,* Democrats, 1992
ABC News/*Washington Post, ABC News/Washington Post Democratic Delegate Poll, 1992* (ICPSR 9935).

Universe: Delegates to the 1992 Democratic National Convention.
Sampling: Random sample of delegates.
Method: Telephone.
Cases: 496.

Washington Post, Republicans, 1988
Washington Post, Washington Post Republican Convention Delegate Poll
(ICPSR 9069).
Universe: Delegates to the 1988 Republican National Convention.
Sampling: Random sample.
Method: Telephone.
Cases: 504.

New York Times, Republicans, 1988
New York Times, New York Times Republican Convention Delegate Survey, 1988
(ICPSR 9218).
Universe: Delegates to the 1988 Republican National Convention.
Sampling: Random sample of delegates.
Method: Telephone.
Cases: 739.

ABC News/*Washington Post,* Republicans, 1992
ABC News/*Washington Post, ABC News/Washington Post Republican Delegate Poll, 1992* (ICPSR 6015).
Universe: Delegates to the 1992 Republican National Convention.
Sampling: Random sample of delegates.
Method: Telephone.
Cases: 511.

Progressive Conservative Delegate Survey 1983
Principal Investigator: George Perlin.
Universe: Delegates to the 1983 PC Leadership Convention.
Sampling: Random.
Method: Mail.
Cases: 933.

Progressive Conservative Delegate Survey 1993
Principal Investigator: George Perlin.
Universe: Delegates to the 1993 PC Leadership Convention.
Sampling: Random.
Method: Mail.
Cases: 1,384.

Liberal Party Delegate Survey 1990
Principal Investigator: George Perlin.
Universe: Delegates to the 1990 Liberal Party of Canada Leadership Convention.
Sampling: Random.
Method: Mail.
Cases: 1,481.

Scale Construction

The scales constructed from the various data sets in order to measure attitudinal feminism are additive scales, which is to say that one point is added to the respondent's score for each response that is coded as "feminist." This is the only type of scale that could be constructed consistently across all of the data sets. Scales were not constructed from every data set, since some surveys did not include enough relevant items to allow scale construction.

Where the survey included at least three items measuring attitudinal feminism, a scale was constructed. Although every effort was made to construct the scales consistently across surveys, the inherent limitations of the data sets made it impossible to construct identical scales. Because questions were repeated in some of the American data sets, it was possible to construct identical scales for the two US parties in any given year and to make comparisons based on these scales. In all other cases, the only comparisons that could be made related to the strength of various factors in determining attitudinal feminism as measured by the scales.

The reliability of each of the scales is measured by an alpha score. Generally, scales with alpha scores over 0.4 are considered reliable. Items included in scales with alpha scores below 0.4 are not sufficiently correlated to permit construction of a reliable scale. With two exceptions, the scales employed in this study fell within the acceptable range. One scale had an alpha score of 0.22, and the other had an alpha score of 0.39. Both these scales were included in order to replicate the scale for comparison across parties.

Party Elite 1984

Five items (scale ranges from 0 to 5):
Respondent's position on abortion:
    1 = "woman's choice"; 0 = "never permitted," "if life in danger," "if hard to care for child."
Respondent's position on women's rights:
    1 = 5-7; 0 = 1-4. (Original item was a 7-point scale, where 1 = "woman's place is in the home" and 7 = "women should have an equal role with men").

Women should be 50 percent of delegates at party conventions:
   1 = strongly agree/agree; 0 = strongly disagree/disagree/uncertain.
Respondent's position on the Equal Rights Amendment:
   1 = pro; 0 = anti.
Respondent's position on equal representation for women at party conventions:
   1 = require equal representation; 0 = promote equal representation or leave it up to state party.
Alpha score: 0.67.

Party Elite 1988
Three items (scale ranges from 0 to 3):
Respondent's position on abortion:
   1 = "never forbid"; 0 = "never permit," "if life of mother threatened," "if difficult to care for child."
Respondent's position on spending on child care:
   1 = increase (5-7); 0 = decrease, remain the same. (Original item was a 7-point scale, where 1 = "decrease" and 7 = "increase").
Women should be 50 percent of delegates at party conventions:
   1 = strongly agree/agree; 0 = strongly disagree/disagree/uncertain.
Alpha score: 0.43.

New York Times 1988
Three items (scale from 0 to 3):
Abortion:
   1 = "legal as it is now"; 0 = "only to save mother, rape or incest," "not permitted."
Federal spending on day care and after-school care for children:
   1 = "increased"; 0 = "decreased," "kept the same."
The United States government's attention to the needs and problems of women:
   1 = "too little"; 0 = "too much"; "about right."
Alpha score: 0.47.

Determinants of Feminism Using Scales

Table A.1

Mean scores on feminism scale by gender and other demographic variables: Democratic party elite, 1984

		Men Score	Men (n)	Women Score	Women (n)
Gender[***]		2.7507	(706)	3.8563	(487)
Race	White	2.7620	(626)	3.9082	(403)
	Black	2.8857	(35)	3.6087	(46)
	Hispanic	2.4667	(30)	3.4091	(22)
Marital status	Married	2.6474	(570)	3.7397	(315)
	Separated/ divorced	3.1136	(44)	4.1324	(68)
	Single	3.2597	(8)	4.2174	(69)
		***		**	
Age group	18-29	3.3056	(36)	4.2188	(32)
	30-9	2.9401	(217)	3.9718	(142)
	40-9	2.7135	(171)	3.9603	(126)
	50-9	2.6069	(145)	3.5983	(117)
	60+	2.5000	(134)	3.7000	(60)
		**		*	
Education	High school/less	2.3000	(140)	3.2045	(88)
	Some college	2.4500	(80)	3.5161	(93)
	College	2.8616	(159)	4.1203	(133)
	College+	2.9937	(317)	4.2182	(165)
		***		***	

* Eta score $p < .05$
** Eta score $p < .01$
*** Eta score $p < .001$
Source: Appendix, calculated from data set: Party Elite 1984.

Table A.2

Mean scores on feminism scale by gender and other demographic variables: Democratic party elite, 1988

		Men		Women	
		Score	(n)	Score	(n)
Gender***		1.5211	(380)	2.1837	(275)
Race	White	1.5294	(340)	2.2093	(215)
	Black	1.5385	(26)	2.0000	(19)
	Hispanic	1.1250	(8)	2.2000	(10)
Marital status	Married	1.5137	(292)	2.2466	(146)
	Separated/ divorced	1.5517	(29)	2.1842	(38)
	Single	1.5098	(51)	2.2439 *	(41)
Age group	18-29	1.4706	(17)	2.4444	(9)
	30-9	1.5056	(89)	2.1961	(51)
	40-9	1.5781	(128)	2.2985	(67)
	50-9	1.4795	(73)	2.0923	(65)
	60+	1.4769	(65)	2.0833	(48)
Education	High school/less	1.2258	(62)	2.3023	(43)
	College	1.6087	(92)	2.1892	(74)
	College +	1.5865 *	(208)	2.1961	(102)
Years in party	< 2	1.3332	(3)	2.4286	(7)
	2-5	1.5500	(20)	2.1154	(26)
	6-10	1.3696	(46)	2.1750	(40)
	> 10	1.5537	(307)	2.1916	(167)

* Eta score $p < .05$
** Eta score $p < .01$
*** Eta score $p < .001$
Source: Appendix, calculated from data set: Party Elite 1988.

Table A.3

Mean scores on feminism scale by gender and other demographic variables: Democrats, 1988

		Men		Women	
		Score	(n)	Score	(n)
Gender***		2.0901	(554)	2.4602	(515)
Race	White	2.0259	(424)	2.4046	(346)
	Black	2.4545	(88)	2.5812	(117)
	Other	1.9375	(32)	2.5577	(52)
		***			
Marital	Married	2.0596	(436)	2.3975	(322)
status	Not married	2.2376	(101)	2.5714	(187)
				*	
Age group	18-29	2.1667	(12)	2.8571	(21)
	30-9	2.3191	(94)	2.5089	(112)
	40-9	2.1031	(194)	2.5976	(164)
	50-9	2.0490	(143)	2.3209	(134)
	60+	1.9010	(101)	2.2436	(78)
		*		***	
Education	High school/less	1.8913	(46)	2.2000	(45)
	Some college	1.8966	(58)	2.4400	(125)
	College	2.2292	(96)	2.4298	(121)
	College+	2.1166	(343)	2.5471	(223)

* Eta score $p < .05$
** Eta score $p < .01$
*** Eta score $p < .001$
Source: Appendix, calculated from data set: *New York Times,* Democrats, 1988.

Table A.4

Mean scores on feminism scale by gender and other demographic variables: Republican party elite, 1984

		Men		Women	
		Score	(n)	Score	(n)
Gender***		1.1441	(687)	1.4255	(416)
Marital status	Married	1.1008	(595)	1.4201	(338)
	Separated/divorced	1.4815	(27)	1.6500	(38)
	Single	1.3889	(54)	1.4000	(20)
		*			
Age group	18-29	1.1538	(26)	1.5714	(14)
	30-9	1.3285	(137)	1.6667	(57)
	40-9	1.2484	(157)	1.5532	(94)
	50-9	0.9457	(184)	1.2950	(139)
	60+	1.1341	(179)	1.4302	(97)
		**			
Education	High school/less	0.9709	(103)	1.0658	(76)
	Some college	1.1250	(104)	1.3496	(123)
	College	1.1423	(239)	1.5385	(156)
	College+	1.2611	(226)	1.7115	(52)
				**	
Housewife	Yes	n/a		1.1776	(107)
	No			1.5036	(274)
				*	

* Eta score $p < .05$
** Eta score $p < .01$
*** Eta score $p < .001$
Source: Appendix, calculated from data set: Party Elite 1984.

Table A.5

Mean scores on feminism scale by gender and other demographic variables: Republican party elite, 1988

		Men		Women	
		Score	(n)	Score	(n)
Gender		0.4119	(403)	0.4207	(145)
Marital status	Married	0.3960	(351)	0.3983	(118)
	Separated/divorced	0.6111	(18)	0.4000	(10)
	Single	0.5000	(26)	0.5000	(6)
Age group	18-29	0.5000	(10)	0.4000	(5)
	30-9	0.2874	(87)	0.7333	(15)
	40-9	0.3544	(79)	0.5116	(43)
	50-9	0.5273	(110)	0.2750	(40)
	60+	0.4364	(110)	0.3784	(37)
Education	High school/less	0.5000	(40)	0.4516	(31)
	College	0.3673	(147)	0.4444	(18)
	College+	0.3709	(275)	0.4237	(118)
Years in party	< 2	n/a	n/a		
	2-5	0.4722	(36)	0.3750	(8)
	6-10	0.3733	(75)	0.4444	(18)
	> 10	0.3709	(275)	0.4237	(118)
Born-again Christian	Yes	0.2100	(100)	0.2629	(26)
	No	0.4849	(299)	0.4655	(116)
		***			
Housewife	Yes	n/a		0.1795	(39)
	No			0.5000	(100)
				*	

* Eta score $p < .05$
** Eta score $p < .01$
*** Eta score $p < .001$
Source: Appendix, calculated from data set: Party Elite 1988.

Table A.6

Mean scores on feminism scale by gender and other demographic variables: Republicans, 1988

		Men		Women	
		Score	(n)	Score	(n)
Gender*		0.7863	(486)	0.9483	(271)
Marital status	Married	0.7861	(416)	0.9300	(200)
	Not married	0.7755	(49)	1.0143	(70)
Age group	18-29	0.5000	(18)	0.5556	(9)
	30-9	0.4865	(74)	1.0000	(19)
	40-9	0.8316	(137)	1.0694	(72)
	50-9	0.8661	(127)	0.9271	(96)
	60+	0.8532	(109)	0.9041	(73)
		*			
Education	High school/ less	0.5161	(31)	0.6889	(45)
	Some college	0.5938	(64)	1.0333	(90)
	College	0.7500	(116)	1.0667	(75)
	College+	0.8849	(252)	0.8667	(60)
		*			
Housewife	Yes	n/a		0.7347	(47)
	No			1.0497	(181)
Years in party	<10	0.7067	(75)	0.9000	(40)
	>10	0.8015	(393)	0.9567	(231)

* Eta score $p < .05$
** Eta score $p < .01$
*** Eta score $p < .001$
Source: Appendix, calculated from data set: *New York Times,* Republicans, 1988.

Notes

Introduction

1   See Bashevkin (1993); Biersack and Herrnson (1994); Brodie (1991); Carroll (1987); Erickson (1991; 1993); Lovenduski and Norris (1993); Studlar and Matland (1994); Young (1991).

2   See Assendelft and O'Connor (1994); Brodie (1988); Bystydzienski (1995); Carroll (1992); Jennings and Farah (1981); Norris and Lovenduski (1988); Skjeie (1988; 1991); Thomas (1994); Welch (1985).

3   For example, Conover (1988); Day and Hadley (1994); Thomas (1994); Young (1996).

4   Socialist feminists adopt a variety of stances on this question. For the most part, they view women's participation in bourgeois parties with considerable scepticism, but they differ in their assessments of the merits of women's participation in socialist parties.

5   There is a socialist feminist component to Gotell and Brodie's argument, in that they single out "mainstream" or non-socialist parties' unwillingness to address the structural sources of women's oppression.

6   The archival research was conducted primarily at the Canadian Women's Movement Archives/Archives canadiennes du mouvement des femmes at the University of Ottawa. Documents housed at this archive are cited as "CWMA," with the relevant file names. Some additional research was conducted at the National Archives of Canada. These documents are cited as "NA," with the appropriate volumes and file numbers.

Interviews were conducted on a confidential basis, and are identified by the date on which they occurred. Sixteen interviews were conducted for the Canadian case and ten for the American.

7   As Vickers et al. (1993, 7) note, francophone feminists in Canada, both sovereigntist and federalist, are committed to decentralization, which would make it possible for them to relate as feminists primarily to the Quebec state. Thus, the primary focus of francophone feminists has been on Quebec politics. Because this research concentrates on the relationship between women's organizations and national parties, it does not consider feminist organizations in Quebec except insofar as they engage with federal parties.

8   See, for example, Rankin and Vickers (1998).

9   For the Canadian research, some of the party documents were found in the Liberal and New Democratic parties' holdings at the National Archives of Canada. These documents are cited as "NA," with the relevant volume and file numbers.

10 The details regarding the data sets employed are found in the Appendix. The Canadian data sets were made available by George Perlin of the Centre for the Study of Public Opinion at Queen's University and by Keith Archer and Alan Whitehorn. The American data sets were made available by Denise Baer and by the Inter-University Consortium for Political and Social Research (ICPSR) at the University of Michigan. The names of the original collectors of the data sets are found in the Appendix. Neither the collectors of

any of the data used in this book nor the ICPSR bear any responsibility for the analyses or interpretations presented here.

Chapter 1: Theorizing Feminist Strategy and Party Responsiveness

1   Because they restrict their analyses to the new social movements that emerged from 1968 on, one might argue that the new social movement theorists are addressing a different phenomenon than the resource mobilization theorists. It is certainly the case that the new social movement theorists do not claim the same explanatory scope as the resource mobilization theorists (whose model should be able to apply to virtually any social movement, not only those that have emerged since 1968). The resource mobilization and political opportunity structure theorists apply their models to the new social movements, and this brings them into conflict with the new social movement theorists. Given the debate between these two schools of thought concerning the mobilization and strategy of contemporary women's movements, it is appropriate to construct these as competing approaches in the context of this study.

2   In a similar vein, Kitschelt (1993, 27) argues that for movements engaged in the politics of identity, "means and ends, processes of mobilization and objective, cannot be clearly differentiated. To a large extent, the objective of the movement's practices is embodied in the process itself. In such groups ... the interdependence between process and goals inhibit[s] instrumental organization in ways instituted by parties and interest groups."

3   For further discussion, see Young (1994).

4   For a further discussion of the emerging party system, see Carty et al. (2000).

5   Both parties were subject to a trend towards nationalization in the 1960s and early 1970s that did strengthen the national party organizations to some extent. In comparative context, however, US national parties remain extraordinarily decentralized.

6   Hanson (1992) found that only 7 percent of delegates to the convention were Wappel supporters, although almost three-quarters of them received assistance in becoming a delegate from pro-life advocates. The party subsequently gave the leader the power to appoint candidates, which Chrétien used to prevent the nomination of Liberals for Life candidates in the 1993 election.

7   It is a matter of some debate among party scholars whether the NDP should be considered a brokerage party.

8   See, for example, Bashevkin (1993) and Burrell (1993a, 1993b).

9   There are also those in both countries who make the normative argument that political parties *should* be more ideological in character, offering voters distinct programs to choose between (Clarke et al. 1991; Brodie and Jenson 1980; APSA 1950).

10   Canadian conservatism has traditionally been "tory" in character, which is to say that it has acknowledged a role for the state in ensuring the welfare of the citizenry. See Bashevkin (1998).

11   Some scholars have tried to quantify the left-right placement of political parties in a range of democratic systems by asking experts in each country to place the parties on a scale from left to right. The results of such efforts are, however, somewhat suspect as they rely on subjective understandings of the scope of the left-right political spectrum. A recent survey of this type found that on a scale from 1 to 10, where 1 is left and 10 is right, Canadian experts placed the NDP at 2.9 (on average), the Liberals at 5.1, and the PCs at 7.3. American experts placed the Democrats at 4.2 and the Republicans at 6.9 (Huber and Inglehart 1995). While confirming the relative placement of the Progressive Conservatives and Republicans on the right, the Liberals and Democrats in the centre, and the NDP on the left, the specific findings are of little comparative validity, as it would be impossible to argue credibly that the Canadian Conservatives are substantially to the right of the US Republicans, at least during the 1980s and 1990s.

12   Pure rational choice approaches privilege self-interested action above all other causal factors, while neo-institutional approaches portray actors as responding rationally to rules embedded in institutional frameworks (see March and Olsen 1989).

13   There are divergent ideological tendencies within the parties, such as the Red Tories in

the Progressive Conservative party or nationalists in the Liberal party, but these tendencies seldom take on the characteristics of a party faction, so conflict remains muted, and it is usually played out in private or in periodic leadership contests.

14 For a discussion of the Christian Coalition's efforts to capture the Republican party, see Penning (1994) and Wilcox (1994a).

15 For a discussion of the co-optation model as applied to Canadian political parties, see Gotell and Brodie (1991).

Chapter 2: Partisan Engagement

1 This is, of course, not the only source of contention or strategic divergence within the movement. Nonetheless, for the purpose of this research, it is the most directly relevant.

2 While it might seem naive by current standards, Friedan took this position prior to the polarization of US politics around feminist issues and before the emergence of an anti-feminist counter-movement with high-profile women speaking on its behalf.

3 Separate Democratic and Republican task forces were formed within the NWPC so that activists affiliated with a party could concentrate their efforts on reforming that party from within.

4 Although WISH List is the most obvious case of this, the Gay and Lesbian Victory fund is also employing EMILY's List's techniques. A more exotic case of imitation is British Labour Party and feminist activist Barbara Follett's effort to create EMILY's List U.K. In an effort to counteract the "radical feminist" EMILY's List contributions to "radical, leftwing, pro-abortion feminist Democratic ... ultra-liberal ... pin-up girls" like Geraldine Ferraro and Diane Feinstein, Phyllis Schlafly in 1992 established an "Eagle List" of endorsees that would be sent to anyone contributing $100 or more to her PAC. In a fund-raising letter, Schlafly explained the practice of bundling to potential supporters, reassuring them that it was not an illicit sexual practice, even though feminists indulge in it (Schlafly 1992).

5 To account for inflation, these figures were adjusted using the Consumer Price Index.

6 According to Bella Abzug (who was a Kennedy supporter), NOW had considered endorsing Edward Kennedy for the nomination against Carter in 1980, but eventually decided against the move. (See Abzug and Kelber 1984, 77).

7 NOW was poised to back Representative Patricia Schroeder's bid for the presidential nomination but, after testing the waters, she decided not to run.

8 This distancing is discussed in Eleanor Smeal's (1991, 72) article in *Ms.* magazine, which endorsed the third party route.

Chapter 3: Power Is Not Electoral

1 Since the late 1980s, the composition and orientation of the FFQ have changed considerably, culminating in support for the sovereigntist option in the 1995 Quebec referendum.

2 Although sometimes termed "neo-conservative," the Mulroney government is more appropriately described as "neo-liberal." The term "neo-conservative" usually refers to an ideology that combines fiscal and social conservatism, while the term "neo-liberal" refers to an ideology that embraces fiscal conservatism but is liberal on social issues.

3 For a discussion of the Canadian suffrage movement, see Cleverdon (1974).

4 This reflects a tendency for radical feminist organizing to take place at the local level, and to be dispersed among a large number of small groups.

5 Directing the movement's development was not the government's primary purpose in funding women's organizations. Rather, as discussed in Chapter 5, national unity and state-building concerns were paramount.

6 This focus on lobbying government officials can be attributed to the distribution of power within the Canadian federal government. Cabinet ministers, their staffs, and senior public servants are the key players in policy development in the Canadian political system.

7 Of the 166 delegates listed in the report, 110 indicated an affiliation. Thirty-one were members of the WPA, 46 were affiliated with status-of-women groups or women's

centres, and two were journalists. Of the 31 who listed political parties as their affiliations, 12 were NDP, 8 were Liberal, 10 were PC, and 1 was Parti Québécois (based on WPA 1973d).

8   For example, the NAC President's Report applauded the candidacies of women for the leadership of the New Democratic and Progressive Conservative parties in 1975 and 1976 respectively. See Marsden (1976).

9   For a thorough discussion of the mobilization around the equality rights provisions of the Charter, see Hošek (1983). The Liberal government's mishandling of the issue is discussed in greater detail in Chapter 5.

10 Vickers et al. (1993) argue that this reflected a deliberate policy of rotation among the three parties. Activists interviewed for this study were divided on this question. Some concurred, while others expressed the view that "nothing in NAC at that time was deliberate."

11 This, of course, stands in sharp contrast to the American women's movement, which became heavily involved in the internal politics of the Democratic party in the early 1980s.

12 This is discussed in greater detail in Chapter 5.

13 In a 1993 interview, former NAC president Judy Rebick (1993: 10) argued that the movement had to take a stand opposing the Charlottetown Accord even if the decision would hurt the movement.

14 For a detailed discussion of feminist policy gains and losses under Mulroney, see Bashevkin (1996).

15 On the implications of the discourse of competitiveness and entry into regional trade arrangements on state capacity, see Abele (1992) and Robinson (1993). There is, of course, considerable debate among both academics and practitioners regarding the extent to which pressures for harmonization have affected the capacity of the Canadian state. What is important to note for the purpose of this argument, however, is that most women's movement activists were also active opponents of both the Canada-United States Free Trade Agreement and NAFTA, and were convinced by the arguments that free trade would constrain the Canadian state. Even if there has not been a measurable trend towards harmonization or erosion of state capacity, activists *perceive* these trends and base their political calculations on them.

16 These changes to the Canadian party system are discussed in greater detail in Chapter 5.

Chapter 4: Polarization

1   For an excellent discussion of the organization of American parties, see Katz and Kolodny (1994).

2   For a discussion of "cycles of protest," see Tarrow (1994, 153-70).

3   Although the platform document is drafted by the platform committee and ratified by the convention, the presidential nominee who must run on the platform exercises considerable influence on its content.

4   It is interesting to note that the Democrats' majority in Congress in the 1970s allowed them to enact many of these measures, even with a Republican in the White House.

5   Ironically, the first attitudinal survey of delegates to American national party conventions was originally conceived as a study of women in politics. In 1970, several academics decided to use women delegates to the two national conventions as a cross-section of women who were active in American politics (Kirkpatrick 1976: xvii). Fortuitously, this decision to survey delegates to the two conventions left a record of the attitudinal characteristics of women at the historic 1972 convention, and created a benchmark against which attitudes of delegates at subsequent conventions could be measured.

6   The eta score for the difference of means on both of these thermometer scales is significant at $p < .001$.

7   The chi-square scores for these differences were not statistically significant.

8   It is noteworthy that the commission was formed and its chairs appointed by Jean Westwood while she was still DNC chair. Both Mikulski and her original co-chair Leonard Woodcock were pro-reform. Woodcock resigned shortly after being appointed, and the

new DNC chair was forced to decide whether to appoint a new co-chair less favourable towards the reforms. In an effort to maintain peace within the party, the DNC Chair allowed Mikulski to chair the commission on her own, but he appointed 21 new members to the 51-member panel in an effort to have better representation of the anti-reform faction on the commission. See Klinkner (1994a, 115).

9   Specifically, this is based on the following calculation: (percent of women who are Democrats – percent of women who are Republicans) – (percent of men who are Democrats – percent of men who are Republicans). See Kirschten (1984).

10 The gender difference on this question was statistically significant (chi-square significant at $p < .01$).

11 There are, of course, exceptions to this. Bill Clinton's vice-president, Al Gore, played a significant role in policy development during the Clinton administration.

12 The chi-square statistic for the gender difference is significant at $p < .001$; the statistic for the difference between women belonging to women's organizations and women not belonging is significant at $p < .01$.

13 Kirk's changes to the internal organization of the DNC were not permanent, however. The system of regional desks has since been dismantled and the position of director of women's outreach has been created at the DNC. This is a relatively junior position and its occupant is expected to fulfil other unrelated tasks.

14 The chi-square statistic for this gender difference was statistically significant at $p < .05$.

15 The eta score for this difference was significant at $p < .001$.

16 The Republicans first adopted a plank supporting the ERA in their platform in 1940.

17 For a discussion of the survey, see Appendix. As was noted in Chapter 3, the Party Elite Survey is not an ideal means of developing a profile of the women active in party women's organizations, but it represents the only available data.

Chapter 5: Moderate Endorsement

1   For a discussion of the rise of the Bloc and Reform, see Carty et al. (2000), Chapter 2.

2   See Flanagan (1995).

3   In the early 1970s, "participatory democracy" of this sort was common practice within the extra-parliamentary party, although its effect on the parliamentary party was at best limited (Wearing 1988).

4   When pressed on the issue of abortion in 1971, Trudeau responded that it would be impossible to pass more liberal abortion legislation in Parliament, and went on to express his own ambiguous stance on the issue, saying, "I was really very influenced by the overwhelming feeling of women on this, because they are making the terrible moral decision of killing ... I think it is a terribly difficult moral question, and I know the ladies, the women, are very severely divided" (Trudeau 1972, 38).

5   Vickers et al. (1993) chronicle several of NAC's efforts to raise money from various schemes. While major national American feminist organizations such as NOW are sustained primarily through membership fees and private contributions, NAC's umbrella structure precluded such an arrangement. NAC did create the non-voting membership category of "friend of NAC" in the 1980s, but this has not proven a route to financial independence. It would, of course, be more difficult for a national feminist organization in Canada to operate solely on private funds than for an American organization, as the Canadian population base is much smaller and there are fewer charitable foundations to fund group projects and office operations.

6   Implementation of this provision was not immediately forthcoming.

7   The Liberal Party of Canada (LPC) had a great deal of difficulty with the issue of mailing lists. Provincial parties were in many cases unwilling to share their mailing lists with the national party. Even though every woman who held a Liberal membership in Canada was technically a member of the NWLC, the Commission's active membership was limited to its mailing list.

8   One is left wondering what feminist readers would make of some of the material in the document, which exhorts readers to "be prepared to deal positively with hostile and

derogatory remarks and questions ... e.g., If you are fortunate enough to have in the audience someone foolish enough to make reference to 'bra burners,' assure them that feminists never burn their bras – the women's movement needs all the support it can get" (NWLC 1982b, 8).

9   After Anderson's resignation, Axworthy appointed Gardner as interim president of CACSW. Several months later, he appointed one of the other executive members – Lucie Pépin – as president of the council. Although Pépin was not a Liberal party member at the time of her appointment as council president, she went on to run as a Liberal candidate in a Quebec riding in the 1984 federal election.

10   The Liberal party's maintenance of the NWLC as a form of quota system for convention delegates, particularly when coupled with the existence of the party's Aboriginal Commission and reserved spots for university clubs and youth delegates, creates a system of "double voting" whereby some party members are given more votes than others. A female party member can vote not only for delegates from her constituency, but also for women's commission delegates. If she is a university student, she can also vote for delegates from the campus club, and so on. This system means that the representational guarantees can be attacked not only as quotas, but also on the grounds that they violate the principle of "one person, one vote." (See, for example, MacIvor 1994, 21).

11   In postmortems of the campaign, the NWLC leadership concluded that a better "media strategy" was needed for the next campaign, and that "the mainstream media is not ready to discuss the real issues of women in politics" (NWLC 1994b).

12   See Young (1996).

13   This study was conducted by Amy Nugent. Clearly, a study of the ridings with executives posted on the Internet is not a scientific sample. Nonetheless, it does give a basic indication of the representation of women in governing Reform constituency associations.

14   The author attended the convention as an observer, and would estimate that around 25 percent of delegates were women.

15   The Bloc's increase might possibly be attributed to the decline in the party's fortunes. Having lost its charismatic founding leader and the 1995 Quebec referendum on sovereignty, the Bloc had clearly become the "B-Team" for Quebec sovereigntists. As a result, Bloc candidacies presumably became less competitive. The party did not take any formal measures to encourage women candidates prior to the 1997 election.

Chapter 6: Can Feminists Transform Party Politics?

1   Vickers et al. (1993) argue that Canadian feminists in the 1970s were committed to "politics as usual" as an operational code.

2   Even trade unions struggle because they are unable to deliver the votes of their members to the political party with which they are affiliated.

3   It should be noted that the cross-national differences in opinion on abortion are more complex than these simple statistics suggest. Rather, as Nevitte et al. (1993, 27-8) observe, more Americans believe that abortion should be legal than express personal approval of abortion. Americans are less likely than Canadians to approve of abortion in discretionary circumstances, although this gap is narrowing over time, and unlike Canadians, Americans are becoming less supportive of abortion to avoid the birth of a child with a severe physical handicap.

4   Somewhat ironically, the greatest success of the Christian Heritage party came in the 1988 election when their candidates took enough votes away from the PCs in five ridings to defeat Conservative incumbents and elect Liberals (Bernard 1994, 78).

5   In the US case, Tolleson Rinehart (1992) finds that gender gaps are created by less than one-third of women – those who identify as feminists.

6   For further discussion, see Darcy, Welch, and Clark (1994) and Young (1991).

7   This phrase was used in the Court's landmark ruling in *Buckley* v. *Valeo,* in which the Court struck down several articles of the Federal Election Campaign Act, leaving Americans with a system of electoral finance regulation in which contributions were controlled, but expenditures by candidates or other political parties were not controlled, on

the grounds that such controls would infringe on constitutional guarantees of freedom of speech. See Alexander (1992).

8   Ironically, the way around this would be to adopt EMILY's List's technique of bundling contributions to candidates. If cheques were made out to the candidate in question, then the candidate would issue a tax receipt directly to the contributor.

References

Primary Sources

Women's Organizations (United States)
BPW USA. 1994a. *Congressional Voting Chart: 103rd Congress.* Washington, DC: BPW USA.
–. 1994b. *National Legislative Platform, 1994.* Washington, DC: BPW USA.
Council of Presidents. 1993. *Council of Presidents: Who We Are.* Washington, DC: Council of Presidents.
EMILY's List. 1995. "Report to Members." Photocopy.
Getting It Gazette. 1996. Distributed at the 1996 Democratic National Convention.
LWV. 1927a. "Data Assembled for the Special Committee of 9 to Present Recommendations for Activities of the League of Women Voters with reference to the approaching general election of 1928," Library of Congress, LWV Papers, Microfiche, Part III, Series A, Reel 10.
–. 1927b. "Women in the Political Parties," Library of Congress, LWV Papers, Microfiche, Part III, Series A, Reel 13.
NOW. 1984. *National NOW Times* (May-June).
–. 1987. *National NOW Times* (April).
–. 1988a. *National NOW Times* (May/June).
–. 1988b. *National NOW Times* (July/August/September).
–. 1988c. *National NOW Times* (December/January).
–. 1992. *National NOW Times* (February).
–. 1996. *National NOW Times* (November/December).
–. 1999. "NOW Update on Impeachment/Action Needed." http://www.now.org/issues/legislat/impeachupdat.htm.
NWPC. 1971. Statement of Purpose. Private paper.
–. 1980. *Democratic Women Are Wonderful: A History of Women at Democratic National Conventions.* Washington, DC: NWPC.
–. 1992. *Women's Political Times* 18, 2 (July).
–. Democratic Task Force. 1992. The DTF Report. Private paper.

Parties and Party-Related Organizations (United States)
Bond, Rich. 1993. "Remarks to 1993 Republican National Committee Winter Meeting." *RNC News Release,* 29 January 1993.
Democratic Leadership Council. 1991. *The New American Choice: Opportunity, Responsibility, Community.* Washington, DC: Democratic Leadership Council.
DNC. 1995. *Reaching Out: The Newsletter of the Women's Leadership Forum* (Winter).
National Democratic Women's Network. 1994. *Action Alert.* Private paper.
NFDW. n.d. *The National Federation of Democratic Women.* Private paper.

–. 1994. *NFDW Communicator* (Autumn).
NFRW. 1981. *Consider Yourself for Public Office*. Washington, DC: NFRW.
–. 1987. *NFRW: Fifty Years of Leadership*. Washington, DC: NFRW.
RFC. n.d.a. "Assorted Poll Results on the Question of Choice." Private paper.
–. n.d.b. "Seven Myths about Republicans for Choice." Private paper.
–. n.d.c. "Talking Points on the 1992 Republican National Convention." Private paper.
–. n.d.d. "What Is Republicans for Choice?" Private paper.
Stone, Ann. 1992. "Testimony before the Republican National Committee Platform Hearings," 26 May. Private paper.
–. 1993. "Testimony for the Republican Majority Coalition," 10 May. Private paper.
Women's Division, RNC. 1971. *Women in Public Service*. Washington, DC: RNC.

Other (United States)
Unofficial Transcript of Christian Coalition Virginia Beach Conference, 1991.
Christian Coalition. 1992. "ActionGram." 26 March. Private paper.
Schlafly, Phyllis. 1992. "Letter to Eagle Friends," April 1992.

Women's Organizations (Canada)
FPC. n.d. "The Feminist Party of Canada." Typed manuscript. Canadian Women's Movement Archives/Archives canadiennes du mouvement des femmes at the University of Ottawa (hereinafter CWMA), file: FPC.
–. 1979. "Towards a Canadian Feminist Party" (April). CWMA, file: FPC.
–. 1981a. *Newsletter* (February). CWMA, file: FPC.
–. 1981b. *Newsletter* (April). CWMA, file: FPC.
–. 1981c. *Newsletter* 3, 3 (June 1981). CWMA, file: FPC.
Marsden, Lorna. 1976. "President's Report." NAC Annual Meeting, National Archives of Canada (hereinafter NA), MG 31 K7, vol. 10, file 11 (Elsie Gregory McGill Collection).
NAC. 1972a. "Report of the Strategy for Change Convention of Women in Canada." CWMA: NAC – Formation.
–. 1972b. "Submission to the Government of Canada." February, Laura Sabia, Chair. CWMA, file: NAC.
–. 1972c. "Minutes of Steering Committee Meeting," Sunday, 17 April, CWMA: NAC – Minutes.
–. 1976. "Minutes of NAC Executive Meeting," 21 November. CWMA: NAC Executive Minutes.
–. 1979. "Memo to NAC Executive and Member Organizations, from Lynn McDonald, re: Appointments to Boards, Commissions etc." 7 November. CWMA, file: NAC – Correspondence 1976-1979.
–. c. 1980. "Election Activity." NA, MG 31 K7, vol. 10, file 16. (Elsie Gregory McGill).
–. 1980. "NAC President's Report, March 1980." NA, MG 31 K22, vol. 8, file 8 (Ruth Marion Bell).
–. 1984. Memo. (April).
–. 1985. "Minutes, Executive Meeting, June 15-16, 1985." CWMA, file: NAC Executive Minutes.
–. 1986a. "Minutes, Executive Meeting, 22-23 February 1986." CWMA, file: NAC Executive Minutes.
–. 1986b. "Minutes, Table Officer's Meeting, October 24, 1986." CWMA, file: NAC Executive Minutes.
–. 1986c. "Minutes, Executive Meeting, November 21, 1986." CWMA, file: NAC Executive Minutes.
–. 1988a. "Minutes, Executive Meeting, February 4-5, 1989." CWMA, file: NAC Executive Minutes.
–. 1988b. "Minutes, Executive Meeting, April 9-10, 1988." CWMA, file: NAC Executive Minutes.
–. 1988c. "Is the NAC Election Campaign Partisan?" Memo from Alice [staff person] to NAC Executive, 14 October. CWMA, file: NAC Executive Correspondence.

–. 1989. "Minutes of NAC Executive Meeting," 4-5 February. CWMA, file: NAC – Minutes.
–. 1997. "Press Release," 3 June.
REAL Women of Canada. 1998. *REALity* (November/December). http://www.realwom-enca.com/html/newsletter.
Women for Political Action. 1972. "Aline Gregory: Independent for Rosedale." CWMA, file: WPA file #1.
–. 1973a. "Policy Statement"; CWMA, file: WPA file #1.
–. 1973b. "Notice of meeting, February 3, 1973." CWMA, file: WPA file #1.
–. 1973c. *WPA Newsletter* 2, 1 (April). CWMA, file: WPA file #1.
–. 1973d. "Women in Politics: National Conference 1973." CWMA, file: WPA file #1.
–. 1975. *WPA Newsletter.* CWMA, file: WPA file #1.
Women's Commission of the League for Socialist Action. 1972. "Which Way for Women's Political Action?" CWMA, file: WPA, file #2.

Liberal Party (Canada)
Liberal Party. c. 1984. "Some Thoughts and Notes for Speeches and Other Communication Materials on Equality for Women." NA, MG 28 IV 3 1587, file: 1984 General Election – Issues Affecting Women and Statistics on Women.
LPC. 1966. "Liberal Policy Convention Report." NA, MG 28 IV 3, vol. 1077, file NLF National Meeting 1966.
–. 1972. "Final Report of the Liberal Party Task Force on the Status of Women." NA, MG 28 IV 3 1178, file: Status of Women 1972.
–. 1975a. "Summary Notes, National Convention Policy Committee Meeting." NA, MG 28 IV 3 1175, file: Convention '73.
–. 1975b. "Minutes of July 17, 1975 National Convention Policy Committee Meeting." NA, MG 28 IV 3 1175, file: Convention '73.
–. 1980. Discussion Paper for the National Convention of the Liberal Party of Canada, July 4, 5, and 6, 1980. Ottawa.
–. 1984. "Women's Issues Book for Televised Debate." NA, MG 28 IV 3 1587, file: 1984 General Election, Debate on Women.
–. 1988. "Women in the Campaign."
–. 1992. *The Chrétien Report* (September).
NWLC. 1974. "Minutes of Meeting, November 1-2, 1974." NA, MG 28 IV 3 1253, file: Meeting WLC November.
–. 1975. "Minutes of Executive Meeting, 3-4 May." NA, MG 28 IV 3 1253, file: 136; Réunion de la Commission libérale feminine tenue le 15 février 1974.
–. 1978a. "Open Letter to All Women Liberals," 29 May. NA, MG 28 IV 3 1295, file: Irma Melville 1979.
–. 1978b. "Election '78: Information on Issues of Particular Concern to Women." NA, MG 28 IV 3 1377, file: 1.4.20 WLC National Executive Meeting, 1978.
–. 1980. "NWLC Action Plan." NA, MG 28 IV 3 1607 1.3.11, file: NWLC Executive 1981.
–. 1981. "Report to Members of National Executive," March. NA, MG 29 IV 3 1407, file: Irma Melville, President WLC 1981.
–. 1982a. "Programme, Women's Liberal Commission Meeting at Convention '82: Women for Canada." NA, MG 28 IV 3 1607 1.3.11, file: NWLC Executive 1982.
–. 1982b. "Guidelines for Political Action." NA, MG 28 IV 3 1377, file: 4.1.8: Guidelines for Political Action.
–. 1982c. "WLC Initiatives since Convention '80." NA, MG 28 IV 3 1594, file: NWLC Executive 1982.
–. 1984. "Minutes of Meeting, May 26, 1984." NA, MG 28 IV 3 1295, file: NWLC Meeting.
–. 1987. "Background Notes on the National Women's Liberal Commission." Private paper.
–. 1991. "Presentation of the National Women's Liberal Commission to the Reform Commission of the Liberal Party of Canada." 20 April. Private paper.
–. 1993. *Walk, Knock and Talk.* Private paper.
–. 1994a. *Women Changing the Face of Canada.* Private paper.

–. 1994b. "Communiqué." Private paper.
WLFC. 1966. "Liberal Policy Convention Report." NA, MG 28 IV 3 1064, file: NLF National Meeting 1966.
–. 1967. "Resolutions Adopted." NA, MG 28 IV 3 1064, file: NLF National Meeting 1966.
Wylie, Torrance. 1972. "Memorandum to Bob Andras re: Presentation to Caucus," 12 June. NA MG 28 IV 3, vol. 1052, file: Caucus Presentation.

New Democratic Party (Canada)
BC POW Committee. 1974. *BC Women's Manifesto*. NA, MG 28 IV 1, vol. 458, file: Literature, 1962-80.
Bernard, Elaine. 1994. "Labour, the NDP and Social Movements: What Political Parties Do and Why We Need Each Other." Paper distributed to NDP Party Renewal Conference, Toronto, December.
Brown, Rosemary. 1974. "Speech to NDP Women's Conference." NA, MG IV 1, vol. 547, file: 574-29 (1974 National Women's Conference).
DeWitt, Ann. 1974. Letter to Nancy Eng, 5 December. NA, MG 28 IV 1, vol. 463, file: Participation of Women Committee, 1970-76.
–. 1975a. Letter to Clifford Scotton, 5 January. NA, MG 28 IV 1, vol. 458, file: Correspondence: Ann DeWitt (Federal Coordinator) 1974-76.
–. 1975b. Letter to POW Committee, 16 January 1975. NA, MG 28 IV 1, vol. 463, file: Participation of Women Committee, 1970-6.
–. 1975c. Memorandum to Robin Sears Re: Women's Organizer, POW Committee, 5 August. NA, MG 28 IV 1, vol. 458, file: Correspondence: Ann DeWitt (Federal Coordinator) 1974-6.
–. 1976. Memo to Robin Sears, 2 March 1976. NA, MG 28 IV 1, vol. 458, file: Correspondence: Ann DeWitt (Federal Coordinator) 1974-6.
Eady, Mary. 1970a. Letter to Members of POW Committee, 11 February. NA, MG 28 IV 1, vol. 463, file: Participation of Women Committee, 1970-6.
–. 1970b. "Text for Women's Leaflet." Presented to Federal NDP Council, Ottawa, 19 September. NA, MG 28 IV 1, vol. 458, file: Literature, 1962-80.
Eng, Nancy. 1974. Memo to all POW Committee Members and representatives of NDP Women's Committees, 30 October. NA, MG 28 IV 1, vol. 463, file: Participation of Women Committee, 1970-76.
Federal Women's Committee of the NDP. 1965. "Report to Federal Executive." NA, MG IV 1, vol. 426, file: Women's Activity in the NDP.
Hartman, Grace. 1967. Letter to Grace MacInnis MP, 23 January. NA, MG IV 1, vol. 463, file: Correspondence, RCSW, 1964-8.
Latham, Eva. 1967. Letter to Laura Sabia, 26 January. NA, MG IV 1, vol. 463, file: Correspondence, RCSW, 1964-8.
Laxer, Krista Maeots. 1970. "The Burdens of Discrimination." Presented to Federal NDP Council, Ottawa, 9 September. NA, MG 28 IV 1, vol. 458, file: Literature 1962-70.
Lewis, David. 1974. Letter to Eleanor O'Connor and Myrna Phillips, 24 December. NA, MG 28 IV 1, vol. 426, file: Women's Rights, 1962-76.
NDP. 1962. "Women's Committees, New Democratic Party." NA, MG IV 1, vol. 426, file: Women's Activity in the NDP.
–. 1968. "Brief to the Royal Commission on the Status of Women in Canada." NA, MG IV 1, vol. 463, file: Correspondence, RCSW, 1964-8.
–. 1974. "Women Voters." NA, MG IV 1, vol. 426, file: Women's Activity in the NDP.
NDP POW. 1970. *POW Bulletin*. NA, MG 28 IV 1, vol. 463, file: Participation of Women Committee, 1970-6.
–. 1975. "Minutes of POW Committee Meeting," 16 January. NA, MG 28 IV 1, vol 463, file: Participation of Women Committee, 1970-76.
–. 1976. "Minutes of POW Committee Meeting," 26-7 January. NA, MG 28 IV 1, vol. 463, file: Participation of Women Committee, 1970-76.
No author. 1970a. "NDP Women's Liberation Movement: Our Aims." NA, MG 28 IV 1, vol. 458, file: Literature 1962-70.

–. 1970b. "The Canadian Women's Movement and the New Democratic Party." NA, MG 28 IV 1, vol. 458, file: Literature 1962-70.

–. 1974. "Report on Women's Conference." NA, MG 28 IV 1, vol. 461, file: National Women's Conference 1974.

Scotton, Clifford. 1974. Letter to David Stewart, 16 October. NA, MG 28 IV 1, vol. 458, file: Correspondence: Carla Funk, Coordinator.

Progressive Conservative Party (Canada)

Bowerman, Joyce. 1973. Speech. NA, MG 28 IV 2, vol. 645, file: Women's Association (1) 1972-73.

Chong, Gladys. 1975. Letter to Michael Meighan, National President, 16 June. NA, MG 28 IV 2, vol. 645, file: Women's Association (3).

Clark, Joe. 1980. Transcript of Remarks by the Rt. Hon. Joe Clark, PM, to a meeting of the National Action Committee on the Status of Women, 2 January. NA, MG 28 IV 2, vol. 660, file: Campaign 1980, Policy, Women's Issues.

Einarson, Pearl. 1973. Letter to Liam O'Brian, National Director, 20 February. NA, MG 28 IV 2, vol. 645, file: Women's Association (1) 1972-73.

Federal PC Women's Caucus of Ottawa. 1989. *Newsletter* (November/December). NA, MG 28 IV 2, vol. 477, file: Federal PC Women's Caucus of Ottawa.

Ford, Barbara. 1981. Women's Bureau: Objectives, Timetables and Budget. NA, MG 28 IV 2, vol. 651, file: Organization, Women's Caucus, general.

Ford, Barbara, Ruth Archibald, Françoise Guenette, and Valerie York. 1989. Report: Evaluation and Recommendations on Women's Bureau. NA, MG 28 IV 2, vol. 477, file: Ad Hoc Committee on Women in the Party, 1989-91.

Harrison Smith, H.S. 1964. Report of the National President. NA, MG 28 IV 2, vol. 477, file: Annual Meeting 1964.

Holt, Alene. 1973a. Speech to Fundraising Banquet and Dance, 21 September. NA, MG 28 IV 2, vol. 623, file: Holt, Alene.

–. 1973b. Letter to May Lambert, 10 July. NA, MG 28 IV 2, vol. 645, file: Women's Association (1) 1972-3.

MacAulay, Isobel. 1968. Letter to Gene Rheaume, 15 February. NA, MG 28 IV 2, vol. 477, file: MacAulay, Isobel.

MacKinnon, Millie. 1976. Letter to Michael Meighen, National President of PC Party, 9 March. NA, MG 28 IV 2, vol. 641, file: PC Women's Association, 1975-6.

Ontario PC Women's Association. 1977. Resolutions. NA, MG 28 IV 2, vol. 641, file: PC Women's Association 1976-7.

PC Party. 1972a. Campaign Document – Women in Society. NA, MG 28 IV 2, vol. 713, file: Women – Research (1) 1971-4.

–. 1972b. PC Policy Statement: The Role of Women. NA, MG 28 IV 2, vol. 713, file: Women – Research (1) 1971-4.

–. 1980. The Progressive Conservative Response to the Advisory Council on the Status of Women Questionnaire. NA, MG 28 IV 2, vol. 660, file: Campaign 1980, Policy, Women's Issues.

–. 1982. Summary, Access to Power. NA, MG 28 IV 2, vol. 477, file: Access to Power Symposium (first).

–. 1984. A New Partnership. NA, MG 28 IV 2, vol. 477, file: Conference – Initiatives '84.

PCWAC. 1974. Minutes of the Annual Meeting of the Progressive Conservative Women's Association of Canada. NA, MG 28 IV 2, vol. 477, file: Annual Meeting 1974.

Pringle, Don. 1981. Memo to Don Mazankowski and Paul Curley re: Roles of PC functions as they relate to Special Interest Groups. NA, MG 28 IV 2, vol. 645, file: Organization, National Pre-Writ Strategy.

Quart, Josie. 1961. Report of the National President. NA, MG 28 IV 2, vol. 477, file: Annual Meeting 1961.

–. 1962. Memo to Allister Grossart, National Director PC Party of Canada, 31 July. NA, MG 28 IV 2, vol. 107, file: Correspondence.

Secondary Sources

Abele, Frances. 1992. "The Politics of Competitiveness," in *How Ottawa Spends: The Politics of Competitiveness*, ed. Frances Abele, 1-22. Ottawa: Carleton University Press.

Abzug, Bella, and Mim Kelber. 1984. *Gender Gap: Bella Abzug's Guide to Political Power for American Women*. Boston: Houghton Mifflin.

Adamson, Nancy, Linda Briskin, and Margaret McPhail. 1988. *Feminist Organizing for Change: The Contemporary Women's Movement in Canada*. Toronto: Oxford University Press.

Alberts, Sheldon. 1999. "NAC Serenades, Then Berates MPs." *National Post* (Toronto), 9 June.

Aldrich, John H. 1995. *Why Parties? The Origin and Transformation of Political Parties in America*. Chicago: University of Chicago Press.

Alexander, Herbert. 1992. *Financing Politics: Money, Elections and Political Reform*, 4th ed. Washington: Congressional Quarterly Press.

Allen, Judith. 1990. "Does Feminism Need a Theory of the State?" in *Playing the State: Australian Feminist Interventions*, ed. Sophie Watson, 21-38. London: Verso.

American Political Science Association Committee on Political Parties (APSA). 1950. "Toward a More Responsible Two-Party System." *American Political Science Review* 44 (supplement).

Andrew, Caroline. 1984. "Women and the Welfare State." *Canadian Journal of Political Science* 27:667-83.

Archer, Keith, and Faron Ellis. 1994. "Opinion Structure of Party Activists: The Reform Party of Canada." *Canadian Journal of Political Science* 27: 277-308.

Assendelft, Laura van, and Karen O'Connor. 1994. "Backgrounds, Motivations and Interests: A Comparison of Male and Female Local Party Activists." *Women and Politics* 14:245-62.

Baer, Denise. 1991a. "National Federation of Democratic Women," in *Political Parties and Elections in the United States: An Encyclopedia*, ed. L. Sandy Maisel, 682. New York: Garland.

–. 1991b. "National Federation of Republican Women," in *Political Parties and Elections in the United States: An Encyclopedia*, ed. L. Sandy Maisel, 683. New York: Garland.

–. 1992. "Who Has the Body? Party Institutionalization and Theories of Party Organization." *American Review of Politics* 14:1-38.

–. 1993. "Political Parties: The Missing Variable in Women and Politics Research." *Political Research Quarterly* 43:547-76.

Baer, Denise, and David A. Bositis. 1988. *Elite Cadres and Party Coalitions: Representing the Public in Party Politics*. New York: Greenwood Press.

–. 1993. *Politics and Linkage in Democratic Society*. Englewood Cliffs, NJ: Prentice-Hall.

Balz, Dan. 1988. "Democrats Take up Platform." *Washington Post*, 11 June, A5.

Barakso, Maryann. 1996. "Playing with Fire? Social Movements and Electoral Politics – The Case of the National Organization for Women." Paper presented at the 1996 Annual Meeting of the American Political Science Association, 2-5 September, San Francisco.

Bashevkin, Sylvia. 1989. "Free Trade and Canadian Feminism: The Case of the National Action Committee on the Status of Women." *Canadian Public Policy* 15:363-75.

–. 1993. *Toeing the Lines: Women and Party Politics in English Canada*, 2nd ed. Toronto: Oxford University Press.

–. 1996. "Losing Common Ground: Feminists, Conservatives and Public Policy in the Mulroney Years." *Canadian Journal of Political Science* 29, 2 (June): 211-42.

–. 1998. *Women on the Defensive: Living through Conservative Times*. Toronto: University of Toronto Press.

Bendyna, Mary E., and Celinda C. Lake. 1994. "Gender and Voting in the 1992 Presidential Election," in *The Year of the Woman: Myths and Realities*, ed. Elizabeth Adell Cook, Sue Thomas, and Clyde Wilcox, 237-54. Boulder, CO: Westview Press.

Biersack, Robert, and Paul S. Herrnson. 1994. "Political Parties and the Year of the Woman," in *The Year of the Woman: Myths and Realities*, ed. Elizabeth Adell Cook, Sue

Thomas, and Clyde Wilcox, 161-80. Boulder, CO: Westview Press.

Black, Naomi. 1985. "Where Does the Gender Gap?" *Canadian Woman Studies* 6:33-6.

Blustein, Paul. 1988. "Domestic Advisor to the Bush Campaign Stalking the Female Vote." *Washington Post*, 8 August, C1.

Briskin, Linda. 1991. "Feminist Practice: A New Approach to Evaluating Feminist Strategy," in *Women and Social Change: Feminist Activism in Canada*, ed. Jeri Dawn Wine and Janice L. Ristock, 24-40. Toronto: Lorimer.

Brodie, Janine. 1988. "The Gender Factor and National Leadership Conventions in Canada," in *Party Democracy in Canada: The Politics of National Party Conventions*, ed. George Perlin, 172-87. Scarborough, ON: Prentice-Hall.

–. 1991. "Women and the Electoral Process in Canada," in *Women in Canadian Politics: Toward Equity in Representation*, ed. Kathy Megyery, 3-60. Toronto: Dundurn.

–. 1992. "Choice and No Choice in the House. " In *The Politics of Abortion*, ed. Janine Brodie, Shelley A.M. Gavigan, and Jane Jenson, 57-116. Toronto: Oxford University Press.

–. 1998. "Restructuring and the Politics of Marginalization." In *Women and Political Representation in Canada*, ed. Manon Tremblay and Caroline Andrew. Ottawa: Ottawa University Press.

Brodie, Janine, and Jane Jenson. 1980. *Crisis, Challenge and Change: Party and Class in Canada*. Toronto: Methuen.

Brown, Rosemary. 1988. "Women and Electoral Politics." *Resources for Feminist Research*, 17:106-8.

–. 1989. *Being Brown: A Very Public Life*. Toronto: Random House.

Bruce, John, John A. Clark, and John H. Kessel. 1991. "Advocacy Politics in Presidential Parties." *American Political Science Review* 85:1089-105.

Buechler, Steven M. 1990. *Women's Movements in the United States*. New Brunswick, NJ: Rutgers University Press.

Burrell, Barbara. 1993a. "John Bailey's Legacy: Political Parties and Women's Candidacies for Public Office," in *Women in Politics: Outsiders or Insiders*, ed. Lois Lovelace Duke, 123-34. Englewood Cliffs, NJ: Prentice-Hall.

–. 1993b. "Party Decline, Party Transformation and Gender Politics: The USA," in *Gender and Party Politics*, ed. Joni Lovenduski and Pippa Norris, 291-308. London: Sage.

Burt, Sandra. 1995. "Gender and Public Policy: Making Some Difference in Ottawa," in *Gender and Politics in Contemporary Canada*, ed. François-Pierre Gingras, 86-105. Toronto: Oxford University Press.

Bystydzienski, Jill M. 1995. *Women in Electoral Politics: Lessons from Norway*. Westport, CT: Praeger.

Cairns, Alan C. 1968. "The Electoral System and the Party System in Canada 1921-1965." *Canadian Journal of Political Science* 1:55-80.

Canada. Chief Electoral Officer. 1973. *Report of the Chief Electoral Officer on the 29th General Election*. Ottawa: Minister of Supply and Services.

Canada. Royal Commission on the Status of Women. 1970. *Report*. Ottawa: Minister of Supply and Services.

Carabillo, Toni, Judith Meuli, and June Bundy Csida. 1993. *Feminist Chronicles: 1953-1993*. Los Angeles: Women's Graphics.

Carroll, Susan J. 1987. *Women As Candidates in American Politics*. Bloomington: Indiana University Press.

–. 1992. "Women State Legislators, Women's Organizations and the Representation of Women's Culture in the United States," in *Women Transforming Politics*, ed. Jill M. Bystydzienski, 23-41. Bloomington: Indiana University Press.

Carty, R.K. 1991. *Canadian Political Parties in the Constituencies*. Toronto: Dundurn.

Carty, R.K., and Lynda Erickson. 1991. "Candidate Nomination in Canada's National Political Parties," in *Canadian Political Parties: Leaders, Candidates and Organization*, ed. Herman Bakvis, 97-190. Toronto: Dundurn.

Carty, R.K., William Cross, and Lisa Young. 2000. *Rebuilding Canadian Party Politics*. Vancouver: UBC Press.

Castro, Ginette. 1990. *American Feminism: A Contemporary History.* New York: New York University Press.

Center for the American Woman and Politics. 1988. *Fact Sheet: Women and the Democratic and Republican National Conventions.* New Brunswick, NJ: CAWP.

Chafe, William H. 1991. *The Paradox of Change: American Women in the 20th Century.* Oxford: Oxford University Press.

Christian, William, and Colin Campbell. 1989. *Political Parties and Ideologies in Canada,* 3rd ed. Toronto: McGraw-Hill Ryerson.

Clarke, Harold D., Jane Jenson, Lawrence Le Duc, and Jon Pammett. 1991. *Absent Mandate: Interpreting Change in Canadian Elections,* 2nd ed. Toronto: Gage.

Cleverdon, Catherine. 1974. *The Woman Suffrage Movement in Canada,* 2nd ed. Toronto: University of Toronto Press.

Cohen, Marcia. 1988. *The Sisterhood: The Inside Story of the Women's Movement and the Leaders Who Made It Happen.* New York: Fawcett Columbine.

Cohen, Marjorie. 1992a. "NAC: When Women Count." *Broadside* 10 (5): 12-14.

–. 1992b. "The Canadian Women's Movement and Its Efforts to Influence the Canadian Economy," in *Challenging Times: The Women's Movement in Canada and the United States,* ed. Constance Backhouse and David Flaherty, 215-24. Montreal: McGill-Queen's University Press.

Cohodas, Nadine. 1984. "Divided Republican Women Seek to Counter Gender Gap." *Congressional Quarterly Weekly Report,* 25 August, 2088.

Congressional Quarterly. 1995. *Players, Politics and Turf in the 104th Congress.* Washington, DC: Congressional Quarterly.

Conover, Pamela Johnston. 1988. "Feminists and the Gender Gap." *Journal of Politics* 50:985-1010.

"A Convention Bush Won't Pass Up." 1988, *Washington Post,* 7 July 1988, A6.

Cook, Elizabeth Adell, Ted G. Jelen, and Clyde Wilcox, eds. 1992. *Between Two Absolutes: Public Opinion and the Politics of Abortion.* Boulder, CO: Westview Press.

Cook, Elizabeth Adell, Sue Thomas, and Clyde Wilcox, eds. 1994. *The Year of the Woman: Myths and Realities.* Boulder, CO: Westview Press.

Costain, Anne, and Douglas Costain. 1987. "Strategy and Tactics of the Women's Movement in the United States: The Role of Political Parties," in *The Women's Movements of the United States and Western Europe: Consciousness, Political Opportunity and Public Policy,* ed. Mary Fainsod Katzenstein and Carol McClurg Mueller, 196-213. Philadelphia: Temple University Press.

Cott, Nancy F. 1990. "Across the Great Divide: Women in Politics before and after 1920." In *Women, Politics and Change,* ed. Louise A. Tilley and Patricia Gurin, 153-76. New York: Russell Sage Foundation.

Courtney, John. 1995. *Do Conventions Matter? Choosing National Party Leaders in Canada.* Montreal: McGill-Queen's University Press.

Cross, Michael. 1971. "Third Class on the Titanic: The NDP Convention." *Canadian Forum* (April-May): 2-5.

Dalton, Russell. 1994. *The Green Rainbow: Environmental Groups in Western Europe.* New Haven: Yale University Press.

Darcy, R., Susan Welch, and Janet Clark. 1994. *Women, Elections and Representation,* 2nd ed. Lincoln: University of Nebraska Press.

Day, Christine, and Charles D. Hadley. 1994. "The Power of Feminism: Policy Attitudes among Southern Political Party Activists." Paper presented at the Annual Meeting of the American Political Science Association, 1-4 September, New York.

Day, Shelagh. 1993. "Speaking for Ourselves," in *The Charlottetown Accord, the Referendum and the Future of Canada,* ed. Kenneth McRoberts and Patrick J. Monahan, 58-72. Toronto: University of Toronto Press.

Diamond, Sara. 1989. *Spiritual Warfare: The Politics of the Christian Right.* Boston: South End Press.

Downs, Anthony. 1957. *An Economic Theory of Democracy.* New York: Harper and Row.

Duerst-Lahti, Georgia. 1989. "The Government's Role in Building the Women's

Movement." *Political Science Quarterly* 104:249-68.

Duverger, Maurice. 1954. *Political Parties.* New York: Wiley.

Edwards, India. 1977. *Pulling No Punches: Memoirs of a Woman in Politics.* New York: G.L. Putnam's Sons.

Ehrenreich, Barbara. 1996. "Why I Didn't Vote for Clinton." *Ms.* 7, 3 (November/December): 20-1.

English, Deirdre. 1992. "Through the Glass Ceiling." *Mother Jones* 24, 6 (November/December): 29-31.

Erickson, Lynda. 1991. "Women and Candidacies for the House of Commons," in *Women in Canadian Politics: Toward Equity in Representation,* ed. Kathy Megyery, 101-24. Toronto: Dundurn.

–. 1993. "Making Her Way In: Women, Parties and Candidacies in Canada," in *Gender and Party Politics,* ed. Joni Lovenduski and Pippa Norris, 60-85. London: Sage.

Erwin, Lorna. 1993. "Neoconservatism and the Canadian Pro-Family Movement." *Canadian Review of Sociology and Anthropology* 30:401-20.

Everitt, Joanna. 1996. "Changing Attitudes in Changing Times: The Gender Gap in Canada, 1965-1990." Ph.D. diss., University of Toronto.

Feit, Rona. 1979. "Organizing for Political Power: The National Women's Political Caucus," in *Women Organizing: An Anthology,* ed. Bernice Cummings and Victoria Schuck, 37-51. Metuchen, NJ: Scarecrow Press.

Ferree, Myra Marx, and Beth B. Hess. 1985. *Controversy and Coalition: The New Feminist Movement.* Boston: Twayne.

Findlay, Sue. 1987. "Facing the State: The Politics of the Women's Movement Reconsidered," in *Feminism and Political Economy,* ed. Heather Jon Maroney and Meg Luxton, 31-50. Toronto: Methuen.

Flanagan, Tom. 1995. *Waiting for the Wave: The Reform Party and Preston Manning.* Toronto: Stoddart.

Frankovic, Kathleen A. 1988. "The Ferraro Factor: The Women's Movement, the Polls and the Press," in *The Politics of the Gender Gap,* ed. Carol Mueller, 102-23. Newbury Park: Sage.

Franks, C.E.S. 1987. *The Parliament of Canada.* Toronto: University of Toronto Press.

Frappollo, Elizabeth. 1973. "The Ticket That Might Have Been: Vice President Farenthold." *Ms.* 1, 7 (January): 74-6.

Freeman, Jo. 1975. *The Politics of Women's Liberation.* New York: David McKay.

–. 1987. "Whom You Know versus Whom You Represent: Feminist Influence in the Democratic and Republican Parties," in *The Women's Movements of the United States and Western Europe: Consciousness, Political Opportunity and Public Policy,* ed. Mary Fainsod Katzenstein and Carol McClurg Mueller, 215-46. Philadelphia: Temple University Press.

–. 1994. "Feminism vs. Family Values: Women at the 1992 Democratic and Republican Conventions," in *Different Roles, Different Voices: Women and Politics in the United States and Europe,* ed. Marianne Githens, Pippa Norris, and Joni Lovenduski, 70-83. New York: HarperCollins.

Friedan, Betty. 1976. *It Changed My Life: Writings on the Women's Movement.* New York: Random House.

Gagnon, Alain, and Brian Tanguay, eds. 1988. *Canadian Parties in Transition: Discourse, Organization and Representation.* Scarborough, ON: Prentice-Hall.

Galipeau, Claude. 1989. "Political Parties, Interest Groups, and New Social Movements: Toward a New Representation?" in *Canadian Parties in Transition: Discourse, Organization, Representation,* ed. Alain Gagnon and Brian Tanguay, 404-26. Toronto: Nelson.

Gamson, William. 1992. "The Social Psychology of Collective Action," in *Frontiers in Social Movement Theory,* ed. Aldon Morris and Carol McClurg Mueller, 53-76. New Haven: Yale University Press.

Garner, Roberta, and Mayer Zald. 1985. "The Political Economy and Social Movement Sectors," in *The Challenge of Social Control,* ed. Gerald D. Suttles and Mayer Zald, 119-48. Norwood: Ablex.

Gelb, Joyce. 1989. *Feminism and Politics: A Comparative Approach.* Berkeley: University of California Press.

Gidengil, Elisabeth. 1995. "Economic Man – Social Woman? The Case of the Gender Gap in Support for the Canada-US Free Trade Agreement." *Comparative Political Studies* 28:384-408.

Gotell, Lise, and Janine Brodie. 1991. "Women and Parties: More Than an Issue of Numbers," in *Party Politics in Canada,* 6th ed., ed. Hugh Thorburn, 53-67. Toronto: Prentice-Hall.

Gottleib, Amy. 1993. "What about Us? Organizing Inclusively in the National Action Committee on the Status of Women," in *And Still We Rise: Feminist Political Mobilizing in Contemporary Canada,* ed. Linda Carty, 368-85. Toronto: Women's Press.

Graham, Sara Hunter. 1996. *Woman Suffrage and the New Democracy.* New Haven: Yale University Press.

Granat, Diane. 1984. "Democrats Hope Ferraro, Gender Gap Will Lure Women Voters in Fall Races." *Congressional Quarterly Weekly Report,* 21 July, 1722.

Gray, Charlotte. 1994. "House-Breaking." *Saturday Night* (December): 27-32.

Gray, Elizabeth. 1981. "Women's Fight to Get in from the Cold Political Wind." *Globe and Mail,* 30 January, 7.

Hanson, Lawrence. 1992. "Contesting the Leadership at the Grassroots: The Liberals in 1990," in *Canadian Political Party Systems: A Reader,* ed. R.K. Carty, 426-35. Peterborough, ON: Broadview Press.

Hošek, Chaviva. 1983. "Women and the Constitutional Process," in *And No One Cheered: Federalism, Democracy and the Constitution Act,* ed. Keith Banting and Richard Simeon, 280-300. Toronto: Methuen.

–. 1984. "President's Message." *Status of Women News* 9, 3 (Fall): 1.

Huang, Agnes, and Fatima Jaffer. 1993. "Interview with Judy Rebick." *Kinesis* (June): 10-11.

Huber, John, and Ronald Inglehart. 1995. "Expert Interpretations of Party Space and Party Locations in 42 Societies." *Party Politics* 1:73-112.

Jennings, M. Kent, and Barbara G. Farah. 1981. "Social Roles and Political Resources: An Over-Time Study of Men and Women in Party Elites." *American Journal of Political Science* 25:462-82.

Jonasdottir, Anna. 1988. "On the Concept of Interests, Women's Interests, and the Limitations of Interest Theory," in *The Political Interests of Gender,* ed. K.B. Jones and A.G. Jonasdottir, 33-65. London: Sage.

Katz, Richard, and Robin Kolodny. 1994. "Party Organizations as an Empty Vessel: Parties in American Politics," in *How Parties Organize: Change and Adaptation in Party Organizations in Western Democracies,* ed. Richard S. Katz and Peter Mair, 23-50. London: Sage.

Katz, Richard, and Peter Mair, eds. 1992. *Party Organizations: A Data Handbook on Party Organizations in Western Democracies, 1960-90.* London: Sage.

–. 1995. "Changing Models of Party Organization and Party Democracy: The Emergence of the Cartel Party." *Party Politics* 1:5-29.

Katzenstein, Mary Fainsod, and Carol McClurg Mueller, eds. 1987. *The Women's Movements of the United States and Western Europe.* Philadelphia: Temple University Press.

Kelber, Mim. 1994. *Women and Government: New Ways to Political Power.* Westport, CT: Praeger.

"Kemp Loses Endorsement." 1988. *Washington Post,* 3 March, A15.

Keone, Miriam. 1999. "Regionalism and Restructuring in the Progressive Conservative Party." Paper presented to the Conference on Regionalism and Party Politics in Canada, University of Calgary, 11-13 March.

Kessel, John H. 1980. *Presidential Campaign Politics: Coalition Strategies and Citizen Response.* Homewood, IL: Dorsey.

Kidd, Varda. 1971. "Sexism Prevailed at the NDP Convention." *Canadian Dimension* 8 (1): 8-10.

Kinsley, Michael. 1992. "The GOP's Abortion Trap." *Washington Post,* 5 June, A31.

Kirkpatrick, Jeane. 1976. *The New Presidential Elite: Men and Women in National Politics.* New York: Sage.

Kirschten, Dick. 1984. "The Reagan Reelection Campaign Hopes 1984 Will Be the Year of the Woman." *National Journal,* 6 June, 1083.

Kitschelt, Herbert. 1993. "Social Movements, Political Parties and Democratic Theory," in *Citizens, Protest and Democracy,* ed. Russell J. Dalton, 13-29. Annals of the American Academy of Political and Social Science 528. Newbury Park: Sage.

Klinkner, Philip. 1994a. *The Losing Parties: Out-Party National Committees 1956-1993.* New Haven: Yale University Press.

–. 1994b. "Party Culture and Political Behaviour," in *The State of the Parties: The Changing Role of Contemporary American Parties,* ed. Daniel M. Shea and John C. Green, 275-88. Lanham, MD: Rowman and Littlefield.

Kolodny, Robin, and Richard S. Katz. 1991. "The United States," in *Party Organizations: A Data Handbook on Party Organizations in Western Democracies, 1960-90,* ed. Richard S. Katz and Peter Mair, 23-50. London: Sage.

LaMarsh, Judy. 1968. *Memoirs of a Bird in a Gilded Cage.* Toronto: McClelland and Stewart.

Larkin, Jackie. 1971. "Status of Women Report: Fundamental Questions Remain Unanswered." *Canadian Dimension* 7, 7 (January/February): 6-9.

Lavigne, Yves. 1981a. "Minister 'Manipulated' Votes to Halt Meeting, Women's Head Charges." *Globe and Mail,* 13 January, 9.

–. 1981b. "Loses Decisive Vote, Women's Head Quits." *Globe and Mail,* 21 January, 9.

–. 1981c. "MPs Rake Axworthy over Coals for Turmoil in Women's Group." *Globe and Mail,* 23 January, 1-2.

Léger, Huguette, and Judy Rebick. 1993. *The NAC Voters' Guide.* Hull: Voyageur.

Lerner, Gerda. 1986. *The Creation of Patriarchy.* Oxford: Oxford University Press.

Lewis, S.P. 1993. *The Life of Grace MacInnis.* Madeira Park, BC: Harbour Publishing.

Lovenduski, Joni, and Pippa Norris, eds. 1993. *Gender and Party Politics.* London: Sage.

McCall, Christina, and Stephen Clarkson. 1994. *Trudeau and Our Times: The Heroic Delusion.* Toronto: McClelland and Stewart.

McGlen, Nancy, and Karen O'Connor. 1995. *Women, Politics and American Society.* Englewood Cliffs, NJ: Prentice-Hall.

MacIvor, Heather. 1994. "The Leadership Convention: An Institution under Stress," in *Leaders and Leadership in Canada: An Introduction,* ed. Maureen Mancuso, Richard Price, and Ronald Wagenberg, 13-27. Toronto: Oxford University Press Canada.

MacKinnon, Catharine. 1989. *Toward a Feminist Theory of the State.* Cambridge: Harvard University Press.

McLaughlin, Audrey. 1992. *A Woman's Place: My Life and Politics.* Toronto: Macfarlane, Walter and Ross.

McLeod, Ian. 1994. *Under Siege: The Federal NDP in the Nineties.* Toronto: Lorimer.

McSweeney, Dean, and John Zvesper. 1991. *American Political Parties.* London: Routledge.

Maillé, Chantal. 1990. *Primed for Power: Women in Canadian Politics.* Ottawa: CACSW.

Makinson, Larry. 1992. *Open Secrets: The Encyclopedia of Congressional Money and Politics,* 2nd ed. Washington, DC: Congressional Quarterly.

March, James G., and Johan P. Olsen. 1989. *Rediscovering Institutions: The Organizational Basis of Politics.* New York: Free Press.

Maroney, Heather Jon. 1988. "Contemporary Quebec Feminism: The Interrelation of Political and Ideological Development in Women's Organizations, Trade Unions, Political Parties and State Policy, 1960-1980." Ph.D. diss., McMaster University.

Maslove, Allan M. 1992. "Reconstructing Fiscal Federalism," in *How Ottawa Spends: The Politics of Competitiveness,* ed. Frances Abele, 57-78. Ottawa: Carleton University Press.

Matlack, Carol. 1991. "Abortion Lobbyists Striking a Vein of Gold." *National Journal,* 16 March, 43.

Melich, Tanya. 1996. *The Republican War against Women.* New York: Bantam Books.

Melucci, Alberto. 1980. "The New Social Movements: A Theoretical Approach." *Social Science Information* 19: 199-225.

–. 1985. "The Symbolic Challenge of Contemporary Movements." *Social Research* 52:789-816.

–. 1989. *Nomads of the Present: Social Movements and Industrial Needs in Contemporary*

Society. Philadelphia: Temple University Press.

Michels, Roberto [1915] 1962. *Political Parties: A Sociological Study of the Oligarchical Tendencies of Modern Democracy.* New York: Crowell Collier.

Miller, Arthur. 1988. "Gender and the Vote: 1984," in *The Politics of the Gender Gap,* ed. Carol Mueller, 258-82. Newbury Park: Sage.

Miller, Warren E., and M. Kent Jennings. 1986. *Parties in Transition: A Longitudinal Study of Party Elites and Party Supporters.* New York: Sage.

Morton, Desmond. 1986. *The New Democrats 1961-1986: The Politics of Change.* Toronto: Copp Clark Pitman.

Mundy, Alicia. 1992. "It Happened One Night: Is WLN a Big Tent Alternative – or Just a Sideshow Distraction?" *Campaigns and Elections* (November): 17.

Myers, Patricia A. 1989. "A Noble Effort: The National Federation of Liberal Women of Canada 1928-1973," in *Beyond the Vote: Canadian Women in Politics,* ed. Linda Kealey and Joan Sangster, 39-62. Toronto: University of Toronto Press.

Nelson, Candice J. 1994. "Women's PACs in the Year of the Woman," in *The Year of the Woman: Myths and Realities,* ed. Elizabeth Adell Cook, Sue Thomas, and Clyde Wilcox, 181-96. Boulder, CO: Westview Press.

Nevitte, Neil, William P. Brandon, and Lori Davis. 1993. "The American Abortion Controversy." *Politics and the Life Sciences* 12, 1 (February): 19-30.

Newman, Christina. 1976. "Despite Meaty Policy Sessions, PC Convention's Style Is High Fakery." *Globe and Mail,* 21 February, 1-2.

Norris, Pippa, and Joni Lovenduski. 1988. "Women Candidates for Parliament: Transforming the Agenda?" *British Journal of Political Science* 19 (1): 106-15.

Offe, Claus. 1990. "Reflections on the Institutional Self-Transformation of Movement Politics: A Tentative Stage Model," in *Challenging the Political Order: New Social and Political Movements in Western Democracies,* ed. Russell Dalton and Manfred Kuechler, 232-50. Oxford: Oxford University Press.

Pal, Leslie A. 1993. *Interests of State: The Politics of Language, Multiculturalism and Feminism in Canada.* Montreal: McGill-Queen's University Press.

Penning, James M. 1994. "Pat Robertson and the GOP: 1998 and Beyond." *Sociology of Religion* 55 (3): 327-44.

Perlin, George. 1997. "The Constraints of Public Opinion: Diverging or Converging Paths," in *Degrees of Freedom: Canada and the United States in a Changing World,* ed. Keith Banting, George Hoberg, and Richard Simeon, 71-107. Montreal: McGill-Queen's University Press.

Peterson, Bill, and Gwen Hill. 1988. "GOP's Female Delegates Scoff at Gender Gap." *Washington Post,* 16 August, A17.

Phillips, Susan D. 1990. "Projects, Pressure and Perceptions of Effectiveness: An Organizational Analysis of National Canadian Women's Groups." Ph.D. diss., Carleton University.

Pierson, Ruth Roach, Marjorie Griffin Cohen, Paula Bourne, and Philinda Masters, eds. 1993. *Canadian Women's Issues.* Vol. 1, *Strong Voices.* Toronto: Lorimer.

Rae, Nicol C. 1989. *The Decline and Fall of the Liberal Republicans from 1952 to the Present.* Oxford: Oxford University Press.

–. 1994. *Southern Democrats.* Oxford: Oxford University Press.

Raney, Tracey. 1998. "Redrawing the Map of Canada: Identity and Community Constructions in the Citizenship and Nationalist Discourses of the Reform Party of Canada." M.A. thesis, Carleton University.

Rankin, Pauleen, and Jill Vickers. 1998. "Locating Women's Politics," in *Women and Political Representation in Canada,* ed. Manon Tremblay and Caroline Andrew. Ottawa: University of Ottawa Press.

Rapoport, Ronald B., Walter J. Stone, and Alan I. Abramowitz. 1991. "Do Endorsements Matter? Group Influence in the 1984 Democratic Caucuses." *American Political Science Review* 85:193-203.

Razack, Sherene. 1991. *Canadian Feminism and the Law: The Women's Legal Education and Action Fund and the Pursuit of Equality.* Toronto: Second Story Press.

Rebick, Judy. 1992. "Unity in Diversity: The Women's Movement in Canada." *Social Policy* 44:47-55.

–. 1993. "Interview with Judy Rebick," by Agnes Huang and Fatima Jaffer, *Kinesis* 3:10-11.

–. 1994. "Interview with Judy Rebick" by Pat Armstrong, *Studies in Political Economy* 44:39-72.

Rebick, Judy, and Kike Roach. 1996. *Politically Speaking*. Vancouver: Douglas and McIntyre.

Reform Party of Canada. 1999. *Blue Book*. Available at http://www.reform.ca.

Reid, T.R. 1988. "Democrats' Platform Is Short, Subtle." *Washington Post*, 24 June, A4.

Rimmerman, Craig A. 1994. "New Kids on the Block: The WISH List and the Gay and Lesbian Victory Fund in the 1992 Elections," in *Risky Business: PAC Decisionmaking in Congressional Elections*, ed. Robert Biersack, Paul S. Herrnson, and Clyde Wilcox, 214-23. Armonk, NY: M.E. Sharpe.

Rinehart, Dianne. 1997. "Women's Group Laments Lack of Election Clout." *Vancouver Sun*, 16 May, A3.

Ritchie, Laurell, and Marjorie Cohen, eds. 1981. "Pierre Trudeau on Women." Partial transcript of meeting between Trudeau and representatives of NAC, *Canadian Forum* (March): 9-13.

Robinson, Ian. 1993. "The NAFTA, Democracy and Continental Economic Integration: Trade Policy As If Democracy Mattered," in *How Ottawa Spends: A More Democratic Canada?* ed. Susan D. Phillips, 333-80. Ottawa: Carleton University Press.

Rosin, Hanna. 1995. "Invasion of the Church Ladies." *The New Republic*, 24 April, 20-7.

Russell, Peter. 1993. *Constitutional Odyssey: Can Canadians Become a Sovereign People?* 2nd ed. Toronto: University of Toronto Press.

Sangster, Joan. 1989. *Dreams of Equality: Women on the Canadian Left, 1920-1950*. Toronto: McClelland and Stewart.

Sartori, Giovanni. 1976. *Parties and Party Systems: A Framework for Analysis*. Cambridge: Cambridge University Press.

Seltzer, Richard, Jody Newman, and Melissa Voorhees Leighton. 1997. *Sex As a Political Variable: Women As Candidates and Voters in U.S. Elections*. Boulder, CO: Lynne Rienner.

Shafer, Byron. 1983. *Quiet Revolution: The Struggle for the Democratic Party and the Shaping of Post-Reform Politics*. New York: Sage.

Sharpe, Sydney. 1994. *The Gilded Ghetto: Women and Political Power in Canada*. Toronto: HarperCollins.

Sherill, Martha. 1992. "The GOP's Abortion-Rights Upstart." *Washington Post*, 4 April, D1.

Sigurdson, Richard. 1994. "Preston Manning and the Politics of Post-Modernism in Canada." *Canadian Journal of Political Science* 27, 2 (June): 249-76.

Simeon, Richard, and Elaine Willis. 1997. "Democracy and Performance: Governance in Canada and the United States," in *Degrees of Freedom: Canada and the United States in a Changing Global Context*, ed. Keith Banting, George Hoburg, and Richard Simeon, 150-86. Montreal: McGill/Queen's University Press.

Simpson, Peggy. 1988. "Why They'd Rather Fight Than Switch." *Ms.* (November).

Skjeie, Hege. 1991. "The Rhetoric of Difference: On Women's Inclusion into Political Elites." *Politics and Society* 19:233-63.

–. 1988. *The Feminization of Power: Norway's Political Experiment. (1986-)* Oslo: Institute for Social Research.

Smeal, Eleanor. 1984. *Why and How Women Will Elect the Next President*. New York: Harper and Row.

–. 1991. "Why I Support a New Party." *Ms.: The World of Women* 1, 4. (January/February): 71-4.

Stanbury, W.T. 1991. *Money in Politics: Financing Federal Parties and Candidates in Canada*. Toronto: Dundurn.

Stanley, Harold W., and Richard G. Niemi. 1994. *Vital Statistics on American Politics*, 4th ed. Washington, DC: CQ Press.

Steed, Judy. 1988. *Ed Broadbent: The Pursuit of Power*. Toronto: Viking.

Studlar, Donley, and Richard E. Matland. 1994. "The Growth of Women's Representation in the Canadian House of Commons and the Election of 1984: A Reappraisal." *Canadian Journal of Political Science* 27 (1): 53-79.

Tarrow, Sidney. 1989. *Struggle, Politics, and Reform: Collective Action, Social Movements and Cycles of Protest.* Western Societies Papers. Ithaca, NY: Cornell University.

–. 1990. "The Phantom at the Opera: Political Parties and Social Movements of the 1960s and 1970s in Italy," in *Challenging the Political Order: New Social and Political Movements in Western Democracies,* ed. Russell J. Dalton and Manfred Kuechler, 251-75. New York: Oxford University Press.

–. 1994. *Power in Movement: Social Movements, Collective Action and Politics.* Cambridge: Cambridge University Press.

Taylor, Paul. 1988. "No-Shows from GOP." *Washington Post,* 24 January, A9.

Thomas, Sue. 1994. *How Women Legislate.* New York: Oxford University Press.

Thomlinson, Neil. 1992. "Intra-Party Caucuses and NDP Leadership Selection in 1989." M.A. thesis, University of Saskatchewan.

Tolleson Rinehart, Sue. 1992. *Gender Consciousness and Politics.* New York: Routledge.

Trudeau, Pierre. 1972. *Conversations with Canadians.* Toronto: University of Toronto Press.

Tsebelis, George. 1990. *Nested Games.* Berkeley: University of California Press.

Vickers, Jill. 1980. "Coming up for Air: Feminist Views of Power Reconsidered." *Canadian Women's Studies* 2 (4): 66-70.

–. 1989. "Feminist Approaches to Women in Politics," in *Beyond the Vote: Canadian Women in Politics,* ed. Linda Kealey and Joan Sangster, 16-38. Toronto: University of Toronto Press.

Vickers, Jill, Pauline Rankin, and Christine Appelle. 1993. *Politics As If Women Mattered: A Political Analysis of the National Action Committee on the Status of Women.* Toronto: University of Toronto Press.

Vienneau, David. 1991. "PM Criticizes Tories against Violence Study." *Toronto Star,* 20 June.

Ware, Alan. 1985. *The Breakdown of Democratic Party Organization, 1940-1980.* Oxford: Clarendon.

–. 1996. *Political Parties and Party Systems.* Oxford: Oxford University Press.

Ware, Susan. 1987. *Partner and I: Molly Dewson, Feminism and New Deal Politics.* New Haven: Yale University Press.

Wearing, Joseph. 1988. *Strained Relations: Canadian Parties and Voters.* Toronto: McClelland and Stewart.

Wearing, Peter, and Joseph Wearing. 1991. "Does Gender Make a Difference in Voting Behaviour? in *The Ballot and Its Message,* ed. Joseph Wearing, 341-50. Toronto: Copp Clark Pitman.

Welch, Susan. 1985. "Are Women More Liberal Than Men in the U.S. Congress?" *Legislative Studies Quarterly* 10:125-34.

Whitehorn, Alan, and Keith Archer. 1995. "The Gender Gap amongst Party Activists: A Case Study of the New Democratic Party," in *Gender and Politics in Contemporary Canada,* ed. François-Pierre Gingras, 2-30. Toronto: Oxford University Press.

Wilcox, Clyde. 1994a. "Premillennialists at the Millennium: Some Reflections on the Christian Right in the Twenty-first Century." *Sociology of Religion* 55:243-61.

–. 1994b. "Why Was 1992 the 'Year of the Woman'? Explaining Women's Gains in 1992," in *The Year of the Woman: Myths and Realities,* ed. Elizabeth Adell Cook, Sue Thomas, and Clyde Wilcox, 1-24. Boulder, CO: Westview Press.

Williams, Marjorie. 1988. "The Women in Bush's Brigade." *Washington Post,* 11 August, D1.

Winsor, Hugh. 1976. "I Had to Gamble, Proud Flora Says." *Globe and Mail,* 23 February, 11.

Witt, Linda, Karen M. Paget, and Glenna Matthews. 1994. *Running As a Woman: Gender and Power in American Politics.* New York: Free Press.

Young, Lisa. 1991. "Legislative Turnover and the Election of Women to the Canadian House of Commons," in *Women in Canadian Politics: Toward Equity in Representation,* ed. Kathy Megyery, 81-100. Toronto: Dundurn.

–. 1994. *Electoral Systems and Representative Legislatures: Consideration of Alternative Electoral Systems*. Ottawa: Canadian Advisory Council on the Status of Women.

–. 1996. "Fulfilling the Mandate of Difference: Women in the Canadian House of Commons," in *In the Presence of Women: Representation in Canadian Governments*, ed. Linda Trimble and Jane Arscott, 82-105. Toronto: Harcourt Brace.

Zaborszky, Dorothy. 1988. "Feminist Politics: The Feminist Party of Canada," in *Feminist Research: Prospect and Retrospect*, ed. Peta Tancred-Sheriff, 250-62. Montreal: CRIAW/McGill-Queen's University Press.

Index

Set in Stone by First Folio Group

Printed and bound in Canada by Friesens

Copy editor: Kate Baltais

Indexer: Patricia Buchanan

Proofreader: Darlene Money